Away from this World

THE AFGHAN HOUND

ACKNOWLEDGEMENTS

Life is short and problems are everywhere, going to washroom is problem, shaving and eating are the biggest problems. I have problems and my parents might have had five times more problems as I do. If this world was not made of problems we should have never known what the meaning of pleasure is.

Honest thanks to my siblings, particularly Mr. Ramin who had encouraged me to write this novel, Special thanks to Professor Dr. Ali Mohammad Rajput who is the falcon of Khorog, Tajikistan mountains. Thanks to those professors, and teachers for their understanding and educating. I have the warmest feeling towards people of intelligence and education.

I love to create, to learn and love people on the same field. Loving humanity, diverse culture, experiencing and understanding the concept of pluralisms within nation's cultural value is a great pleasure of knowledge to grasp. I kiss my parents hands one more time, for educating and enabling to leave a few words behind.

Please read "Away from this World" the Afghan-hound and leave comments, which will be a need for next Novel.

Thanks.

_Away from this World

Fardin Azizzada

One

I must have been five years old, I think, because my baba (grandfather) had given me shiny new marbles. I was excited and restless because I was eager to show my cousins my new colourful marbles. Sharouch was the first one to notice them; he knocked the marbles out of my hands. I watched as the marbles fell and scattered into the snow. Angrily, I pushed him hard and he fell onto the snow. He got up quickly and grabbed me with both hands. I tried to pull away from him, but he grabbed my left leg with his right hand. I got one arm loose and tried to push his shoulder away, but he countered by locking both his arms around my waist. I put my arm back over his head and tried to pull his chin back. We remained locked into this position for some time when suddenly, my *engay* (aunt) saw us and pulled us apart. Once Sharouch was free, he yanked my jacket, and a button ripped off and fell into the snow. 'This is *my* house, Aftab,' he shouted. 'Go back to Bamyan!' I never found that button.

That afternoon, my *abbay* (mother), and his abbay had a big fight over it. I heard them yelling at each other from the hallway. Late in the evening, as my mother tucked me into bed, I asked her, 'Why do we have to stay here? What happened to Attay?' (Father). I remember seeing the tears welling up in her eyes as she let out a sigh, and then she started rubbing my cheek with her palm. She told me the story of why we had come to Baba's place, and the story of how we lost father.

My father had been a wheat farmer back in Bamyan, Afghanistan where we used to live. My mother told me what had happened: 'A few of the Pashtun shepherds would often graze their sheep in Father's wheat. Your father would protect his wheat and run them off his field. One day, your father took offence to some particularly aggressive Pashtun shepherds. He had seen these men before, but this time these men did not back down. This time they came well prepared with knives and swords, and your father tried to protect himself using a shovel. We are the native people of Bamyan'.

I had been two years old then, and she had been six months pregnant with my sister. Just then my baby sister woke up and started crying. My mother wiped the tears off her face. I looked up at her and saw that she was weeping quietly. Without a word, she turned around to check on the baby. Behind her, my baba was standing in the doorway. 'Pashtuns are worse than dogs,' he said. 'I hate those fucking Pashtuns.' Then he walked into the room. 'Sleep,' my mother said. 'I will buy you more shiny and colourful marbles, *Bachem'* (my son).

Two

The house was made of clay, and there were about thirteen people living in it all together. It had four bedrooms, a kitchen, and a bathroom. The biggest room in the house was on the north side, where my eldest uncle (*kakky*), Ghulam, and my aunt Zeynab slept with their two sons, Murad and Sohrab, and their daughter, Shreen. Murad was six years older than me; Sohrab was four years older, and Shreen was three years older. Uncle Ghulam owned a shop in town where he sold groceries. Uncle Rustam and Aunt Laily slept across the hall from Uncle Ghulam. They had a daughter named Ziba and a son name Sharouch. Ziba was two years older than me, and Sharouch was a year older. Uncle Rustam worked at Baba's store. My youngest uncle was Ali. He was younger than my father and was not married. He slept in the room with my baba and my grandmother, Ajjay, at the back of the house on the east side. We always ate in Baba's room. I enjoyed being around my cousin Sohrab. Every time Sohrab played with his kites, he would ask me to help him. When he had money, he would take me to the shop and buy me juice and chewing gum.

The kitchen was located at the end of the main hallway where the hallway narrowed and continued to the right. The bathroom was on the right side of the narrow hallway, with a small window. At the back of the house, across from the bathroom, was a very small room with a window. This was where I slept with my mother and my younger sister, Mina. The house was surrounded by a fairly large yard, completely bare, save for Baba's vegetable plants in the summer. The yard was surrounded by tall clay walls on all sides. The toilet was in the corner of the yard. There was a rusty red gate in the middle of one of the walls in front, facing the main street. There was a smaller turquoise-coloured door built into the gate; the paint had long since faded with age. Usually we just used the smaller door to go in and out. The gate was used only when Baba's car left in the morning and came back in the evening. The house was located in the Taymani district in the northeast part of Kabul in Afghanistan. The majority of the people in the Taymani district were Tajiks. There were also Pashtuns, and only a few Hazara families, like mine. It was not a rich neighbourhood.

Baba imported hardware goods from China and Hong Kong in large quantities. He had a store in town where he sold different types of nails, hammers, locks, door handles, and other hardware materials. In the same building where his store was he rented a warehouse in which he stored his goods. Uncle Rustam also worked in Baba's business; they sold and delivered hardware materials in large quantities to other stores.

One night, during the first week of Hafizullah Amin's government in 1979, Uncle Ali never came home. We waited all night for him, but he never came home. My grandmother, Ajjay, didn't sleep the entire night. In the morning, the first thing I heard was Ajjay nervously rocking back and forth in her chair, whispering over, and over to herself, 'Ali, my son, when are you coming home? When are you coming home?' Ajjay cried all the next night. I woke up in the morning to find Baba sitting on his favourite chair listening to the radio. Then Ajjay started shouting at him, 'Find Ali! Find Ali! Do something. Don't just sit there!' She started crying again. Baba looked at her, but said nothing. He just turned back to the radio and stared at it without moving, and without saying anything. It must have taken Baba a few minutes to notice me standing next to him. He turned his head, looked at me, and in a weak voice, he asked me to serve him a cup of black tea. Several minutes passed in silence, without anyone saying anything. The only thing I could hear was the sound of the radio and the rustling of the leaves in the backyard. I served him the cup of tea. He had a sip. 'It is not hot enough,' he said. 'Go and prepare fresh black tea for me, Bachem.' By the time I had prepared the fresh tea, it was midmorning and the sunlight covered much of the room, dividing it into two parts. Suddenly someone knocked at the door. Ajjay looked up. 'It's my Ali,' she said. 'My Ali has come home?' Baba took the cup of hot tea from me and took a very slow and thoughtful sip, and said nothing more. A few minutes later, Murad came into Baba's room to tell us it had only been one of our neighbours at the door.

Uncle Rustam walked into the room. 'We should go to Kabul University to find out if Ali was there yesterday,' he said.

Baba stroked the tip of his grey beard and looked up at Rustam. He sighed. 'Ne, Bachem,' he said softly (No, my son). 'When Hafizullah Amin came into power, I should have forbidden him to teach.' He paused. 'It's my fault.'

Since that day, every time there was a knock at the door, Ajjay would say, 'It's my Ali. My Ali has come home?'

One time I asked my mother why she had to work around the house so much. 'It is because they are providing the food, and this is how I compensate ... by working around the house,' she explained. 'Everything is fine here; they all love us.'

'No, not Aunt Zeynab,' I protested. 'She does not want us to be here. She is always fighting with you.'

'She wants us to go back to Bamyan, and I do not want to because there is no school for you,' she said.

My baba was literate, and he was the one who took the time to help me with my schoolwork. By the age of seven, in my second year of school, I was able to read and write in the Dari language. During annual holidays in the winter season, my grandfather would teach me how to read and write. If I did not do the assignments he gave me, he would punish me. His punishments were different. He would stand me against the wall and tell me to put my hands up and to open my mouth. Then he would put a shoe into my mouth. If I did not continue to bite on the shoe and keep my hands up, then he would hold the tips of my ears and twist them from left to right and pull them up and down until I was able to bite on the shoe and keep my hands up at the same time. Meanwhile, he would stare into my eyes, always with his Muslim rosary (*tasbih*) in hand, and he would lecture. 'Didn't I tell you to do your homework? All of it? You are always out playing with kites and marbles, or going to see chicken fights with your friends. If you do not learn this, you will never be able to go for higher grade. You want to be stupid, is this it?' He would repeat 'Is this it?' over and over until I cried and cried while I held onto the shoe with my teeth and kept my hands up.

My sister was really sweet. Every evening she would wait in anticipation of my return from school. She had olive skin; glassy almond eyes; and straight, long, brown hair. And she smiled all the time. Her beauty radiated throughout the house.

Most of the time we ate cooked vegetables; sometimes we had beef, lamb, or chicken, and sometimes we had fish. We sat around on a big plastic tarp and always ate together. Baba didn't like it if we spoke while we were eating. Baba always asked me to sit next to him while we had dinner. My mother washed the dishes outside when it was not cold or raining. My little sister helped her by pouring water as she was washing the dishes. Mina kept her pretty almond eyes on my mother's fingers, and poured water. Once, the wind blew my mother's scarf all the way across her face and covered her eyes. As she was holding a dishpan in her left hand and the towel with a bowl of soup in her right hand, she asked my sister to pull her scarf away so she could see. Mina was an angel. At the age of five, she had the talent to calm down Abbay. She was able to sing. Every time she sang for us, she would bow down after her performance and bounce back up with a big smile that captivated everyone.

When I was nine years old, uncle Ghulam's wife, aunt Zeynab had a new baby boy. Baba named him Timur. A year later, my other uncle Rustam's wife, aunt Laily gave birth to twin girls. This was exciting to see. Everyone was happy, but the babies cried a lot.

Three

One time, my aunt Sakina, my mother's sister, came to visit us from Bamyan. Usually when we received guests at our house, the guests would spend the night in Grandpa's room while Grandpa slept in Uncle Rustam's room and Grandma slept in Uncle Ghulam's room. But this time Aunt Sakina spent the night in our room with my mother. A few days later, Aunt Sakina came back from the city and showed us the brand-new, ruby-red shoes she had purchased that day. They looked very expensive. She was excited and told us how happy she was for the price she had paid. She was going to take them back to Bamyan and show all her friends. Two days later, her new shoes went missing from the hallway. She was in an absolute rage. My mother tried to calm her down, but Aunt Sakina wouldn't listen. 'They were right here!' she said, and gave accusing glances to Laily. 'They just couldn't have disappeared by themselves. Someone must have taken them!'

'What are you trying to imply?' said Aunt Laily.

'You tried my shoes yesterday, and you said how much you liked them,' Aunt Sakina replied.

'You think just because I said I liked them, I would steal them? My husband can buy me any shoes I want. Probably you have misplaced them,' Aunt Laily said.

Aunt Zeynab sneered and said, 'Maybe you left them somewhere.'

'I left them right here,' Aunt Sakina repeated.

'You're just a poor, ignorant, young farmer girl from Bamyan, and we're from the city. You don't even know what good shoes are,' Aunt Zeynab refuted. 'Laily just gave you a compliment to make you feel good.'

'You want shoes?' Aunt Laily said. 'Here, take mine.' She went into her room and came back with a pair of her shoes and shoved them onto Aunt Sakina's hands. 'Take them; I already have another four pairs of shoes a hundred times more expensive than yours.'

'I don't need your ugly shoes!' yelled Aunt Sakina. 'I want *my* shoes!' Aunt Sakina threw Aunt Laily's shoes against the wall in the hallway. Aunt Laily then just glared at Aunt Sakina for a few seconds, then turned to my mother in frustration for help, raising both palms in the air, as if saying, what's wrong with your sister? Then she took one more look at Aunt Sakina and went back into her room.

Before my mom could say anything, Aunt Zeynab snickered loudly. My mom gave her an angry look. Aunt Zeynab turned around and walked into her room. Aunt Sakina started crying. My mother put her arms around her and pulled her into our room and closed the door. I stayed in the hallway; I could hear my mother trying to comfort her from inside but couldn't make out any words. An hour later my mother and Aunt Sakina came out of the room, but no one mentioned anything further.

The next day, Aunt Sakina left and went back to Bamyan. The day after that, Aunt Zeynab walked into our room and threw a muddy pair of shoes onto the floor. 'Take your sister's shoes,' she said. 'I found them outside.' And then she went back to her room. My mother nearly dropped my baby sister. She put down Mina and rushed out of the room after her, screaming and swearing at Aunt Zeynab, accusing her of intentionally stealing the shoes.

I grabbed my sister's hand and went into the hallway. My mom was pounding on Aunt Zeynab's door fiercely, as if she was going to break it down. Grandpa came out of his room and grabbed her arm and asked her to calm down. My mother stopped banging on the door, but then, not knowing what to do, started crying. Mina, sensing something was wrong, started crying too. My mom looked down, took her from me, and picked her up in her arms. Mina put her small arm around my mom's neck and with her soft little palm, wiped the tears off of our mother's face.

'Please tell me what is wrong, Soraya,' Grandpa said. 'I will help you.'

'I want to talk to Zeynab,' my mother said. The door opened, and Uncle Ghulam came out. Uncle Rustam also came out of his room, wondering what the commotion was about. Grandpa asked her again what was wrong.

But all mother would say was, 'I want to talk to Zeynab.' Grandpa asked Ghulam to get his wife and bring her to his room.

A few minutes later, we were assembled in Grandpa's room waiting for Ghulam and Zeynab. Grandpa sat against the wall on his mattress. My sister crawled up beside him and held onto his arm, sucking her thumb. My mother's head was down; she looked frustrated and tired. Ghulam walked into the room with Aunt Zeynab. Aunt Zeynab went to sit in the front near Grandpa, but Grandpa asked her to sit next to her husband. She had no sooner sat down than my mother picked her head up. 'How could you do this to my sister?'

'I didn't do anything to your sister. I found those shoes right next to the tomato plants when I was on my way to the toilet,' Zeynab said. My mother leaned forward and looked straight at Aunt Zeynab. 'You are lying, you arrogant woman,' she cried, pointing a finger at Zeynab. 'I have been looking for my sister's shoes everywhere for the last two days. Look at these shoes. They're covered in mud! Why would you do such a thing? Why?'

Grandpa put his hand up for silence. He took one of the shoes from my mother and looked it over carefully. He turned to my mother and smiled. 'You are right.' Turning back to the others, he said, 'These shoes were deliberately hidden in the mud.' Aunt Zeynab looked as if she was about to protest, but before she could, Murad started giggling in the back. Everyone turned around. Murad stopped giggling when he saw Grandpa looking at him in annoyance.

'Murad, come here,' Grandpa ordered. Murad didn't move. 'I am talking to you. Come here and sit next to me.' Instead, Murad got closer to his father, leaning on him, but his father pushed him forward. Murad sat down next to Grandpa.

Grandpa asked him to explain why he was laughing. Murad replied, 'I don't know.'

'Prophet Mohammed, peace be upon him, has said do anything, but do not lie,' Grandpa said, shaking his head up and down. Murad started giggling to himself again. Bewildered, everyone looked at one another, not understanding what Murad found so funny. My mother looked at Murad curiously. Grandpa was furious. 'You are fourteen years old! Stop acting like a child! Tell me, did you do this?' he shouted angrily.

Murad stopped giggling. He just looked at Grandpa.

'Answer me, child!' Murad put his head down and slowly shook it from side to side. He was pulling his sleeves down, as if his sleeves had suddenly grown too short to cover him 'Did you do it?' Grandpa asked again.

'No, no, no, I swear,' Murad said.

'Then who did? Tell me now!'

Murad put his head up and looked at his mother. Aunt Zeynab pulled her scarf off her face and sat up straight, but her eyes were down. Sohrab, Murad's brother, turned red and was playing on his Mother's arm. Murad pointed towards his younger brother, Sohrab.

Sohrab was ten years old. He pushed himself into his mother's arm and buried his head into his mother's breast. 'No, I did not do it,' he whimpered.

'I was on the roof flying my kite, and I saw you were hiding the shoes in the yard, near the plants,' Murad said.

Everyone else stared at Sohrab, and other kids laughed. I laughed too. 'Soh-rab! Soh-rab!' we started mocking. Grandpa told us to be quiet. Aunt Zeynab looked at my mother. Her daughter Shreen walked in front of her and stood there blocking her view. Aunt Zeynab pulled her aside and told her to sit down. Aunt Zeynab turned back to my mother, 'You, widow! Listen to me,' she said shaking her right index finger at her. 'You are very lucky that you only have to wash the dishes, and we have a lady to wash our clothes; otherwise, you'd have to wash our clothes too. And also, for next time, we don't want your sister to come here and stay for weeks on end.' My mother looked taken aback.

Grandpa stood up and looked at Aunt Zeynab. He grabbed Sohrab by the ear and pulled him out of Aunt Zeynab's arms. He took Sohrab to the wall and stood him against it. Grandpa kept twisting his ear and trying to push the muddy shoe onto his mouth, but Sohrab had his mouth shut and kept turning his head away. Grandpa twisted his ear even harder, pulling his head, and said, 'Open it, you ignorant child!' Sohrab complied, and Grandpa shoved the muddy shoe into his mouth, then told him to bite on the shoe and keep his hands up. 'And keep one leg up in the air! Don't let it touch the floor.' Aunt Zeynab then got up and fixed her scarf around her head and without another word grabbed Shreen and left the room.

Grandpa paced back and forth in front of Sohrab. With both hands he played with his rosary behind his back. 'I want you to keep your hands and leg up!' he shouted into Sohrab's ear. Sohrab looked as if he couldn't breathe from his mouth since the shoe was in it. The other kids and I laughed and ran around the room, chanting 'Soh-rab did it … Soh-rab did it …'

Sohrab had tears coming out of the corners of his eyes now. He kept sniffing as if he was trying to breathe from his nose, but now it looked like his nose was instead trying to drain out his tears, as small streams of yellow sticky liquid were bubbling out of his nose and pouring down over his lip.

My sister jumped up and shouted, 'Ohhhhhh,' then she grabbed my mother's head over her torn, chocolate-coloured scarf. My mother smiled and with tears in her eyes and looked at Mina as an angel coming down to promise her hope. She looked at Grandpa and took my sister's hand, 'Let's go,' she whispered to her and left.

Finally, Murad spoke up and told Grandpa that it was his mother who had asked him to do it. He would not do it, so she asked Sohrab to do it. Grandpa turned to Murad and paused. Then a few seconds later he went over to Sohrab and took the dirty shoe away from his mouth. 'Next time, don't be stupid, my son,' he said, and hugged him.

Four

Grandpa built another house in the Kolola Pushta district, about fifteen minutes' walk from the Taymani district. It had two floors; each floor had four bedrooms, a dining room, a bathroom, and a kitchen. There was even a basement. Two years later my uncles moved into their new house.

It was at this time that I started the fourth grade. In my class there were two other Hazara boys, besides me, in a class of about thirty-five students. There was a Hindu and an Uzbek student too. The rest were Tajiks and Pashtuns. On the first day of school, we got a new teacher. The new teacher was Pashtun. She asked the captain of the class to come forward. Since I was the captain, I stood up and started to walk to the front. But the teacher stopped me, 'What? No way is another Hazara the captain of this class.'

A little surprised and not knowing what to do, I stood at attention and introduced myself to her. 'My name is Aftab. I am the captain.'

Making a funny face, the teacher cut me off by holding up her hand. She twisted her nose up and scoffed, 'In every school I have taught, there were always three to four Hazara in each of the classes, and apparently they happen to always be the captains of the classes. Why is that so?' she asked. She waved me to sit down. She snatched the attendance sheet from my hands and gave it to the Pashtun who sat next to me. She spoke to him in his language. Then she announced to the class, 'This year, from now on, Abdullah is the captain. He will make sure you all have your required text books for next week.'

After school I told Mother and Grandpa how the teacher had treated me. 'Abdullah can't even read and write properly, and she made him captain! It's because of these stupid Pashtuns that we Hazara people cannot speak openly,' I complained. 'These Pashtun are the cowards who killed father!'

Grandpa rolled his head back and started to laugh, '*Mash'Allah!* Mash'Allah, Bachem,' he said (in the name of God). 'You are not a fool; you are learning.' And he started laughing again.

My mother stopped washing the dishes and wiped her hands. 'That's it! You are not going to that school any more,' she said. 'Tomorrow we are going to sign you up in a new school.' Grandpa suggested the German school in Wazerakber Khan District. The next day Grandpa took me to that school and enrolled me.

From the fourth grade onwards I attended the German school. The school had been built by the Germans in 1924, and every subject was taught in the German language with the exception of Islam, which was taught in the Dari and Pashto languages. Boys and girls attended from grade one to grade four, but only boys were permitted to attend from grades five to twelve. The school was surrounded by the rich and important districts in Kabul. The majority of the students lived in these surrounding neighbourhoods. They were mostly rich kids, and their parents were elites who worked in high-paying professions, belonged to political parties, or had business backgrounds.

The school was surrounded by fences all around, with one gate. In front of the gate there was a canteen next to the bicycles. An old security guard kept his eyes on the bicycles. On the school grounds were the most beautiful Shegofa trees that I had ever seen. Every year, for the first few weeks of school, these trees would blossom with white flowers, and their perfume would fill the school's classrooms and corridors for weeks on end. There was a huge outdoor football field where we played football early in the morning before class and during breaks and even sometimes after school. There were even a handball court, two basketball courts, and a volleyball court, where the older kids played. There was a small mosque in the middle of the schoolyard. There was also a toilet at the back of the yard for the use of teachers and students. There were a total of ten buildings where the classes were held, and each building had four floors. Inside, the tables and chairs were top-quality wood. Everything was imported from Germany, including the chalk. On every floor there were two classrooms. Each classroom had a sink with running water, and there was modern lighting on the ceiling. There were also a gymnasium, a conference room, an event hall, and a separate chemistry and biology building.

In 1984, at the age of eleven, I began the fifth grade. By this time, the communist government had ordered all the West German teachers to leave Afghanistan. 'The Germans steal the intelligent Afghan students from us,' the government said. 'They teach them the German language, and then they give out higher education scholarships to bring our Afghan students back to West Germany, and then manipulate them to stay there and not come back. They pollute our blood by tricking them into marrying local German women.'

I never had a German teacher, but the German language survived as the school's official foreign language. In the upper grades, called the Amani High School, every student had to learn the German language. However, after the German teachers left, classes were taught in the Dari language. Additionally, we had to learn the Pashtu language. The majority of the students were

Dari native speakers; others spoke Pashto. Other minority groups spoke Hazaragi, Uzbek, Hindi, and Turkish, among others.

A school similar to the Amani High School was built and funded by France in Kabul. Called Istiglal High School, this school's language was French. Every other school's foreign language was English, but during the Afghan communist regime, these schools gradually changed to the Russian language. Many young students did leave to study in Russia; some students from our school left for the communist state of East Germany to continue for higher education.

Five

When Grandpa went out, he usually dressed in black, and wore *qaraqul* hat, as is the Afghan custom. A qaraqul hat is made from the skin of baby lamb. Indoors he liked to dress in white, and wear a thin, small, white hat. We would often have guests that came from Bamyan. They would come spend a few nights just so they could discuss things with Grandpa. Sometimes, if Grandpa left his door open, I could overhear some of their conversation. I would pretend to play, but would actually be trying to hear what was being said. I remember a very nice man who always smiled at me. The Pashtuns had stolen sixteen of his sheep back home in Bamyan. 'Nobody would do anything,' he said. 'Even though the majority of people there are Hazara people, the government is Pashtun.' A week after this incident, another man complained about the same thing; he had gotten himself into a big fight with a government official over paying an absurd and unfeasible tax to the Pashtuns.

For some reason, the Hazara people from Bamyan respected Grandpa. One day I got the courage to ask him about it. 'I even have seen people who are older than you kiss your hand and call you *Khan Sahib*' (a formal title of honour).

'Bachem, our ancestors used to be *khans*,' he said, meaning they had been leaders. 'This means our own people led our tribe in the last few centuries.' He looked at me affectionately for a few minutes, then asked me to come sit next to him, and he held me. 'Do you know why your father went to Bamyan?' I replied no. Grandpa pulled up his right leg, placed his right hand on his kneecap, played with his rosary, and sighed. He leaned his back against the pillow that was attached to the wall he looked straight ahead and sighed again. 'Your father and I were born in Kabul. Your father left because he fell in love with your mother. Your mother was guest in our house in Bamyan. She had come to stay with us one afternoon with her parents. And your father was probably only twenty years old. Your father was the smartest son I had; however, at that time he had nothing in Kabul to care about, so there was no reason for him to stay in Kabul.'

"I don't understand. Why he couldn't he stay Kabul?" I said, needing an answer.

'Patience, Bachem,' Grandpa replied. 'Let me finish. From the first grade to twelfth grade, your father was the captain of his class, and he got a full scholarship to Kabul University to study medicine. And he was going to go too. He was very excited to go; his application had already been accepted by the university. A month before classes were to begin, he received a refusal letter from the Ministry of Education to study medicine.'

'But, why?' I asked.

'He was Hazara. For them, that is often enough reason.'

'Couldn't Father contest?' I asked.

'With whom?' Grandpa said. 'The governments are all Pashtun. He did try, though deep down he probably knew nothing would come of it. Finally they told him that the registration was full for that year and he would have to wait another year before he could reapply.'

'Did he reapply after? I want to know.'

'I think he wanted to, at first anyway.' Grandpa sighed again. 'In the meantime he continued to study the Dari literature. He was also a good poet. He wrote many poems about his love of justice, and of Allah. He was very devoted to his studies. Then your father met your mother.' Grandpa paused. I looked at Grandpa, impatiently waiting for him to continue. 'When he met your mother, his favourite subject changed,' Grandpa continued. 'Now everything was about your mother. Your father lost interest in his studies. He loved only your mother from that point forward. Then finally he quit studying, married your mother, and moved to Bamyan with her.' Also, your father had a conflict with one of his professors, a Tajik who did not like the Hazara people,' he said. The Tajiks are Iranian in origin. 'It was his last year of his studies when he fell in love. Your father said, "These Pashtuns hate Hazara, but why are these stupid Tajiks racist towards Hazara people?"'

As the years passed, Grandma never recovered. She seemed to get weaker, and her skin never returned to the vibrant colour it used to be. Because Uncle Ali went missing, Grandma remained silent. Some days I never heard her talking. We heard her voice only when she coughed, or sighed. Some days she never left her room; neither did she eat or even drink water or tea.

Six

During the communist regime, every member of the Afghan male population between the ages of eighteen and forty had to serve in the military service for two terms. In 1985, when I was in eighth grade, a new policy for serving the military came into practice; because of this new policy, most of our male teachers disappeared from the school's premises. Some of them had to serve in the military service; some of them joined the Mujahideen fighters, a radical Islam group; and some left the country. According to this new policy, every male Afghan citizen had to serve in the military for at least one term. In this era, the Afghan government also extended the military age obligation from the age forty to age fifty. Those who were between forty and fifty and had served two terms had to serve an additional term. Teachers, civil workers, doctors – it really did not matter which professions people were practising. Probably was because of the shortage of soldiers to fight the Mujahideens. On the other hand, some Afghans from Kabul joined the Mujahideen fighters to fight the central government – the communists.

Female teachers substituted for the male teachers who had left for military service. Every teacher we had was a female, except for a few male teachers who were above the age of fifty. Our female teachers were not even qualified to teach; instead of teaching, these women were recruiting the students to join the communist school of thought. Our school opened an office for those students who had joined the communist party. A classroom was turned into a game room with two ping-pong tables, a foosball table, and a few chess tables. Only members were allowed to use this room. Some of these students were sponsored by the communist party from Russia to continue their education in Russia; this was part of the agreement to return to Afghanistan and serve the Afghan communist government. I was told by Grandpa to stay away from anything that dealt with the communists.

I was riding a Chinese bicycle between school and home, which was about twenty-five minutes each way. I had a friend named Jawed; he had lost his father when he was thirteen years old in Panjshir Valley. His father had been a soldier on his first term. We did enjoy each other's company. Sometimes after school, I gave him a ride from school to the bus stop; he sat on the handlebars. Jawed had family members in New York in the United States. Once he showed me his family picture, which had been taken in the States. He always looked forward to emigrating to the States. Jawed had two younger sisters. He was very concerned about his sisters. He was only fourteen years old, but acted mature. He was responsible, and he was the man of the house.

Once Jawed and I were sitting in the shade of a Shegofa tree in the schoolyard in the afternoon. This was in the fall 1986 before the school was closed for the three-month winter holiday. The Shegofa trees were as old as school; their beautiful white flowers bloomed in the spring with exotic perfume. The leaves were light green in the spring. As the temperatures became warmer and warmer, the light green colour gradually transformed to dark green. In the fall, the leaves became colourful – yellow, caramel, red, ruby. On the other hand, the colour of the bark on the trunks and branches transformed through out the year from caramel colour, to chocolate colour, and darker chocolate colour, and eventually turned to black in the winter. That afternoon, Jawed and I diligently discussed whether we wanted to serve in the Afghan communist military, join the Mujahideen fighters, or emigrate to neighbouring countries. Although we were quite young to face any of these unwanted destinies, we had no other option but to take this matter seriously. Jawed was expecting to receive some money from his uncle who lived in New York. He planned to emigrate to Pakistan. From there he was hoping to emigrate to the States and merge with his family members.

For one of the Islamic holidays (Eed), my uncles with their families and two of our cousins came to celebrate. When we had guests in the house, the females stayed in the other rooms. This was in the winter 1986 when Dr. Mohammad Najib was in power. After having dinner one evening, we ate pomegranates. Jamal and Rahim were brothers and third cousins to Grandpa. The guests were between twenty-five and thirty-five years of age. Rahim was the eldest, married with two kids. Jamal had finished his first military service, in the Helmand Province. Jamal was concerned; he had two more years to go before going for his second term. He said, 'Helmand is very dangerous.' He considered himself very lucky to be back alive. 'Khan Sahib, as you are aware, many Afghans emigrated out of the country. What are your thoughts on that?' Jamal asked.

Grandpa was using a white towel to clean the pomegranate juice from his hands. He rested his elbows on his legs while sitting on the mattress. 'It is Allah's decision when and how we will die,' Grandpa said. Then Jamal asked Grandpa's thought on emigrating to Iran. 'Bachem, everyone is a lion in his home town,' Grandpa said. Rahim was playing with a brown rosary. He had a half-full glass of tea in front of him on the carpet. He shook his head said, 'Even the Hazara people have the same Islamic doctrine and practice as the Iranian Shia Muslim, yet are discriminated against because of their physical appearances. The Iranians look down on the Hazara people living in Iran, and consider them as Mongols. The Hazara work very hard to make a living. Most of them work for the construction companies for very low wages. Not only that, the Hazara have difficulties obtaining work permits too. On the other hand, when Tajiks and

Pashtuns emigrate to Iran, they are treated humanely by the Iranians. Even though they are Sunni Muslim, it is much easier for them to obtain work permits.'

'Bachem, you are right,' Grandpa said. 'Wherever we go as minority we will be discriminated against. If we emigrate to India, it is very different. People are open-minded there and respect every religion. I had a friend who lived in India for one year, then emigrated to Canada. I have never heard from him ever since.'

Ghulam was sipping tea. 'The Western world is a much better to live in, and to work in, I agree. I have served in the military for two terms – a total of six years,' he said. 'I cannot believe that, according to this new policy, I have to join the military for the third time. And my eldest son, Murad, and second son, Sohrab, have to join the military in a few months too.' Ghulam shook his head and then stared at Grandpa.

Jamal looked at Ghulam, then at Grandpa, and then looked back at Ghulam, who said, 'Why don't you go? If this was in my hands, I would emigrate to Iran with my family tomorrow, and wait there until the right regime takes over. Only then would I return Kabul.' He looked at Grandpa, and then left the room.

'Because of the war,' Grandpa said, 'million, and millions of Afghan people emigrate to the neighbouring countries. These displaced Afghans want to save themselves from being killed, or having to kill … from being punished, or punishing others. Most of the Hazara people favour emigrating to Iran, because Iran is the only majority Shia Muslim country among the bordering countries. For this reason they prefer to start their new lives in Iran. In contrast, Pashtuns, Tajiks, Uzbeks, Turks, and other ethnic groups emigrate to wherever they can.'

Uncle Ghulam was a tall man. He never grew his beard longer than the length of his neck. He had darker skin than the others, and was very creative in conversation as well as physical movements. Uncle Ghulam loved to laugh, and enjoyed making others laugh at the same time. Any time he had a joke, he would look for people to share it with. Sometimes he told jokes that were not even funny. Most of the time, when he told those jokes, he was the only one who was laughing. Then everyone else laughed at him and asked what was so funny. He would laugh and say, 'Okay, okay, I have another joke.' For example, one of his jokes was this, if I remember it clearly: Once up on time, there were three men in a boat crossing the Persian Gulf – an American, an Afghan, and a Russian. The American pulled a gun out from his under shirt and threw it into the river, saying, 'We have a lot of guns in America.' The Russian man looked at both parties then unlaced his military boots and threw them into the river, saying, 'We have too many military boots in Russia.' The American and the Russian waited to see if the Afghan man had anything to say. All of a sudden, the Afghan man grabbed the Russian man by the back of his neck and threw him into the river, saying, 'We have too many Russians in Afghanistan!' (This joke made everyone laugh.)

Sometimes Uncle Ghulam used expressions and told myths in order to reveal his points. Grandpa never got along with him. He thought of Ghulam as ignorant and looked down on him. Uncle Ghulam at all times thought the only way we could be saved from the discrimination by the Pashtuns was to get out of the country. He told Grandpa that we had enough money, and we must get out; otherwise, we would be killed by the Pashtuns, one by one. But Grandpa was against this idea. Grandpa believed we should wait for the right regime to take over Afghanistan. When this new policy came into force, Ghulam was forty-seven years old and was forced to stay at home (meaning he was hiding from the government officials). Uncle Rustam had another three months before serving the military for the third time. The government of Afghanistan searched for soldiers on the street. House-to-house and shop-to-shop searches were conducted by organized groups of three to four soldiers and a lieutenant to lead them. They wore dark green uniforms and were armed. They had the right to ask for the identification from anyone who appeared to be between the ages of eighteen and fifty years old.

Aunt Laily knocked on the door early one morning. She was shaking. Once Grandpa locked the door behind her, she said, 'My husband did not come home last night.' Poor Grandma was not expecting to hear that Rustam was missing. 'I wanted to report him missing last night,' Laily continued, 'but we were expecting him to come, and he never did.'

Grandpapa asked, 'Where is Ghulam?' and then he looked at Grandma.

'Ghulam has been home since early in the morning' Aunt Laily said.

Grandpa asked me to open the gate. He left our home driving his red Toyota pickup. After twenty minutes or so, Grandpa returned to our house, having picked up everyone from the other house. 'No one is allowed to leave the house,' he ordered, 'and no one is allowed to open the door for anyone. Rustam had another three months.'

Since this new policy had come into practice, Ghulam had been concerned about his situation about going into the military for the third time. In the last few months, Uncle Rustam, with one of Uncle Ghulam's employees, had been taking care of Uncle Ghulam's store. This was in the winter 1986; I was fourteen years old. His oldest son, Murad, who was twenty years old, was a second-year university student. And Sohrab was a seventeen-year-old high school student. We were in the old house again, every one of us, plus three young kids – Timur, Ghulam's youngest son, and Aunt Laily's twin girls. After they had all left for their new house, I had moved to the biggest room.

Grandpa had both hands behind his back, and he played with his rosary as he walked around in his room. His dark-brown eyes reflected his big heart. 'This communist regime will destroy the noble families, especially those of the Hazara people,' he said. Then he took his white hat off and passed his right hand over his thinning gray hair. 'We wait until tomorrow morning,' he said. 'Then we think what we can do.'

Ghulam walked in with his wife and smiled. 'Rustam is young, and I know he loved a girl whose father is very wealthy.' Grandpa shook his head. 'No,' he said. Grandpa did not say much more that morning.

Just as Grandpa walked out from the house to the yard Aunt Laily unexpectedly screamed, 'Grandma!' I ran to see what was happening and saw Grandma lying still on the floor, her green scarf spread out next to her. Aunt Laily carried her from the hallway to her bed.

Ghulam said, 'I know that girl's father. If you want, I can find out if he is with her.'

'You are stupid,' said Grandpa. 'Don't you know Rustam is a revolutionary? He is not stupid. I know that girl's father too. It has been a while since Rustam has seen her.'

Aunt Laily did not know that her husband had a girlfriend. Once she heard that, her body started to tremble. She became very pale, and her eyes were glassy. Wearing a white scarf on her head, she started to walk around in the hallway. She looked at Aunt Zeynab, and Aunt Zeynab smiled at Aunt Laily as if she had been aware of her husband's affair. Then Aunt Laily sighed. She said, 'Oooh, Allah,' and walked into my room.

Grandpa gave a hundred Afghani bill to Sharouch and told him to get six loaves of bread from the bakery around the corner. 'Make sure they are fresh,' he said. Then he looked at me. 'Lock the door behind him, Bachem,' he said.

Grandpa went to his room, and everyone else followed him. He sat on his mattress and repeated his previous words: 'No one is allowed to leave the house, or open the gate for anyone.'

Ghulam sat next to Grandpa. 'We need to go to the city and ask other shopkeepers and friends,' he said.

Grandpa looked at him and said, 'If you go, do you think you will return? They will take you too. You are Hazara. According to this new policy, you must serve for one more term.'

My mother unrolled the plastic tarp (*dastarkhan*) on the carpet; everyone sat around it to have breakfast. My cousin Shreen had the teapot in her hand as she walked into the room, and then my sister Mina walked right behind her holding a tray full of glasses, some with sugar in them. We heard a knock on the door in the yard. I got up to open it. 'Make sure it is Sharouch before you open,' Grandpa said, 'and lock the door behind him.'

Before I opened the door, I asked, 'Who is it?' There was so response, so I asked again.

Then I heard Sharouch say, 'Open the door, you fatherless bastard.' Sharouch had the bread wrapped in a white towel.

I locked the door behind him. 'What do you want from me?' I asked. He walked quickly inside with the bread, and I followed him. Once he arrived in the room and saw everyone sitting around the plastic tarp he threw the breads onto the tarp.

'You stupid *heywan*' (animal), Aunt Zeynab said. 'Have some respect. That is food!' Then Sharouch turned around, and he knew I was right behind him.

Shreen looked at Mina said out loud, 'Heywan!' Then Mina and Shreen laughed. I smiled and said, 'Animal,' and then the kids kept on saying, 'Animal, animal, animal.' Everyone laughed, including Grandpa. It was his first smile that morning.

I passed by Sharouch to sit; he watched everyone laughing at him. His face turned red, tears came out from eyes, and he screamed, 'Where is my mother?'

Aunt Zeynab was pouring the black tea into my glass. 'Your mother is praying for your father to come back home from his other wife,' she said.

'You should go, and take Murad with you,' Uncle Ghulam said to grandpa . 'I need to know if my store is open.'

'Your store – I told you not to give your store keys to your employee,' Grandpa said.

'But Rustam went there only in the evening to pick up the money,' Uncle Ghulam said. 'Then who would have opened my store, if not my employee?'

Grandpa roared, and then uttered 'Ooooof' as he brought out his keys and placed them in front of Ghulam's eyes. 'These are my keys,' he said. 'Almost the keys for everything I own. Rustam worked for me for probably twenty years, and I never gave him my keys, even though he is my son. You are ignorant. I told you this many times. You should have rented out your store instead of leaving someone in charge that you don't know. You are dull. Didn't I tell you I knew someone who was trustworthy who wanted to give a year's rent in advance? But you, idiot, told me, "Oh, no, my employee has an old mother and a young sister to feed." What is wrong with you, idiot? Tell me what do you have? You have a small store, four children, and a wife to feed. If you rented your store, at least you would have money for the next few months to buy food.'

Although, Ghulam was quite naughty with everyone else, he respected his father. He shook his head put his hands up. 'Allah, please save us from this ruthless situation!' He looked at his wife. 'Where is my tea?'

'Tea, tea, tea … Can you stop drinking tea? Find your keys! Find Rustam! Why can't you stop drinking tea? All you do is stay at home and eat, shit, sleep, and drink tea!' Aunt Zeynab protested.

'Can you stop yelling at each other?' Grandpa said.

Aunt Zeynab pointed at Ghulam. 'You see? You see? This old man does not like us. Let's go!' she said.

Grandpa was sitting on his mattress holding a cup of tea in his hand. Suddenly, he smashed that cup against the wall. Sharouch stood up and passed his hands over his clothing. 'Ohhhhhh, glass, glass,' he said. Ghulam and his wife left the room. My mother ran after them and whispered to them in the hallway and took them into the other room.

Usually we kids spent our time running around the house and in the yard playing with marbles or flying kites, but on that day everyone was quiet. Grandpa's radio batteries were dead, so he went out to purchase new ones. He came back after a short while, put in the new batteries, changed his white clothes to black, and left the house without his car. 'I am going to the house of a Pashtun who knows a few people in the government,' he told us. 'If I am not back in two days' time,' he said to Ghulam, 'leave for Bamyan Province.' Then he looked at Murad. Ghulam opened the small door in the gate. Grandpa took off his watch, turquoise ring, and his qaraqul hat and gave them to me. 'They do not like wealthy people,' he said. 'Do not open this door for anybody but me.' And he left our home.

Seven

I had created a library by collecting every book I could find around the house. Interestingly, the most popular book, which was loved by everyone, especially Uncle Ghulam, was a book of Hafiz's poetry; he knew many Hafiz poems by heart. I had gathered about fifty-two books, with both hard and soft covers, small, and big. Some were in Farsi (Dari); others were in English and German. And there were a few dictionaries and magazines. The Arabic books I found were the holy book of Quran, the history of Islam, and a philosophy book. These books had been printed in Iran and had been translated into Farsi. In the house I had found books by Mawlana Jalal-ud-Din Balkhi-Rumi, Nasir Khusrow, Sadi, Firdausi, Attar, Khayyam, and literature from many other Persian scholars and novelists. We did not have any books written in the Pashto language. All the Farsi books had been published in Iran. A few had been published in Kabul, and those were the books my father and uncles had studied during their school years.

I did try to read some of those books, but I did not have the knowledge to understand them. I enjoyed just looking at them and protecting them. I finished reading one interesting novel, which was published in Iran. After I finished reading I realized I had discovered a new pleasure. It was a pleasure that made me smile and made me think creatively. This book was a small book, about 150 pages. It was about a boy who lived with his stepmother after he lost his own mother in a bus crash. Grandpa had quite good knowledge about those books, so when I didn't know words in Farsi, I asked Grandpa. He taught me how to use a Farsi dictionary.

Uncle Ghulam walked into my room and asked his wife to bring him green tea. Uncle Ghulam saw all the books on the shelves against the wall. He scratched the back of his head and looked at me and smiled. 'Wow, all these books,' he said. He lowered his body and knelt on the carpet. He pulled out the book of Hafiz from the shelf. His son Sohrab walked into my room, our cousin Sharouch in tow. Uncle Ghulam stood up with the book in his hand. 'Hafiz … ooh … Hafiz,' he said. He sat on my mattress and lay his back against the wall. Sohrab was holding a cup of tea. 'Is it my tea, Bachem?' Uncle Ghulam asked him.

'No,' Sohrab replied. And then Uncle Ghulam recited a poem in Hafiz and laughed.

While Sharouch was cleaning his teeth and looking at himself in the mirror from all angles, he saw the stereo on my desk. Grandpa's friend had brought it as a gift from Dubai, and Grandpa had given it to me. Sharouch came into my room and began pressing the buttons on the stereo; he didn't want to stop touching the machine. I told him, 'There is no electricity.'

'This belongs to Grandpa,' Sharouch said. Then he touched the tapes. He was holding his tea. I got close to him, then Sohrab passed his tea cup from his right hand to left hand and threw his right hand between us and started giggling. 'No!' he said, and then the tea spilled on Sharouch. He suddenly threw a right punch, but I stepped back. Our cousin Sohrab had been standing in the doorway watching, and could not stop laughing. Sharouch's punch landed on the middle of Sohrab's chest. Sohrab quickly pushed Sharouch with both hands. Sharouch bounced down, and his right elbow hit the left corner of the stereo and cracked it. I grabbed him and threw him against the wall, holding him by his throat.

Uncle Ghulam interfered and a separated us. Aunt Zeynab walked in carrying tray with a teapot and several empty glasses on it. Her eyes grew wide when her foot got tangled in Sharouch's jacket, which he'd let fall to the floor. She lost her balance, screamed, and let the tray go. The tray hit the floor against the carpet, the glasses collided with each other and smashed, and Aunt

Zeynab fell too. The steam from the spilt tea was dancing up. Everyone was quiet – except Uncle Ghulam, who was laughing louder and louder.

Aunt Zeynab had cut her left palm on a few pieces of smashed glass. She started to cry. Surprisingly, Uncle Ghulam stopped laughing and showed a little smile. Aunt Zeynab looked at her palm and continued with her baby crying. Ghulam looked back at three of us, moving his eyeballs from left to right. 'It is because of you,' said. He picked up the jacket, which was still wound around Aunt Zeynab's foot, and threw it against the wall. Then he walked around the smashed glass carefully and put both hands under Aunt Zeynab's shoulders and pulled her up into a sitting position. Holding her palm delicately, he removed the smashed glass pieces one by one. Then he passed his hands over her palm, and helped her to her feet gently, making certain there was no glass nearby. He stared at three of us and motioned with his jaw towards the door. 'Sharouch,' he ordered, 'go and get a pair of sandals for your aunt.'

Just then, Sharouch's mother, Aunt Laily, walked into the room and saw the mess. Sharouch returned with a pair of sandals in his hand. He stared at me. 'We will see,' he said. Aunt Zeynab heard his comment. As she passed her sleeve over her face to wipe her tears, she said, 'That is your jacket, Sharouch,' she said. Sharouch was about to say something, but his mother slapped him on the face very hard. 'Your father is missing! Can you understand? I did not sleep last night, I have lost my appetite, and I feel weak.'

I left my room. My mother walked towards me in the hallway. 'What is wrong between you two?' she asked. 'Every time you get together you must fight.'

Uncle Rustam had served his second military term by the time the new policy came into effect. He was forty-two years old; therefore, he was required by the government to serve in the military for a third time. Rustam was helping Grandpa with business affairs; Grandpa was a wholesaler, a professional businessman. He imported hardware materials, and Rustam delivered them from one store to another. Uncle Rustam looked very much like Grandpa in appearance, but was shorter. He never talked as much as Uncle Ghulam did, and was quite confidential about his private and family lives. Rustam never grew a beard, but he did have a thick moustache.

It was not that late when I heard a knock on the door in the yard. Uncle Ghulam put his right palm on top of his half-full cup of tea, slipped off the mattress onto the carpet, and asked, 'Who could be here?' His son, Murad, had the keys in his hand.

'Maybe it is Rustam,' Ghulam said.

Grandma felt much better when we heard the knock for the second time. 'It is Grandpa,' she said. Ghulam left the room to open the door.

Grandpa walked in and sat on his mattress. He seemed very nervous. 'Insha'Allah, he will be safe,' Grandpa said. God willing. And he asked my cousin Sohrab to put the radio on the news.

Winters in Kabul were not very cold; we received snow only three to five times each winter. It rained in the spring. Also, snow melted on the peaks of mountains, and the water ran down to the valleys creating ponds. Summer in Kabul was dry; it did not rain that much. The tall black mountains surrounded the city of Kabul. The flat planes of the rocks on the mountainside reflected the sunshine into the city of Kabul, which made it even drier and warmer. Most of the houses were made of clay; houses in the rich district were made of concrete and were painted in different colours. We could see the houses on the mountain in the night only, and only if they had electricity. On both sides of the streets in the rich neighbourhoods, old trees grew, creating shade; the roots of those trees reached down towards the water in the land. These huge trees were probably older than Grandpa; otherwise, they would die off in the dry summer of Kabul. Every fruit has its season. For example, in spring we had lots of cherries; in summer, sweet melons were popular. In the fall, we found grapes and pomegranate attractive. In winter, we fed on dry fruits and nuts such as apricots, raisins, almonds, walnuts, and other types of dried fruits. Most of the fruits and vegetables came from outside of Kabul, especially from the southern part of the country.

Every neighbourhood had a spot to dump their trash. The goats, sheep, and donkeys ate what they could from the trash. During the night the street dogs would fight over what was left over, then the dusty wind would come and pick up all the light-weight plastic and paper, and blow it all around the city. Sometimes people searched in the garbage for items to recycle. I never saw a mountain of garbage; it all disappeared before the next morning routinely.

Sometimes Grandpa took us to the towns of Garga and Pagman, and other picnic places, where we gathered and ate kebabs and fruit. We would sit on carpets and drink our tea. In the evening Grandpa would create wrestling matches between us. Uncle Rustam and his friends enjoyed the wrestling. The city was dying. People no longer went to Shari Now Park, where we use to eat sandwiches, kebabs, French fries, ice cream, fresh fruit, and fresh juice. The crowds had vanished from the cinema park and the Zeinab Cinema where they used to line up to purchase tickets for newly released Indian movies. A drastic change had repainted the portrait of a dry

Kabul society. On the corner of every main road there was now a checkpoint, where soldiers searched for young men to serve in the military. And in every corner of the city military bases were established. From time to time, the Russian military trucks and tanks passed through. The Russian soldiers were blond, with blue eyes and green eyes. Some kids would run after the military vehicles, calling out, *'Chocha Shittan!'* (children of devils). The communist regimes were losing power. The Russian soldiers and their military leaders were killed every day; so were the Afghan soldiers. At least one soldier lost his life in our neighbourhood almost each week. Interestingly, the discrimination towards minority groups became less intense. The tension among members of the public was about who was communist (infidel), or who Mujahideen (Muslim). Every ethnic group had created its own political party in the provinces of Afghanistan to fight the communist government.

Eight

As soon as Uncle Rustam vanished, everyone had to stay home, including Uncle Ghulam and his sons, Murad and Sohrab. Even Uncle Rustam's son, Sharouch, who was sixteen years old, had to stay. Grandpa took me with him to the city now and then. Once, as we were driving home, at the checkpoint before entering the Taymani district, a lieutenant, after looking at Grandpa's identification, looked into the pickup truck at me. 'Who is the boy?' he asked with dense Pashtu accent.

'He is my grandson,' Grandpa said.

'How old is he?' the lieutenant enquired.

'Fifteen years old,' Grandpa replied.

The lieutenant pointed the beam of his flashlight onto my face and stared. 'He looks much older than fifteen years,' he whispered, and then he reached into the car through the window. 'Give me his birth certificate,' he said.

'He is just a boy,' Grandpa said. 'He does not have to carry his birth certificate.'

The lieutenant leaned his head through the car window and looked into Grandpa's eyes. 'A boy,' he said. He looked right at me. 'Come out of the car,' he ordered. The lieutenant was a tall Pashtun man with a bushy moustache all the way down to his lower lip. He had green eyes and a big nose. He tapped on the roof of the vehicle. 'Come out!' he shouted.

Grandpa was shocked and got out of the car himself. 'Sir, please, listen, he is just a kid. I watched through the car window. In the dark I could see the lieutenant putting his hand in front of Grandpa's face and pressing his thumb and index finger together, rubbing them back and forward. Grandpa pulled a bundle of cash from his left vest pocket and gave to him, and then the lieutenant shook hands with Grandpa. Just as Grandpa sat in his seat and prepared to drive away, the officer walked back towards us and put both hands on the edge of the open truck. Then he put his head through the window and said, '*Karbalayee (*Karbalayee refers to Shia elders that have visited the Karbala pilgrimage in Iraq*)*, wait.' Grandpa had both hands on the steering wheel. The man looked at Grandpa's watch. 'What time is it?' he asked.

Grandpa looked at his watch. 'It is 9:37 pm.' Then Grandpa pulled his left hand off the steering wheel. The lieutenant bent at his waist. He had the biggest smile on his face, and he looked at another soldier on his right as he tapped his left side coat pocket. Then he said in Pashto, '*Zaa Karbalayee, Zaa!*' (Go, Karbalayee, go!)

This was first time I had ever seen Grandpa scared. He was driving on a bumpy road, and the truck was bumping up and down. He made a fist of his right hand, and ground his white teeth. In the dark, he looked at me. 'Haramzada, haramzada, haramzada!' he said (bastard!). 'He even wanted my watch! I gave him all the cash I had on me.' And then smiled as he faced the road. 'It is over now,' he said. 'This is the last time I will bring you out to the city, and this is last time I will drive to the city.' We arrived at the front gate. He honked on the horn two times, and then Uncle Ghulam ran outside and opened the gate. Through the windshield I could see that Uncle Ghulam had changed. He looked older, thinner, softer, and sadder. He seemed very worried. As I was about to step out from the vehicle, Grandpa said to me, 'Don't say what happened.' I entered the house and saw Aunt Zeynab crying because she wanted to go back to her house, but Uncle Ghulam would not let them walk home. He wanted them to wait so that Grandpa could drive them home. On the other hand, everyone had waited for the whole day to hear from Grandpa about Rustam. Still no one knew where Uncle Rustam had disappeared to.

Grandpa had made a small hiding spot in the outdoor kitchen near the *tandoor* (clay oven). Grandpa had made that spot large enough for three people to fit in. In the beginning of the spring of 1986, in the middle of the day, someone knocked on the door in the yard. Ghulam was working in the yard; his son Murad was in the house, his son Sohrab was eating in the kitchen, and his nephew Sharouch was on the roof playing with his kite. Uncle Ghulam ran into the house when he heard the knocking, and waved at Sharouch to come down from the roof. Ghulam, Murad, and Sohrab ran from the hallway and ran out the back door to the outdoor kitchen. Sharouch descended from the roof. I heard the knocking again, much louder this time. Sharouch was terrified. 'Where should I hide?' he said, and then looked at me.

His mother took his hand and said, 'It is okay. Stay with me.' Then she pointed to me. 'Go open the door before they become suspicious,' she said.

From the yard, I called, 'Coming! Coming!'

When I opened the door, a lieutenant said, 'House search for soldiers.' Then he wrinkled his forehead. 'Are you deaf? Why didn't you open the door?' He walked in through the door, followed by three soldiers. He pointed towards the main entrance of the house. 'Soldiers, go and search,' he said. Pointing his finger towards me, he said, 'Come here. How old are you?'

'I am fifteen years old.'

'Show me your birth certificate.'

'It is in my room; I will go and get it for you.'

'Wait – bring a glass of water too,' he said. I got my birth certificate from my room. Then I went to the kitchen, opened the fridge, and poured glass of water. Aunt Laily was in the hallway holding Sharouch's hand, and one of the soldiers was looking at Sharouch's birth certificate. I walked past them out into the yard with the birth certificate in my left hand and the glass of water in the other hand. I was about to give him my birth certificate when he said, 'No. Water first.' He drank the water. 'Ohhhhhh, cold,' he said. 'Do you have fridge?'

'Yes, yes, we have,' I replied. He took my birth certificate. 'Go get me another glass of water,' he said. I took the empty glass from him walked back to refill his glass. Sharouch's mother was about to cry as she held Sharouch's hand in the hallway. 'He is too young. He is only sixteen years old,' she was saying to the soldier over and over.

I got the second glass of water, and then the officer said, 'You will be sixteen in two months.'

'Yes, sir,' I replied. At that moment, one of the other soldiers came out to the yard waving Sharouch's birth certificate in his hand. He smiled at the officer from a distance. The officer smiled back. 'Do you go school?' he asked me.

'Yes. I am in my ninth grade,' I replied.

'Which school do you go to?' he asked.

'I go to Amani High School.'

'Wow, Hazara in Amani High School,' he said. The soldiers approved Sharouch's birth certificate and gave it to the officer. 'There is another one in the house. He will be seventeen years old in two months,' he said. The officer pointed his chain towards the house and said in Pashto, 'Go and bring him.'

When the soldier got close to the main door he shouted at Sharouch, 'Hazara, Bachem, come out!' When Sharouch got close to the door from the hallway, the soldier grabbed him by the back of his neck and pushed him to the yard. Aunt Laily was holding Sharouch's left hand and was following. 'He is just a boy!' she said. 'He is only sixteen! Let him go!' The officer put his hand under Sharouch's chin and then looked into his eyes. 'This is good,' he said.

The other two soldiers came out of the house to the yard. One of them pointed towards a window of the house. 'There is another room behind this room. There are an old women and two young girls. We didn't see anyone else,' he said.

'Did you go around the house?' the lieutenant asked the soldier.

'Yes. There is an outdoor kitchen and a tandoor. No one is inside,' the soldier replied.

The lieutenant looked at Grandpa's vehicle. 'Whose truck is this?'

'This is Grandpa's,' I replied. He returned my birth certificate to me and put Sharouch's birth certificate in his pocket. Aunt Laily started to cry. 'No, no, no … my husband disappeared three weeks ago, and now my son …'

'Shut up, and stop crying, you ugly Hazara,' the soldier said. Then he tried to open the passenger's door of the vehicle, but it was locked. 'Where is your grandpa?' he asked.

'He is in the city at his store,' I replied.

'Why didn't he take his car?' he asked.

'He could not find gas,' I replied.

'Ohhhhhh, that is true these days. It is not easy to find gas,' he stated.

The two soldiers stood, one on each side of Sharouch, and the lieutenant said, 'Let's go.'

Sharouch's mother, Aunt Laily, was not able to stop crying. She held onto the officer's right arm with both hands. 'Officer, please, please, I beg you. His father disappeared, and I am sure the soldiers have taken him. Please let my son go. He is only sixteen. In two years he will join the military, but not now.'

The officer looked at Aunt Laily. 'Now it is seventeen years old,' he said. 'No.' Then he took off his hat, scratched the back of his head, and then leaned his back against the vehicle and faced Sharouch. 'What grade are you in?'

Sharouch replied, 'I will start my tenth grade.'

'Which school?' he asked

'Omer Shaheed High School.'

Then he smiled. 'Who was your mathematics teacher last year?'

'His name is Allam Khan,' Sharouch answered.

The officer pressed his teeth together. 'He was a good friend of mine,' he said. 'He died last winter fighting the *ashrars* in Kandahar' (gorilla fighters).

Sharouch eyes blinked. 'No way,' he said.

'Yes. I use to be geography teacher in Habibya High School. I do not want to serve the military either, but I have to because of this new policy.' Then he asked one of the soldiers to pull Sharouch's pyjamas up to his knee. 'Look at all the hair on his leg, and look at his moustache,' he said. 'And you think you are a boy!'

The soldier standing to the left of Sharouch laughed. 'For a Hazara boy, he has a lot of hair on his legs,' he said. 'Some Hazara men have no hair.' The other soldiers started to laugh at his comment.

Sharouch's mother had both eyes on the officer. She put her hands on her face. 'Please, please don't take him.' And she kept on repeating the same words.

'Okay, okay, okay. Because he is student of that school, I will leave him, but only if you make one promise.

'Sure, sure,' she said.

'In two months your son will officially be eligible to serve in the military,' he said. 'Even so, my superior ordered us to bring in even those who will not officially be eligible to serve for another five months. I will let him go, firstly because his mathematics teacher was a good friend of mine, and secondly because his father went missing – if you are not lying,' the lieutenant decided.

'God bless you,' Aunt Laily said. 'I swear my husband had another three months before being eligible, and one night he never came home.'

The officer shook his head. 'Yes, I understand,' he said. 'The soldiers take them before their time to train them at the military base. Once they are officially eligible, they give them two options. The first option is called *Maharibee*, and the second option is *Germaharabee*. The Maharibee is two years of service, but outside of Kabul. The Germaharabee is four years of service in Kabul; they are not sent into war.

She sighed. 'Thank you. I pray to Allah to give long life to you and to your children,' she said. Then she went inside and came back with two hundred Afghani. 'Officer, please take this and buy yourself a cold drink or whatever,' Aunt Laily said. 'Thank you very much for your understanding. I think you are a very good person.'

The soldier who had been standing with his back against the wall walked closer. 'Only two hundred? What about us?'

The other soldier said, 'Yes, yes. Especially these days the price for everything has gone much higher. No, no, sister. It is true. With two hundred we cannot even purchase food or soft drinks for four of us. Keep your money.'

The same soldier who was saying that the price had gone up then said something to his command officer in Pashto, which I did not understand. Then he lifted his right hand into the air and turned his body towards the door. The officer looked at Aunt Laily and smiled.

'Wait, wait,' she said. 'I will ask Grandma if she has money.' She walked into the house.

One of the soldiers taped Sharouch on the shoulder. 'Son, bring me a glass of water,' he said.

Then the commanding officer said, 'Son, bring water for everyone. We have been walking all day. The officer looked at me and said, 'You are young, and Amani High School has a good programme that gives students scholarships to get out of the country. Use this opportunity,' he recommended.

Aunt Laily appeared with another 250 Afghani, in total, 450 Afghani. 'This is all we have,' she said.

The officer was laughing. 'It was not necessary,' he said.

Then the same soldier who had turned his body to the gate said, 'I will take it. Thank you, sister.'

Sharouch came out of the house with four glasses of water on a tray and handed them around. The commander had a sip. 'Ho, it is not cold!' he said.

'We lost electricity this morning at around ten,' Sharouch explained, 'and there is no more cold water in the fridge.' The commander did not drink the water. He left the glass on the roof of the car, and finally they left.

Once I locked the door behind them, Sharouch ran to the outdoor kitchen to let Uncle Ghulam and his sons know it was safe to come out of their hiding place. Right after I unlocked the door, his daughter Shreen left to go to her house to inform her mother what had happened. An hour later, we heard knocking at the door again. We were sitting in Grandpa's room sipping tea. Murad stood up. 'Oh, no, again …' he said.

'Wait, wait,' Grandma said. More knocking. 'It is Zeynab,' she said, and she kept on coughing. Grandma was almost always able to tell who was behind that gate, just by the way the person knocked. I unlocked the door for Zeynab. Uncle Ghulam left the room.

Once Zeynab came in we all spread around the house in different rooms. She was loud and seemed miserable. 'Ghulam, Ghulam, come here. We need to talk,' she said.

Uncle Ghulam had a book in his hand as he walked into Grandpa's room. 'Be quiet, you stupid woman!' he said to his wife, then he raised his voice. 'I know what you want to say. You want us to go Bamyan. What we going to do there? There is nothing but mountains, rocks, and sheep. I cannot live in Bamyan. If you miss your parents, go, go … take the children and leave.' I had never seen my uncle that angry or as loud. 'I want to go to Iran, but you don't want to. And this stupid, stubborn Grandpa won't allow us to leave for Iran.' He pointed at Murad. 'Tell me … tell me what else you want to say, huh, huh? When your stupid girl, Shreen, left this house today, she did not even ask my permission,' Uncle Ghulam said. He punched on the door next to him. 'I am tired. Can you see? For almost five months I have not even been able to even go next door!' he said.

Aunt Zeynab stood up. 'You cannot even make decision,' she said. 'Yes, I will go to Iran. Let's go, let's go.'

Aunt Laily walked into the room. 'Please don't fight,' she said. Then she pointed her finger towards Zeynab. 'You must be very thankful to Allah,' she said. 'My husband disappeared, and soldiers came and almost took Sharouch with them today. You have your husband and your children, yet you are not happy.'

Aunt Zeynab got closer to Aunt Laily. 'Your husband … oh, your husband, who has many girlfriends, and does not want to talk about anything … always quiet … no one knows what other thing he does. Maybe he has another wife and children, and he has left you!'

Aunt Laily screamed, 'Be quiet, you whore!' Then Aunt Zeynab attacked Aunt Laily and pulled her hair down. Sharouch put his hand on Aunt Zeynab's hand to release his mother's hair from Aunt Zeynab's hand. But Ghulam broke up the fight.

Aunt Zeynab spoke: 'You calling me whore! Ah, you are younger than I. You should have respect for me. I have treated you like a younger sister at all times.'

Uncle Ghulam smiled at Aunt Laily. 'It is okay,' he said to Zeynab. 'It is okay. She talks like that at all the time.'

'What I am concerned with and what she is concerned with,' said Aunt Laily, 'are two very different things.' Then she left for the other room.

Aunt Zeynab looked at her son, Sohrab. 'Bachem, gather all the dirty clothes. I will take them to the other house to wash. I am scared in that big house with the children. Please help me to bring them.'

However, Uncle Ghulam said. 'He is not going anywhere. He is seventeen years old. With this new policy, soldiers are allowed to take even seventeen-years-old too.'

She sighed. 'Why did I have all these children if they cannot help me?' These fights, arguments, and discussion were not new in the family, but they were happening a lot more, and they were a lot more extreme, especially, since Uncle Ghulam had started staying at home and Uncle Rustam had gone missing.

In the evening, once Grandpa arrived, Aunt Laily explained everything that had happened that day to him, word for word. Ghulam and his two sons were looking at Grandpa as if it all was his fault. Aunt Zeynab, who did not want to spend time in our house, actually came that night with her children and had dinner with us. After dinner that night, we drink tea. Grandpa and Uncle Ghulam and his immature children had a serious discussion. In Grandpa's presence almost no one was able to say anything against him, or his decisions. This time, however, Aunt Zeynab blamed Grandpa by saying, 'Every bad thing which happens in this house is because of you.'

Grandpa was not expecting to hear this. 'What? What? What did you say?' he screamed at Aunt Zeynab.

Then Ghulam said, 'Yes, yes, Father. It is your fault, because you do not allow us to get out of this horrible country. A year ago we wanted to emigrate to Iran, then Murad had a chance to go to Russia to study. Even Rustam wanted to serve his third military service in the Baghlan Province where he knows a family. One of the family members is a general, and Rustam is a friend of the general's brother. And you did not let him. Now he is missing!'

Grandpa calmed down and took up his rosary. Then he put it back down and looked into Ghulam's eyes. 'Listen, both of you.' Then looked into Aunt Zeynab's eyes. The whole family was on one side of the room, all leaning against the wall. Grandpa looked back at Ghulam. 'Yes, two years ago you wanted to go to Iran, but your wife wanted to go to Bamyan. In the case of Murad going to Russia, I am against that, because we are Muslim. This war is about Islam and communism. Why do you think I listen to Iran radio? When I went to Iran for the first time, about fifteen years ago, I was lost. I had never seen such a big city in my life.'

'Why did you not let him to go to Russia?' Zeynab said.

All of a sudden, Murad got up and screamed out loud, 'Why, why, why?' His voice became louder. Then his father, Uncle Ghulam, slapped him really hard. Then he touched the face of his other son, Sohrab. Then he got up and pushed Sohrab too. Sohrab's arms were open, and he went down onto the carpet.

I was sitting next to Grandpa, and he was laughing. He kept on laughing and laughing. But then Sohrab's right hand hit the light, and the room became dark. The other light was still on at the end of the room. Grandpa got close to the other Chinese light, and kept on laughing. When Murad got up and attacked Sohrab, Ghulam stopped the fight. Grandpa was over his laughter and had begun to cough. He returned to his mattress and resumed his laughter. And then Grandpa asked me to bring the other lantern from the hallway. When I got back with the light, I saw that Sohrab's face was scratched and bleeding. Little Timur, son of Guhlam and Zeynab, came and sat on our side of the room between Grandpa and me. After a few minutes, no one was angry with Grandpa. Everyone was quiet. Grandpa asked where Laily and her children were. Timur pointed towards the wall and said, 'In that room.' Shreen left for the other room. Her mother yelled at her, telling her not to go there, but she left any way.

Ghulam was shaking his head, and he smiled at Grandpa 'Three of us hidden in that hole for almost forty-five minutes!' he exclaimed. 'They almost took Sharouch, but his mother bribed the officer. Then Murad farted in the hole. We could not move. There was no oxygen. I was out of breath, then I choked!

All of sudden, Murad started screaming, 'That was not me! That was Sohrab, and look he is fat!' Sohrab had a towel on the scratch part of his face. He just smiled.

Sharouch came from the other room and stared at everyone trying to figure out what was going on. Grandpa asked Sharouch to sit down. 'You are blocking the light.'

Murad was thin and tall like his father, but was not as talkative as his father. Then Ghulam shook his head. 'Your grandpa is right. Russians do not have faith in Allah, and they are against Islam. If I were in your grandpa's shoes I would have made the same decision, Bachem. Most Pashtuns and Tajiks do send their children to Russia, but we are Shia Muslim.' Then Ghulam looked at Grandpa and said, 'Father, I can no longer live like this. Either I have to go to Iran with my family, or I have to join the military.'

His wife, Aunt Zeynab, interrupted and said, 'You do not like anybody.'

Ghulam yelled at her to be quiet. Aunt Zeynab turned her face and left the room. Ghulam, acting very humbly, said, 'Okay. Zeynab does want to go to Iran. She admitted that today.'

'It is much harder and a lot more expensive these days to find a trustworthy smuggler,' Grandpa said. 'Most of the food comes from outside of Kabul, and the price for everything has gone up. On the other hand, there is no business here. I have the stock stored in the city, and no one wants to buy anything. Now Rustam is missing also, and your store is locked too. If you go Iran, you will not have enough money to open a shop, and your kids cannot work for those Iranian construction companies. The work would be too harsh for them. Look at them – they have never worked in their lives! They are spoiled *Kabuli* boys.'

Sohrab threw a piece of cloth onto the carpet. 'Of course I can work hard,' he said.

Ghulam taped on Sohrab on the back. 'Good for you, my son,' he said. Then Ghulam put both of his elbows on his knees and looked at Grandpa. 'How much does the smuggler charge?'

'It is not about the money, Bachem,' said Grandpa, 'it is about trust. Some smugglers take families and leave them on the mountains, or in the desert, and steal everything they own. Sometimes even they kill the families or sell the children in Pakistan. So it is matter of trust, Bachem.'

Aunt Laily was refilling Grandpa's tea cup. 'Ohhhhhh ya, Allah,' she said.

'Anyway, I will keep this in mind, Bachem,' Grandpa said.

'I know my neighbour knows a good smuggler,' Ghulam said. 'He smuggle people into Pakistan. I don't know if he could smuggle to Iran. Should I ask him?'

'No, no, no. This is not a joke,' Grandpa said. 'You have to know the person. Only then can you trust him. I will speak to a good friend of mine who is Hazara, Shia. I am sure he will find me a good smuggler.'

Grandpa asked Aunt Zeynab to prepare him some water so that he could wash and pray. Ghulam touched his face and pushed up his moustache. 'Yes,' he said, 'Pakistan. Pakistan is good too. There are some Shia there. We should go there, and then find the community, and a mosque. There are many Afghan and Pakistani Shia in Peshawar. I also know a family who are waiting to emigrate to Canada. That is a very good opportunity. At least there is a hope, and we would have our Pakistani Shia brothers and sisters. I am sure it is better for everyone, and at least there is no war there.'

When Grandpa got back from praying, this is what Ghulam proposed: 'This is very good idea. Of course, there are many Shia mosques.'

Grandpa passed the rosary from one hand to the other, then polished the rosary against the carpet. 'I visited Pakistan twenty years ago,' he said, 'and I attended the mosque.'

Uncle Ghulam had a half-full teacup in his hand, and he emptied it on the carpet.

'What are you doing?' said Grandpa. 'Watch the carpet! This is a twenty-five-year-old Turkmen carpet! The older it gets, the better it becomes. It's top quality!' Grandpa eyeballed Uncle Ghulam.

Uncle Ghulam sighed and said, 'I cannot even go to the mosque to pray. Praying is good. I love it.'

Boys from the age of six started to attend the mosque in our family. It is place to worship Allah. By the age of seven I had learned the five pillars of Islam, and had memorized the Ten Commandments. We were taught how to read the Holy Quran in Arabic, and how to recite prayers. In the winter season, the schools were closed annually for a three-month holiday. On Friday evenings, special prayers were held in our mosque. Only the male population of the Shia members attended our mosque. When the new military service policy came into effect, we were not even able to attend Friday evening prayer ceremonies, because our praying ceremony took place at around seven in the evening, when soldiers were out on the streets looking for young men to serve in the military. On every corner of the main streets, and at all intersections, there were military posts. Kabul was about to die. There were two other Shia mosques, but we did not attended them, because Grandpa had conflicts with their Shia practices and doctrines. Grandpa attended the new mosque, which was linked to the council at the Shia headquarters in Pakistan; the leaders of this new mosque were Hazara. Three different mosques followed three different doctrines and practices. The majority of the worshipers of these three different mosques were Hazara from different provinces of Afghanistan, while there were thousands and thousands of Sunni Muslim mosques across Kabul.

Since Rustam disappeared, Grandpa's attitude had changed towards Ghulam. Grandpa actually listened to him. When Zeynab was absent, Grandpa advised Ghulam not to listen to his wife. 'Pakistan is a much better place than Iran for your family to live in, because – Insha'Allah – you will be fine. You should realize that we are not rich. My business and many other businesses are closed down. This new policy has changed everything. The prices for food have gone up, and the value of Afghani currency has gone down. I use to have a lot more money four years ago than I have now. I built the house you and Rustam live in four years ago. These days no one will buy a house. Even if I could find a buyer, I couldn't get even half the money back that I spent building that house. I have come to a decision. I will keep the house, and I will manage to pay your expenses in Pakistan. Whatever merchandise is have left in your shop, I will sell. I will try to rent your store. If I cannot find anyone to rent it, it is always better to keep it locked rather than have employees run the business, Bachem.'

Aunt Laily was a quiet lady, and she became much quieter after Uncle Rustam disappeared. When there was nothing to do around the house, she spent her time praying in a quiet room. A few days after our serious conversation, Grandpa started to look very nervous. From the day Uncle Ghulam decided to go Pakistan, every evening he waited for Grandpa's arrival; most of the time it was Ghulam who opened the door for him. In the dark I noticed him smoking cigarettes sometimes. It was not safe to go into the yard during the day. Most of the time we asked Shreen to go on the roof as a lookout before we went out to the yard to use the toilet. It was because of our neighbours. We could not trust anyone. Four of us had to stay in the same house day and night. Uncle Ghulam played his *Danboora* and sang for us. The Danboora is our traditional stringed musical instrument, which has a base and long neck. Two long strings extend from the base all the way to the end of the neck. He placed the base right between his legs and held the end of the neck in his left hand. He used his two right fingers to pluck the strings of the instrument. Uncle Ghulam sang Hafizes poetry and Hazaragi traditional songs. He was very good at playing Danboora.

Aunt Laily was the chef in the house; she was a very good cook, especially when we had guests. Then Aunt Laily cooked the best rice and meat curry with spinach. Sometimes she added carrots, raisins, almonds, and pistachio nuts to the rice. It was super tasty, and we called it *Pallow*. She always asked for help when she wanted to prepare *Mantoo* or *Ashak*. She made the dough and then divided it into small balls. She flatten each ball of dough and then used a rolling pin to make the dough as thin as possible. Then she used the lid of the teapot to cut the dough into small circles on the plastic tarp. We would help by placing small portions of cooked food right in the middle of the dough circle; this food was made of ground beef, onion, garlic, salt, pepper, and other spices. Then we would close the circle of dough around this mixture, pinching the dough together so it wouldn't come apart. After that, we would boil them in water until the dough was cooked.

Nine

Uncle Rustam and Aunt Laily's twin daughters were identical. Paree and Negar grew their hair long, and if they did not wear different outfits, it was not easy to distinguish one from the other. Both were sweet and very tough. I never saw them fighting. They were seven years old when their father went missing. They came to their Grandpa's house two or three times a week. Sometimes both fought with their older sister, Ziba; it was fun to watch them. As soon as the twins mentioned their father's name, everyone became quiet. Then both of them went to sit with Grandpa, one on each side. 'Allah will find your father, Insha'Allah.' Grandpa used the same expression every time we wanted to know about Uncle Rustam.

One summer evening in 1987, Grandpa entered the house carrying a big black bag. In the presence of Grandpa everyone remained silent. We gathered around him every evening, and tea was ready before his arrival. 'Is everyone good in the other house?' Grandpa asked.

'Shreen was here today,' Aunt Laily replied, 'and everyone is good. And we need flour to bake bread.'

'Of course, Bachem. Tomorrow,' Grandpa said, and then he passed his hat to my mother and scratched his head. Uncle Ghulam sat close to me. Grandpa spoke to him. 'Listen to me. It is very important, my son.' Everyone gathered around him to listen. 'Close the door,' he said, and then he looked at every one of us, and sipped his tea. 'This is not hot,' he said. 'Why are you serving me warm tea?'

Sharouch called out loud, 'Grandpa's tea is cold!' He was sitting next to Sohrab. Sohrab pushed Sharouch's head so hard that his head touched the wall and bounced back. Then Sharouch stood and threw a right punch at Sohrab while he was sitting on the mattress. I saw Grandpa laughing out loud. He laughed louder, then Ghulam was laughing. Murad broke up the fight between the cousins. Sohrab's face turned red after he received that punch in the ear. He stood up, but his brother, Murad, grabbed both of Sohrab's hand. 'I saw it. I saw it,' Murad said. Grandpa was laughing.

Ghulam wanted to know what Grandpa wanted to say. He pointed at Murad. 'Take your wrestler outside, and shut the door behind him,' he ordered.

Grandpa looked at Sharouch then laughed. 'Sohrab is a wrestler. Do not play with him. And he is older than you. Have some respect, Bachem.'

'He is older, and a wrestler, but I still can fight him. I can kick!' Sharouch said. Sharouch had a blue belt in taekwondo; actually he was good. On the other hand, Sohrab was a wrestler – a member of the Hazara wrestling team in town.

'Why don't you say something?' Uncle Ghulam asked his father. 'What is this bag for?'

'It is very hard to find a trustworthy smuggler in Kabul,' said Grandpa, 'but in Jalal Abad it's easy to find a trustworthy smuggler. And from here to Jalal Abad there are three checkpoints, and the region from there to Pakistan is controlled by the Mujahideen – then you don't need to show identification. From here to Jalal Abad, I found a smuggler.'

'When are we leaving?' Sharouch asked.

'You are not leaving,' Grandpa said; then Sharouch left the room.

'Shut the door behind you,' Ghulam called. 'When are we leaving?' he asked.

Grandpapa whispered. 'Tonight, Bachem.'

Ghulam was shocked. '*Chi?*' (what).

'Yes, tonight,' Grandpa restated.

Sohrab walked through the door, and Murad was right behind him. Uncle Ghulam moved to the end of the mattress, and Sohrab sat next to him. Grandpa gestured at Grandma to leave the room, and then he looked at me after he looked at everyone else. Grandma walked out, leaving the door wide open. Grandpa pointed at me. 'Go shut the door, Bachem,' he said. He took a piece of black towel from his right side pocket and said to Murad, 'Bachem, bring the big bag that I brought today.' Murad returned with the big bag, Sharouch walking into the room right after him. 'Not you, Bachem,' Grandpa said, 'and close the door behind you.' Sohrab's left ear was still red from Sharouch's punch. Sohrab wanted to ask Grandpa's permission to stay, and Sohrab was about to get up and fight him. He wanted to revenge badly. But Grandpa took his hand. 'Sit, Bachem.' Then he spoke to Sharouch. 'Go and shut the door behind you.' Sharouch slammed the door behind him. Grandpa yelled, 'You animal! You are going to break the door!'

'Let me go and show him, Grandpa. Let me go,' Sohrab said.

Grandpa unzipped the big black bag. We were surprised when he took out two knives, which were wrapped in pieces of cloth. 'Listen,' he said. 'I want you to prepare your family to leave for Jalal Abad. We will leave this morning at around three o'clock. I am going to drive you to Jalal Abad, and the smugglers are going to come with us. They have taken care of the three checkpoints. If the soldiers at the checkpoints ask where are you going, Ghulam, you must say, "My son is getting married in Jalal Abad." The smuggler will be sitting next to me in the front seat,' Grandpa said.

'Are you coming with us?' Ghulam asked.

'Yes,' Grandpa said. 'I am going to drive you until Jalal Abad, and from there your smuggler has arranged for another smuggler to take you into Pakistan.' Grandpa gave his pickup keys to Sohrab. 'Bachem, go and clean inside the truck. Wash the windshield inside out,' he said.

'Father, your vehicle has no gas,' Ghulam said.

Grandpa laughed. 'You don't know your father, Bachem. It is full of gas!' Then he stopped laughing. 'At midnight, I am going to drive to the city to pick up Omer. I will bring him here, and he will explain everything. Then we will leave at three in the morning. I have to clarify a few things first,' Grandpa said.

Grandpa passed one knife to Ghulam and the other knife to Murad. 'Take these,' he said. 'If anything happens to you on the way, use them.' Then he unwrapped the small black towel he had removed from his pocket. There were six black pieces smaller than kidney beans. 'If anything happens which frightens you, or if anyone touches your wife or children, ask your wife and children to swallow one of these, Bachem,' Grandpa said, then he sighed.

'Grandfather, what are these?' Murad asked.

'Bachem, these are poison capsules. It is always good to die rather than to have someone touch you or your sister.' And then Grandpa said, 'Bachem, you have to watch over your sister, your mother, and your brothers.'

Ghulam asked, 'If Zeynab or my children don't want to swallow the poison, what should we do then?'

Grandpa said, 'You have to force them. You are the head of your family, and they have to listen to you.' He looked at Ghulam and his son Murad. 'You two listen to me very carefully. I am going to give each of you three of these. Carry them with you, with your knives. If anything happens to your father, Murad, you are in charge of the family. Hide the knives and the poison somewhere in your clothes, and keep them on you at all times.'

This was serious. As time passed, I discovered more and more about Grandpa, little by little.

'No one should know about the knives or poison – not even Sohrab,' Grandpa said.

Just then Sohrab walked through the door. 'I need someone to hold the flashlight so I can see inside the car to clean,' he said.

'Where is Sharouch?' Grandpa asked.

'He is asleep in the other room,' Sohrab replied.

Grandpa covered the poison capsules with his hand. 'Go wake him up,' he said to Sohrab. 'I need to talk to him.' Then Grandpa looked at Uncle Ghulam and Murad. 'Hide your knives,' he said. Then he put the poison in his pocket. 'Wait, wait – I am not finished,' Grandpa said.

Sharouch felt isolated, and he missed his father, Uncle Rustam. The minute he arrived in the room, he passed his arm towards his face, 'What do you want?' he asked Grandpa.

'Bachem,' said Grandpa, 'go and hold the flashlight for Sohrab, and prepare water for everyone. We need to pray, my son. And close the door behind you.' The minute the door was closed, he again brought out the poison capsules, and counted them one more time. Grandpa gave three capsules to Uncle Ghulam, and then gave the other three to Murad. 'Do not forget what I said,' Grandpa said, and he put his hands up and prayed to Allah, 'Please do not make my children use these.'

Grandpa addressed his son: 'Ghulam, Bachem, after we have finished praying tonight, around ten o'clock, leave for your house. Prepare every member of your family to leave. Be here at three o'clock. Don't walk on the main street. Use the shortcut.' He pointed towards the south side of the room. 'Use that street,' he said. Grandpa, Ghulam, Murad, and I created one straight line, with Grandpa in the middle. He recited a few verses from the Quran, then he asked Allah to take them safely to Pakistan. After praying, Grandpa brought a piece of paper out of his vest coat. 'This is the address of one of our Shia brothers who lives in Peshawar. Once you arrive there, call this number.' Then he asked Murad to write the same address and the telephone numbers, and keep them with him. 'Do not lose these. Be very careful.' Then Grandpa faced me. 'Bring a glass of water, Khan Bachem,' he said. 'I am thirsty. Ghulam leave now. Don't say anything to Sharouch. And, Sohrab, tell them to wash the inside of the truck properly. I haven't driven in almost five months. Bring everyone from the other house to this house,' he said.

After I served him a glass of water, he said to me, 'Go and lock the gate behind your uncle.' By the time I got back, Grandpa was already in the middle of conversion with Sharouch and Sohrab. Grandpa was talking about maturity and unity in the family. For example, he told them, 'We are not even one percent of this country's population, and we are not communist. We don't have a good leader to fight the communist regime. Even if we emigrate to Iran we will be a minority. We just have to survive the way it is, and there is no justice.' Then Grandpa looked at the three of us. 'You are my grandsons,' he said. 'I do not like to see you fight one another.' He looked into Sohrab's eyes 'Bachem, listen to your father, and to your older brother. Anything they say, you must perform accordingly.' Then he said, 'My father had three sons and a daughter. My sister was the oldest. She married an Iranian about forty years ago, and her husband took her to Mashhad, Iran. My other two brothers were killed by the Pashtuns in Helmand Province. The Pashtun, wherever they find the Hazara, will kill them, Bachem. In the last two centuries, the Pashtun have killed the Hazara people not only because they are Hazara. They have also killed them because we are Shia people.' Sohrab lifted up his clothes and started to scratch his body. 'Bachem, go and wash your body,' Grandpa told him. 'You are going on a long journey, Bachem.'

Sohrab was lying on his back on the mattress. He looked at Grandpa as if he had not seen him for a very long time. 'Grandpa, why now?' he asked.

'You are going to Pakistan tonight, Bachem,' Grandpa said. ' Sohrab got up quickly, as he wanted to fight. Then he left. Sharouch tapped on the carpet. 'What about me, Grandpa?' he asked.

Grandpa looked at the door to his left, 'Shut the door, Bachem. You have to be persistent. Leave me alone, Bachem,' Grandpa said, then he sipped his water. 'Tell your mother to cook a lot of food, Bachem.' Grandpa took a nap.

Aunt Laily had a contract with a Tajik baker lady. The deal was that the baker baked our bread and hers in our Tandoor, and we provided the firewood. Luckily, the lady had baked bread that very day. Aunt Laily gathered all the bread, and she cooked mutton curry with rice for dinner. There was a knock at the door. I ran to get the keys from Grandpa, who was asleep. We always had to turn the keys in to Grandpa if he was in the house. 'Bachem wait, let our visitor knock again.' As we heard the knocking again, he passed me the key. 'It is Ghulam, Bachem,' Grandpa said.

Aunt Zeynab had worn the most expensive cloths she had, yet she seemed worried. Murad wore the jacket that Grandpa had given him last year. His sister, Shreen, was thirteen years old at the time. Rustam and Laily's son, Timur, was only a little boy, and he even wore his winter hat. Grandpa took up his rosary and started to play with it. He looked at Ghulam. 'Take all the jewellery from your wife. And Pakistan is much hotter then Kabul; therefore, do not overdress.

'Murad, go and wash your body,' Grandpa said.

Uncle Ghulam stared at Murad, 'I washed my body after you, Father,' Murad said.

Aunt Zeynab wore three rings, earrings, and four gold bracelets. She took them off and passed them to Uncle Ghulam.

'Take your turquoise ring off, Murad, Bachem, and give it to your father,' Grandpa said. 'Ghulam, hide this jewellery. People are thieves.' He handed money to Ghulam. 'Here is twenty-five thousand Calder, which is a lot of money in Afghan currency,' he said. 'This should be enough for four months. Then, Insha'Allah, I will send you more money. But be very careful, and do not lose anything. We live life once, Bachem, we must live with pride,' Grandpa said.

Grandpa looked at everyone in the room, and then he pointed at the big black bag. 'Just fill this bag with whatever is necessary to bring,' he said. He then brought out another bundle of Pakistani money and gave it to Murad. 'Bachem, if you split in two groups, you must lead one group and your father will lead the other group.' He looked at his watch. 'We will pray one more time before I pick up Omer,' Grandpa stated. Everyone prepared to pray. Grandpa sat in the middle, Uncle Ghulam, Murad, and Sharouch sat on his right side. Sohrab and I sat on Grandpa's left side. Timur and Shreen sat beside their mother and made a back row.

Grandma was asleep, Aunt Laily was cooking in the kitchen, and my mother was helping her. We faced to the West as usual and prayed. Grandpa recited the verses of the Quran from his memory and then asked Ghulam to bring the Holy Quran. Grandpa found the verses in the book that were about travelling, and recited them out loud. At the end of praying, we kept our palms up in front of our faces. Grandpa made special request on behalf of the family from Allah, asking Allah to bring his children to their final destination safely. We whispered, 'amen.' Once praying was over, Timur stood up. 'I am hungry. Are we going to eat to night?'

Grandpa started to laugh. 'Come here, my Timur,' he said. We unrolled the dastarkhan onto the carpet, and we ate rice with lamb. Then Grandpa asked Ghulam to gather all the leftovers. 'Your family is going for a long journey,' he said. Then he addressed Sharouch: 'Bachem, go to the other house and stay with the children.' Then he addressed Aunt Laily, Aunt Zeynab, and Shreen: 'Whatever Ghulam and Murad say, you must do accordingly.'

They all nodded their heads. 'Yes, yes,' they said.

'Now go into another room and rest,' Grandpa told them. 'Within four hours, you will leave.'

'Ya Allah, ya Mohammed, in four hours,' Aunt Zeynab said, and then she tapped Shreen's back. 'Bring Timur into the other room,' she said.

Grandpa stood up, 'I am going to get Omer,' he said to me. 'Make sure women do not get out of the rooms. Open the gate, Bachem,' and then he tapped on my left shoulder. When I came back to the house, I noticed that my mother, Aunt Laily, Grandma, and Aunt Zeynab were sitting in a close circle, whispering to each other. When they saw me standing next them, my mother smiled and spoke to me: 'Bachem, go. This is women's talk,' she said.

Murad was walking around in the hallway, and then he went out to the yard. Sohrab was lying on his back on Grandpa's mattress. Uncle Ghulam walked out of the bathroom with a towel on his head, then he touched his face, 'I shouldn't have shaved,' he said. Then he gently kicked the bottoms of Sohrab's feet. 'Bachem, get up and get ready,' he told his son.

At around 12:45 a.m., I heard the sound of Grandpa's truck's horn, and I noticed the reflection of the truck's lights behind the gate. Aunt Laily was passing the broom over the carpet in Grandpa's room. 'No women!' ordered Uncle Ghulam. 'Stop sweeping!' He pointed to another room. 'Stay in that room, and don't come out!' he said. Murad was still in the yard in the dark. Uncle Ghulam opened the gate so that Grandpa could drive in. I saw a huge man in a military uniform sitting next to Grandpa in Grandpa's pickup truck. 'Go and prepare tea, Bachem,' Uncle Ghulam said to me.

In his room, Grandpa offered his mattress to his friend to sit on, and Grandpa sat across from him. The minute Omer sat down, he pointed at Uncle Ghulam. 'I have seen you before,' he said.

'Yes, I have seen you with my father a couple of times,' Ghulam said.

Then Omer waved his hand and asked Ghulam to sit next to him. 'Don't be scared, my son. I have known your father for thirty-five years.' Then he looked at Grandpa. 'It is true, right?'

'Yes, it is true,' Grandpa said.

'Your father is very ambitious, smart, and a very tough old man,' continued Omer. 'We were soldiers in Kandahar Province during King Zahir's reign. Although the Hazara people were not allowed to attain any position higher than soldier, your father became lieutenant in our military base. He was the first – and the only – Hazara lieutenant. I remember he had five soldiers under him, one of whom was Hazara. Two were Tajiks, and three were Pashtuns.' And then he started to laugh. 'I was one of those Pashtun soldiers!' Omer said.

'The stupid one!' Grandpa said. 'Karbalayee … Karbalayee,'

Omer said something in Pashto, and then Grandpa said something in Pashto; both started to laugh. It seemed they had shared interesting adventures together. Omer extended his hand towards Grandpa and shook hands, still laughing. Then he spoke to my uncle. 'Ghulam, listen, your father speaks better Pashto than I speak Dari.' We were sipping tea, then Omer got up. 'I need to use the toilet,' he said. Grandpa pointed at Ghulam to show him the way to the toilet, and to provide Omer with a flashlight. Omer came back with the flashlight and resumed his seat. 'Karbalayee,' he said to Grandpa, 'your house is very clean, and you have covered every inch of the floor with all these beautiful carpets.'

Sohrab had set his feet on the carpet, and leaned his back against the wall. 'Sit properly, Bachem,' Grandpa said.

Then Omer looked at Sohrab and asked, 'What is your name, Bachem?'

'Sohrab,' he said.

'Ohhh … are you a wrestler?' Omer asked. Sohrab looked to his left and then to his right, and then straight ahead. Omar said, 'Your ears are broken from all those training sessions?' Omar's voice was loud, and he spoke Dari in thick Pashto accent. 'Some of you Hazara are incredible,' he said. 'I remember one of you made King Dawood very proud.' He scratched his head. 'Oh yes, Pahlawan Nasser Jowally earned the first gold medal in Afghanistan in a wrestling tournament in Iraq. That was probably fifteen years ago,' Omer said. 'On the other hand, one of you Hazara kids shot one of our kings in his mouth!' And then he stared to laugh. 'Your Grandpa used to be a good wrestler too. I remember when we were soldiers, your Grandpa loved to wrestle. You see how big I am? He was able to pound me!' Omer had a very big nose, and his thick moustache covered his lower lip. His teeth had turned into a dark brown colour, and every fifteen minutes he lit a cigarette and then coughed.

'We are here to do business,' Grandpa said. 'Leave politic aside.'

'Karbalayee, I remember, even back then, you always rejected talking about politics and religion,' said Omer. 'Why, Karbalayee? You are an Afghan, and a Muslim. Why not—'

Grandpa interrupted him. 'Yes, because we will never come to an agreement. Anyway we will be ready at three in the morning. Now explain to Ghulam how you will help him to get from Jalal Abad to Pakistan,' Grandpa suggested.

'Okay, Karbalayee, be tolerant,' said Omer. 'I miss you, and I like you. You used to be my superior in the military,' he said, chuckling.

Then Grandpa touched his beard and said something in Pashto to him. Omer tried to sit properly. He still had the smile on the face. He looked at Grandpa, stopped smiling, and said, 'Okay, okay. Ghulam, Bachem, you are six passengers: three boys, a girl, your wife, and yourself, right?' he said.

Uncle Ghulam nodded his head and said, 'Right.'

Omar placed his right palm on Ghulam's left knee. 'You have to trust me. Your father will drive us from here to Jalal Abad. You and I will sit in the front of the truck. The rest will sit on the backseat of the truck. We will not have any problems at any checkpoint we pass through until we reach Jalal Abad. From Jalal Abad to Pakistan you will have to travel on foot. It is about twenty hours with women and children. The smuggler will provide two donkeys. The first donkey is for your luggage, and the second donkey is for children and women who cannot walk long distances. The people who will be leading you to the Pakistan border are my cousins. For that reason, you do not have to worry. Insha'Allah, three days from now you and your family will arrive in Pakistan. In addition, I have family in Pakistan. They can find you a good place to stay,' Omer stated.

'No, no,' Grandpa said. 'Forget about helping Ghulam and his family in Pakistan. They will be fine once they reach Pakistan.

'It is all about trust, Ghulam,' Omer emphasized. 'You have to trust me.'

'If I did not trust you, do you think I would have invited you in my house?' Grandpa stated.

'Karbalayee, you have a good pickup truck. I always wanted to have vehicle like yours,' Omer said.

'Yes, I have had this pickup truck for seven years, and never had an accident or any mechanical issues,' Grandpa said.

'I know, and it is so convenient,' Omer said. 'Two seats like ordinary cars, plus space in the back to carry whatever.' Then he laughed. Omer spoke some more in Pashto. Ghulam understood and looked at Grandpa.

Grandpa became quiet for a few seconds, and then Omer responded in Pashto: 'Karbalayee, I have been in politics for forty years and more. I am Pashtun. Don't you think I have the potential to pass your family safely to Pakistan?'

Grandpa replied in Dari, 'I have already paid you half of the total amount, and now you want my truck.'

'Karbalayee, in Kabul I am a communist, and outside of Kabul I am a Mujahideen,' Omer said. Then he started to laugh again.

'Yes, I know you Pashtuns are hypocrites,' said Grandpa. 'But my little truck is valued five times more than the amount we agreed on to smuggle my kids to Pakistan.'

'Karbalayee, if you gave me your vehicle, I guarantee your son and his family will appear in Peshawar in two days safely.' Omer thought, and then took his military hat off and scratched his head. 'I will give back the money you have paid, but I want your pickup, and I love the red colour, oh, oh, oh …' Omer said.

Then they spoke in Pashto. Ghulam understood what they were talking about. Grandpa said, 'There is only one condition – that you take these six people to Pakistan safely. Keep the cash I gave you. I will give you the pickup truck. In addition, I will give you a carpet as soon as I hear that Ghulam and his family have arrived in Pakistan in one piece.' Grandpa passed his palm over the carpet and than tapped on it a few times as he eyeballed Omer.

'Karbalayee this is our land, Afghanistan. Even I have cousins who are Pakistani,' Omer said, and then he laughed. Omer took the last cigarette from the pack and asked Grandpa to show him the pickup. Ghulam took the flashlight, and Grandpa followed him. Omer walked out. Murad followed him, and I followed Murad. Omer had the cigarette between his lips and was searching for matches in his pockets. Grandpa passed the keys to Ghulam so he could turn on the truck. Then he left the flashlight in the car.

'Do you hear the engine?' Grandpa asked Omer. Omer had used his last match, and he threw away the empty pack of matches on the driveway. 'No more light,' he said. Omer looked at Murad in the dark. 'Bring me matches,' he said.

'No, no,' Grandpa said, and he opened the front passenger door and pressed on the cigarette lighter. When the cigarette lighter bounced back, Omer lit his smoke and smiled. Omer grabbed Grandpa's hand, and they both walked around the pickup in the dark. In a few minutes, Omer sat in the passenger's seat. Grandpa said to Ghulam, 'Prepare to leave in thirty minutes. Bring your luggage here in the yard, and don't forget the food. Omer and I will go to the city; we will be back very soon.' Grandpa and Omer left for the city in Grandpa's pickup truck.

Timur, Shreen, Sohrab, Murad, Uncle Ghulam, and Aunt Zeynab were ready to take a trip with a nervous sense of right and wrong. Not even twenty minutes passed before we heard the sound of a heavy military truck while we were in the yard. Then someone knocked at the door. Grandpa walked in through the gate, and Omer, wearing his military uniform, was right behind him.

Aunt Zeynab had covered herself from head to toe; so had Shreen. A soldier, who had Kalashnikov rifle on his shoulder, waited in front of the gate. Grandpa asked Ghulam and Murad to follow him to the corner near the tomato plants. I had the flashlight, so Grandpa asked me to hold the flashlight close to his face. 'Bachem, look into my eyes,' he said. 'Do exactly what I have told you. Do not trust anyone. The deal that I have made with Omer is that you do not have to walk long distance in the mountains. Once you get to Pakistan, call my shop. This is the only way, Bachem,' Grandpa said.

Then we walked back towards Omer, who was pulling the black bag. 'It is so heavy! What is inside, gold?' Omer said, then laughed again.

'No,' Uncle Ghulam whispered, 'there are two carpets and some clothes. It is okay. I will carry it.' And Murad picked up the other side of the bag. Sohrab unlocked the door, then Omer exited the door first, then Ghulam exited backwards and faced Murad, who was holding the bag. Murad returned with his father after placing the bag in the military truck.

Grandpa motioned to Sohrab, requesting him to lock the door. 'Listen, all of you,' he said. The curtain of the window moved a little while Grandpa was talking, then Grandma came out of house crying. My mother and Aunt Laily were not happy to see Ghulam and his family leaving. Aunt Laily had big, glossy almond eyes. My mother and Grandma were both crying, as they would never see the family ever again. On the other hand, Aunt Laily had a light in her eyes. She was patient, and even more contented for them to leave for Pakistan. She was playing with her rosary and mumbling to herself.

Uncle Ghulam was standing next to Grandma, holding his mother's right hand and kissing it. 'Ghulam, Ghulam,' Grandma said out loud. It was a quiet and a very dark night. The loudness of Grandma's voice made everyone look at her. Omer knocked on the door said something in Pashto.

Grandpa said, 'Laily, can you calm her down?' Aunt Laily took Grandma's hand and led her towards the house. Then Grandma leaned towards my mother. 'Soraya, Bachem, come inside,' she said. My younger sister, Mina, was twelve years old in 1997; she was standing next to Ghulam and aunt Zeynab, and Shreen were covered head to toe looked like statues, then Grandpa said 'Mina, go inside the house, Bachem.' First, Uncle Ghulam kissed Grandpa's hand, then Murad and Sohrab did the same. Grandpa kept on kissing Timur's cheek.

Omer said something in Pashto behind the door.

'Okay, okay,' Grandpa said. 'All of you listen to Ghulam and Murad.' Then very softly he said, 'Do not tell the smugglers where in Pakistan you will be going. Ghulam, Murad, you have the address. Call first, then find the address. Everything I have told you, do it accordingly.' Grandpa laid out his orders. Murad had tears on his face. 'Don't cry, Bachem,' Grandpa said. 'Men never cry.' He asked me to open the door. When everyone had gone out, I saw a big Russian military truck. Two soldiers were helping the family to climb into the back of the truck. Uncle Ghulam got on last, and the soldiers lowered the cloth tarp and locked the back of the big truck. Grandpa was talking to Omer and showing him his pickup trucks keys. Omer was tapping on his chest in the dark.

Grandpa came back into the house as soon as the military truck left. The way Uncle Ghulam's family left had been like a dream. It had happened so fast; it was not even two in the morning. I thought about the nervous eyes of Aunt Zeynab, the suspicious eyes of Shreen, and the honest smile of Sohrab. The whole family had disappeared.

Ten

Grandpa did not go to the city for a couple of days; he kept on buying new batteries for his old radio, and he listened to the Iran national news. Sometimes the reception on his radio was not clear, the harsh sound of static passed through the house and vibrated the walls. Then he would grind his teeth. Once the voice of the reporter or the sound of the music was clear, he would get excited: 'Oh, oh, oh, it is good now!' Or he would just pray in the corner of his room on the prayer rug.

Two days after Uncle Ghulam and his family had left for Pakistan, after breakfast, Grandpa went out for a walk. He returned after a while and asked me to call Aunt Laily for him. 'Laily,' he said to her, 'go and bring your girls from the other house. Tell Sharouch to stay there and wait for me, even though there are no soldiers on the streets.'

'Okay, Grandpa,' Aunt Laily replied.

Grandpa opened the door for Aunt Laily to leave for the other house. Then he asked me to lock the door behind him. 'I am going to the store to buy groceries,' he told me. 'Lock the door, and don't open it for anyone – and you know what I mean.' In a very short time, someone knocked at the door. 'It is me, Bachem,' Grandpa said. I unlocked the door for him. 'I have to drive to the city, Bachem. We need a lot of food, and fresh food,' he said. He retrieved the grocery list from my mother, and he drove off to the city. I was in my room and noticed that the book of Hafiz was missing from the shelf; therefore, I started to search for it. Finally I could not find it anywhere in the house. Aunt Laily arrived with her children, 'Uncle Ghulam took the Hafiz book with him,' she said. 'That was his book.'

Because of the instability of the middle school and the high school, Grandpa did not allow Laily's daughter, Ziba, my sister, Mina, or I to attend our schools, but Laily's twin girls Negar, and Paree were taken to their primary school every morning, and they were brought back from school by their mother in the afternoon. Their school was in Tymani district, a ten-minute walk from home.

That evening, Grandpa arrived from his shopping expedition. When I opened the gate for him, he expressed happiness, yet he seemed nervous. Once he got out of his vehicle, he asked everyone to see him in his room. As I locked the gate, I saw that Grandpa was washing his hands and face. Mina was pouring water on his hands in the yard. Everyone waited for Grandpa in his room; we knew Grandpa had something important to share. Aunt Laily never stopped praying on her rosary, and she was expecting news from her missing husband. 'Close the door,' Grandpa said. Then he looked at everyone and asked, 'Where is Grandma?'

'She is asleep in the other room,' Laily said.

'It is okay. It is okay,' Grandpa said. 'Ghulam and his family have arrived Peshawar this afternoon.' We were impressed yet anxious to hear more from him. 'Yes, yes, and they are in good hands. They found the address I gave them. I spoke to Ghulam on the phone. They are settled in Pakistan.' Then he took a sip of tea. 'Ghulam told me that Pakistan is not far,' he continued. 'They had to switch vehicles in Jalal Abad, then a few hours later they arrived

Pakistan. Everyone is fine, Ghulam told me.' And then Grandpa said, 'Omer is very powerful. He did not travel with them. I saw Omer in the city hall this afternoon, as I promised him I must give him my vehicle.' Grandpa looked at his watch. 'At ten this evening I have appointment with Omer in town. He will then drop me home, and he will keep the pickup truck.' Finally, he put his hand up and recited a verse from the Holy Quran, and thanked Allah.

After prayers, Grandpa said to me, 'Go, Bachem, roll all the carpets in the house and place them in the back of my truck.' I asked him why. 'Just do what I say. We do not have that much time.' Then he pointed at Aunt Laily. 'We are going to remove every valuable item from this house and take it to the other house. We will leave this house empty for a while. These dogs are hungry. I am afraid they will come tonight or tomorrow to rob us. I can feel it,' Grandpa said.

'Grandpa, we just brought everyone from the other house today, even their clothes. Can we not leave this until tomorrow?' Aunt Laily suggested.

'No, no, it has to be tonight,' said Grandpa, 'because we will not have the vehicle tomorrow, and it is risky to spend the night in this house.' All of sudden, we heard a knocking at the door. Every time we heard that sound, especially at night, we were all frightened. Everyone was silent and looked at Grandpa. The knocking continued. We remained quiet. 'I think it is Sharouch,' Grandpa said. Grandpa walked to the yard and waited for the third knock. 'Ohhhhhh, it Sharouch,' Grandpa said, and he unlocked the door. Once Sharouch got into the yard, Grandpa put his fingers under his chin and tilted his head up. 'Didn't your mother tell you to wait for me?' Grandpa said.

'It's dark, and I was hungry,' said Sharouch. 'I thought you had forgotten about me.'

'Go, go. Help Aftab,' Grandpa said. 'Help him roll up all the carpets in the house and place them in the back of the pickup truck.' Sharouch was hungry, so he went to the kitchen to eat. Grandpa looked at me. 'Bachem, go and start rolling the carpets. Just leave the red Turkmenistan carpet in my room; that is for Omer. I promised him.' And then Grandpa said, 'Wake up your grandma, and tell everyone to wear their shoes. Get ready to leave for the other house, and bring my radio. Put it inside the vehicle.'

Grandma, Aunt Laily, and my mother were searching the house and collecting the valuable stuff. Grandpa saw that my mother had folded all her clothes, my sister's clothes, along with Grandpa, and Grandma's clothes on a bedsheet, and Aunt Laily was helping her to tie it up. Grandpa came up to them. 'Leave these,' Grandpa shouted. 'I said valuables – all the carpets first.'

Sharouch, when he found out that Uncle Ghulam and his family had arrived Pakistan, got upset and kept on asking his mother, 'What about me? Why doesn't Grandpa send me? Do you want me to disappear like my father?' Then his mother, Aunt Laily, slapped Sharouch very hard. Sharouch started to cry. Tears were falling from his eyes, yet he continued to help roll up the carpets and place them in the back of the pickup truck. When we were finished, we had about fifteen carpets in small, medium, and large sizes.

'It is enough,' Grandpa said. 'Not too much. I am afraid the checkpoint soldiers will search, so do not overload the truck. If I have time, I will come and pick up the rest of the stuff,' Grandpa said. Then he walked off with a flashlight and disappeared into the outdoor kitchen. He returned with a locked metal box, which he put into the vehicle. Grandpa asked everyone to get in the truck. 'Sharouch and you, Aftab, Bachem, stay in the house. Do not open the door for anyone. Turn off all the flashlights. Stay in the yard, not in the house, and wait for my arrival. If I am not back in two hours' time, I want you both to leave for the other house. If you see something suspicious, or if anybody climbs the wall, I want you both to go on the roof, then jumped onto the neighbour's roof, and then descend onto the road and go to other house. Run in the dark, Bachem. If they come, they will not come in military dress. They will dress like a bunch of thieves, and they will not run after you or fire their guns at you. Therefore, be aware and keep the main door locked at all times.' Soon, they left the house.

Sharouch had his back against the wall in the dark, and then we went in the house to turn off the flashlights. Sharouch brought out playing cards. 'Let's play a card game,' he said.

No, no. Let's turn the lights off and wait for Grandpa in the yard,' I said. Sharouch did not listen; he kept on shuffling the cards. 'Don't turn off the light,' he said. Then he looked me straight in the eye and smiled. 'If I tell you a secret,' he said, 'would you keep it to yourself?' I had no interest in talking to him, and he pressed the issue: 'Promise me you will not tell anyone,' he said with a smile.

The way he was talking to me made me curios to find out what he had to tell. 'No, no,' I said.

'Just don't tell Grandpa,' he said. 'Last week I won Sohrab's two hundreds Afghani, and the day he left for Pakistan we gambled again, and Sohrab won all my money by cheating. When I punched him on his ear, I did it because I was mad him. I will never raise a hand to the elders in the family,' he said, and then he started to laugh. 'Sohrab is in Pakistan now!' He kept on laughing.

'Yes, Sohrab is in Pakistan.' I repeated, and I tried to turn off the light.

'No, no. Wait! It is too early,' he said. He made a funny face, giggled, and then he smiled. 'Do you want to know something about our cousin Murad?' Sharouch kept on laughing.

'What? Tell me,' I said.

'Don't tell Grandpa.'

'I will not tell anyone.'

'Murad had sex with our lady neighbour,' he said, and he laughed even more. This made me laugh too. Then he put his hand on my right shoulder. 'You are Grandpa's son, and we know he loves you the most,' he stated. He turned off the lights and put his playing cards into his pocket. 'Let's go outside. In the dark, we can lean against the wall, and I will tell you things you don't know, Bachem' Sharouch said.

I had the key in my hand, and I followed him in the dark. He leaned his back against the wall and sighed. 'Khan Grandpa is bullshit!' he said. I was shocked. I had never heard anything like that from any family member. Sharouch started to talk about his father going missing, and about Grandpa not letting Sharouch continue his education in Russia. He spoke about his friend who had shown his family pictures to him, which had been taken in Germany. Sharouch picked up a rock and threw it against the wall. 'It is all Grandpa's fault! He does not allow us to leave Afghanistan,' Sharouch said. It was a quiet night. Then we heard dogs barking and fighting over leftover food in the garbage.

All of a sudden, the dusty wind came and blew the dry dust into our noses and eyes. We were surrounded in swirls of dust and wind within a second. We were under attack! Dust was everywhere; it was impossible to breathe. Sharouch ran into the house, and I followed him. We entered the hallway in the dark. Because of the moonlight outside, we could see a little. In the hallway, we began to shake our clothes to get rid of the dust. Sharouch slammed the outside door hard to stop the dusty wind from blowing into the house. I walked towards Grandpa's room. Before going through the door, I took off my shoes, then I walked towards the big window to see outside. Sharouch came in and stood right beside me. He pointed at the moon. 'Look at the moon,' he said. Plastic bags and papers in different colours were dancing in the light of the moon. 'Look – the kites are flying,' he said, and we started to laugh.

But just then we heard knocking on the door. We looked at each other and started to run, but neither of us had our shoes on. We ran towards the hallway to get our shoes. We heard more knocking. Sharouch ran towards the ladder to climb on the roof. Because I was nervous, I had difficulty in finding my second shoe. I hadn't even been able to tie the one I had found. Then I heard the knocking for the third time, but it was much louder this time. I heard Grandpa's voice: 'It is me! Open the door!' I ran with one shoe on and unlocked the door for Grandpa. When he got in the hallway, he took the box of matches and lit the lantern. Then he noticed that Sharouch was barefoot, and I was wearing only one shoe.

He shook his head. 'Why, why?' he asked. 'What is this?' We tried to explain to him what had happened. First he got really upset, and then looked at us and said, 'Go bring the other light and light it.' Then he said, 'You both have red eyes, and dust in your hair and on your faces. Go and wash your faces and hair. You look like ghosts.'

We cleaned ourselves up, and came to see Grandpa. He was still laughing. Then he took the light, walked into my room, and saw my stereo and tapes. He looked at my bookshelves and sighed. 'Take your stereo,' Grandpa said. He walked into my mother's room; he passed the light up and down around the room. He looked on the shelves, and then saw the two antique swords which were hanging against the wall. He asked Sharouch to take swords down. We followed him to his room, shone the light around and saw the sewing machine. Then he shook his head. 'Okay, let's go.' Then he turned around saw his TV set. 'We forgot to bring the TV, but we took the radio. I will come and bring it to other house tomorrow. It is too dark to carry it all the way,' he said. Then, one by one, we climbed the ladder to our roof. From there we walked onto to the neighbour's roof, then we descended to the street. Because of the moonlight, Grandpa walked in the shade of the walls and houses along the street, and every two or three minutes, he looked behind him to check on Sharouch and me, making sure we also walked under the shade of the walls and the houses. After twenty minutes or so, we arrived the other house.

Early in the morning, I heard grandma talking to Grandpa about their son Ghulam and Ghulam's family. Grandma asked Grandpa, 'Talk to Ghulam today. I want to know how they are.' Grandpa said, 'I do not have their phone number. They have to call me.' Grandpa walked down the stairs, and my cousin Ziba walked into the room in which I had spent the night. 'Breakfast is ready, and my mother told you not to go on the balcony,' she said. I was sleeping in Sohrab's room, on his mattress, and had spent the night under his blanket. I saw a photo of Sohrab against the wall. In it he was wearing his red wrestling uniform. I heard Grandma say, 'Aftab, Bachem, come down.' When I descended to the first floor, I saw that the plastic tarp was unrolled on the floor, and everyone was sitting around it – except Grandpa and Uncle Ghulam and his family. Grandpa walked into the house with some bread. He put the loaves on the plastic tarp, and then he touched the one on the bottom. 'This one is not fresh,' he said.

After breakfast Grandpa talked to Sharouch and me. 'Listen,' he said, 'do not go out of the house. Don't go in the yard or on the balcony or on the roof. Don't trust anyone.' Then he looked at everyone and addressed his daughters-in-law: 'Laily and Soraya, unroll all the carpets and cover my room with those two.' He pointed to the ones he wanted. 'I am going to the city to buy groceries,' he said. He looked at me. 'I need you, Bachem, to bring the TV from the other house tonight.

'Okay, Grandpa,' I said.

'I want to go too,' Sharouch said.

The minute Grandpa left the room for the city, Aunt Laily took his the keys and followed him to lock the door behind him. Sharouch tapped me on my left shoulder. 'Come with me,' he said. I followed him to the second floor. He walked into Murad's room and opened Murad's closet, where he searched through Murad's books and notebooks. 'Maybe he has taken it,' he said. 'I want to show you something you have never seen, Bachem,' he said. Then he walked towards Murad's mattress and pulled it up. He even pulled up the carpet. 'It is not here,' he said. He turned to his right, looked at closet, and opened the other closet door and searched the pockets of Murad's jackets. 'It is not here,' he said. 'I am sure he has taken it with him.'

I was curious. 'What you are searching for so impatiently?' I asked.

'Wait, wait!' he said. Then he put his hand against the back of his head and rubbed it back and forth two or three times. Sharouch looked to the left corner of the room and walked towards it. He picked up the corner of the carpet and pulled it back. 'I found it! I found it!' he said. 'Close the door, Bachem,' he said. When I got close to him, I noticed he was sitting on something. 'No, no. Stay at the door and make sure no one comes in,' he said. I saw him looking at a page of a magazine, then he turned his face towards me. He was all exited. Sharouch had had a big smile on his face, which had turned in red colour.

I heard Aunt Laily called our names. 'Come down and carry a few carpets upstairs,' she said.

I looked at Sharouch and saw him hide the magazine again and replace the carpet. He walked towards me. 'I will show you later. Don't touch that; it is mine,' he said, and then smiled. I followed him down the stairs, and we carried some carpets up the stairs. We made one trip. I followed him back down the stairs. 'Let's bring all of them. That way we can see,' Sharouch whispered into my ear. I had no idea what was he talking about, but he acted totally different, and he walked up the stairs much faster than he had on our previous trip. For the third time we walked down to bring carpets upstairs.

'These two go to your Grandpa's room,' Aunt Laily said. 'And they are heavy, so take one each.' As we were drugging the heavy carpets up the stairs, Sharouch whispered into my ear, 'I can't believe you don't know!' We dropped the carpets in Grandpa's room, then he stood at the door. 'Go and see it,' he said. 'I will watch the door.' I walked into the room and pulled the carpet back. There I saw the pictures of naked blond women on the page of a magazine. This was the first time I had seen the nude body of a woman – everything … I mean everything. Then I heard Sharouch saying, 'You found it! You found it!' And then I heard him again, 'Why don't you talk? You saw it! You saw it!' Then he peeked through the door and saw me sitting on the folded carpet looking at that page. He started to laugh, and then covered his mouth with his right hand and lowered his head. He smiled. 'Now it is my turn, Bachem,' he said. He kept the smile on his face and got close and eyeballed me, and shook his head. He started giggling.

Every time we heard a knock at the door, we remained quiet in our rooms, because the soldiers searched the houses to find men who were eligible for military service. Our childhood days when we were free to eat fresh fruits and play with our marbles and kites and football balls were over. I heard the knocking when we were in the basement. Sharouch was practicing taekwondo, and I was kicking the football ball against the basement wall. Sharouch looked at me. 'Stop kicking the ball!' he said. We even stopped all physical movements and waited to hear the knocking for the second time. When we heard it, Sharouch ran up the stairs, and I ran after him. I saw everyone gathered in the hallway, and Grandma had her finger on her lips. 'Shhhhhhhh,' she said. Then she put her finger up said very softly, 'One more knock.' In the hallway the twins were playing with a ball. Paree was passing the ball to Negar, and Negar was throwing the ball back to Paree; their cousin Ziba was watching them. The small rubber ball suddenly slipped off Paree's finger and rolled and touched Ziba's left foot. Negar stepped forward to pick up the ball. Ziba slapped Negar very hard. 'Stop it!' she said. Then Negar started to cry. Grandma shushed her again as we heard the knocking for the third time. 'It is baba' grandma said, right after, we heard Grandpa calling, 'It is me. Open the door!' Aunt Laily thanked Allah. 'It is Baba,' she said, and as she ran to open the door, she smiled at everyone with her glassy eyes.

Everyone one carried a grocery bag full of food. Grandpa walked into the hallway. 'We are going to eat delicious goat, Sharouch,' he said. Grandpa walked up the stairs to his room. Sharouch and I followed him. Grandpa walked across his favourite carpet. 'The older it gets the better it will become,' he said. My little sister, Mina, walked into the room with a teapot and three glasses on tray. While we were having tea, Grandpa pointed at me. 'We are going to the other house when it gets dark,' said. Then he looked at Sharouch. 'Bachem, you stay home. We must bring the TV from the other house.'

'What are we going to do with TVs?' asked Sharouch. 'There will be two TVs, and uncle's TV is bigger than yours. And there is no electricity!'

'Bachem, I like my TV,' Grandpa said, and he smiled at Sharouch. 'I don't want anyone to find out we are hiding you, Sharouch Bachem. This evening I will go to pray in the mosque. When I return and have eaten dinner, we will leave for the other house. I have something else to bring too, Aftab Bachem,' he said. Before leaving for the mosque, Grandpa advised us pray to Allah.

Right after Grandpa left for the mosque, Sharouch sat close to me. 'Do you want see the sexy photos again?' he said, and he left the room. There was no electricity; we relied on the flashlights. There were two on the second floor, and four on the first floor. We ate *Shorba* when Grandpa came back from the mosque. Shorba is soup. Pieces of bread are soaked in the soup, and the vegetables and the meat are served on top of the soaked bread.

After dinner we drank our tea, and Grandpa started to laugh about what had happened the previous night. He laughed and laughed right after he mentioned Uncle Ghulam. Then he put his hands up, 'Allah, thank you. We are grateful that Ghulam and his family arrived safely in Pakistan. Allah, please find Rustam, and my youngest son Ali, if they are alive.'

Aunt Laily walked out from the room, and Ziba followed her with her long, flowing hair. Little Paree followed Ziba, and Negar stood up and was about to leave the room, but Grandma pulled her down by her arm. Sharouch was leaning against the concrete wall, and had stretched his legs out in front of Grandpa. He looked into Grandpa's eyes. Grandpa opened his right fist towards Sharouch. 'Go call your mother,' he said.

Grandma stood up. 'I will call her,' she said.

Aunt Laily came in and sat close to Grandpa, who then spoke to her: 'Laily, Bachem, I have no idea if Rustam and Ali are alive. It has been almost one year that we do not have news about your husband's wellbeing. People come and go. I know Rustam is literate and physically strong. Maybe he is somewhere outside of Kabul. The only thing that can be helpful in this case is to pray.'

In a very soft voice, Aunt Laily said, 'I pray every morning, and evening.'

'You must pray all the time,' Grandpa said. 'Have a rosary in your hand. Mention the name of Allah, and ask for forgiveness. Ask Allah to send your husband alive.'

Aunt Laily shook her head in silence. Grandpa looked at his watch. 'In ten minutes we go to the other house.' He looked at me. 'Don't forget to wear both shoes,' he said, then started to laugh.

'Last night you two were supposed to be ready to run if the thieves came to the house, but neither of you had no shoes on.' He laughed, then pointed at me. 'Khan had one shoe on!' As he laughed, everyone joined in, even the twins and Grandma.

Grandpa and I managed to walk to the other house safely. When Grandpa took out his key to unlock the main door, we noticed that the door was already unlocked. He pushed me back. 'Stay against the wall,' he said. He peeked through the unlocked door to see if anyone was in the yard or in the house. Then he turned his face towards me. 'Did you lock the door last night?'

'Yes, yes,' I replied. 'I locked it from the inside, and we exited the house from the roof.'

Then Grandpa pointed at me and whispered, 'Silence.' He pushed the door all the way open and walked into the yard. 'There is no one. It is dark,' he said. Then he lit matches. 'They came here last night, Bachem. The main door to the house is unlocked too. He lit another match. 'They have stolen everything,' he said. Grandpa walked around in the house, and then went to the outdoor kitchen, and came back. 'We need to go, Bachem. They have not left us even a flashlight to see. We will come back tomorrow morning before the sunrise,' Grandpa said.

Eleven

Grandpa woke me up early in the morning, then he woke up Sharouch. 'We are going to the other house,' he told us. 'Get up and clean up. We pray first, then we leave.' After we prayed, we left for the other house; it was still dark. Grandpa unlocked the door, and we followed him into the house. It was a mess; they had searched everywhere in the house and had taken everything, whether it was valuable or not – the fridge, TV, sewing machine, winter clothes, shoes, sandals, dishes. They had even taken most of my books. Grandpa walked out into the yard and found a shovel, which he passed to Sharouch. He drew a circle in the dirt in the middle of the yard. Grandpa asked Sharouch to dig in that spot. Then Grandpa asked me to follow him into the outdoor kitchen. Grandpa provided me with a hammer, and then took off the board that was on top of the hiding spot. He asked me to get inside the hiding place and break the surface of the concrete. The hiding place was really small; I was not even able to swing the hammer properly. I kept on hammering on the concrete. 'Bachem, it is not that hard,' he advised me. 'Hit as hard as you can while I go and check on Sharouch.' I started to sweat and was not able to breathe in that hole. After hammering for a few minutes, I stood up in the hole to breathe. The top of the hole didn't even come up to my chest. The tandoor was about two meters away from the hiding spot on the same level. Grandpa came back and saw me standing. He threw a bag to me. 'Put all the smashed concrete in this bag, then come to the yard – and don't say anything to Sharouch,' Grandpa said.

I went back to the yard and saw that Grandpa was digging and Sharouch was standing next to Grandpa. We were sweating. Grandpa threw the shovel on the ground, straightened his back, and passed his arm across his forehead to wipe off the sweat. 'We cannot go to war with empty stomachs,' Grandpa said, and then he pointed towards the kitchen. 'These animals even stole our teapots, tea, and tea cups!' Then he said, 'As long us you two are good, everything will be fine.' Once again he passed the shovel to Sharouch, 'Bachem, keep on digging deeper and deeper, and dig a bit more to the left.'

'Why me?' Sharouch complained. 'Aftab has not even touched the shovel yet.'

Grandpa smiled at me. 'Okay, Khan Bachem,' he said to me. 'Take the shovel and start digging. I will leave for the other house to bring food for us.' Grandpa looked at his watch. 'It is five thirty,' he told us. 'When you reach the rocks, stop digging and wait for me.'

Sharouch had both hands on his waist. He pointed at the spot. 'Why are we digging here? We already have a hiding spot in our outdoor kitchen.'

'We are not digging to make a hiding spot,' Grandpa explained. 'There are two guns down there. I buried them nineteen years ago.' Sharouch and I were shocked when we heard the word *guns*. Grandpa looked at Sharouch and pointed at me. 'His father helped me to bury those guns. We placed a few rocks on top of the guns to protect them from being damaged by shovels. It is time to take the guns out.' Grandpa said it with confidence, then smiled at us. 'That was your father's idea, Bachem, to bury the guns. Now come and lock the door behind me.' Before he turned to leave, he pointed to the spot where Sharouch was standing. 'Make the earth pile there as you dig,' he told us.

I locked the door behind Grandpa and took the shovel to dig. 'Guns … guns,' said Sharouch. 'I have never touched a gun in my life. I want to shoot and kill anyone who enters our house!'

Then, he thrust out his right hand. 'Look, look! My hand is shaking, although I am trying to hold it as still as I can. Still it shakes.' He held out his left hand towards me. 'My left hand does not shake,' Sharouch said, and then he put his right hand on his waist and leaned his upper body back. 'Just from using the shovel for thirty minutes I have no more energy,' Sharouch said. He started to laugh and then giggled. 'Sohrab was right,' he said.

'I don't know what you are talking about,' I said.

'Sohrab did not tell you why he lost the wrestling match in Russia?' He started to laugh again. 'Of course not, because he did not trust you. You are Grandpa's favourite – Khan Bachem.' He laughed some more. 'Masturbation … masturbation! Come out from the spot, and I will tell you what happened to Sohrab in Russia,' Sharouch said. He placed hands on his waist. 'Leave the shovel. Come out. Let's take a break against the wall,' he proposed. He looked at the sky. 'The sun is up, Bachem,' Sharouch said, and then he told me a story: 'Two years ago, Sohrab went to Moscow for a wrestling tournament. He stayed there for three days, and because of those beautiful Russian girls he failed to bring the gold medal. Sohrab told me about what had happened during that tournament. Sohrab told me, "When I got into that arena, those half-naked young girls exhibited and danced for us. They were as pretty as angels. Then I was taken to a huge hotel. Before the Russian wresting coach left my hotel room, he told me to be ready for eight o'clock the next morning. He said that the bus would take me to the arena, and I would have my first wrestling match at ten, and my second at one in the afternoon. He said that, if I made it to the finals, I would compete in two days at ten in the morning." That's what Sohrab told me,' Sharouch said. 'Then Sohrab told me that, that first night, those beautiful girls appeared in his dreams, and he had sex with one!' Sharouch started to laugh. 'Sohrab had sex with Russian girls in his dream!' Sharouch laugh again out loud. 'In his dream!' Sharouch said, 'Then Sohrab won his first and the second wrestling match. However the night before his final match, he had different dream about having sex with another *two* Russian girls. Sohrab swore that his dream felt very real, and when he woke up, he searched for the girls in his hotel room, but they weren't there – he even looked in the bathroom! Sohrab used the shampoo from that hotel's bathroom to masturbate!' Sharouch and I could not stop laughing about what had happened to Sohrab in Moscow. 'Sohrab blasphemed,' Sharouch explained. 'If he had not masturbated, he could have won the final match too. Sohrab told me that he had no strength, which is why he lost. But second place is good too,' Sharouch said. Then shook my hand. 'Don't tell anyone. If Grandpa finds out he might get very upset.' Sharouch once again held out his right hand. 'Look, look … it is out of my control, it shakes!' Then he held out his left hand. 'Look, my left hand is not shaking, because I am right handed.' He kept on laughing. 'Indeed, it is a bad addiction.'

We were laughing, and then Sharouch asked, 'The porn pictures I showed you yesterday – did you like them?'

'Ya, ya, ya,' I whispered.

'Which one did you like the most?'

'All of them,' I said.

'I like the blond girl wearing the long black boots,' he said. 'You can see everything from behind, and she looks back into the camera. She is so pretty.'

I was not sure which one was he talking about. 'I saw four different nude girls in different positions,' I told him, 'but I didn't see a girl wearing black boots.'

Then Sharouch stood up and started to laugh again. 'Really? You did not see that one? Do you know why?' he asked.

'No. Maybe you are talking about another picture,' I said.

He laughed again. 'No, Bachem, that girl is on the other side of the same page!' Now he was giggling.

We heard someone knocking at the door; it was Grandpa. I let him in. He walked to the spot where we had been digging and tapped his shoe on the surface a few times. Then he took the shovel and hit it hard against the earth. 'We are almost there,' he said, and he began to dig. In a short time we heard the shovel hitting the rocks. We brought a few of them out of the hole. When we heard someone knocking at the door, Grandpa said to me, 'It is your mother. Go open the door.' Mina had come along with my mother, and they had brought us food. My mother walked into the house saw there was nothing left. She returned to the yard. 'They have even stolen our winter clothes,' she said.

My sister looked down at her sandals and started to cry. 'My shoes,' she said.

My mother looked at Mina. 'It is okay, my girl. Grandpa will buy you another pair of shoes,' she said.

They were about to leave the house. 'Bring food for two people,' Grandpa told them. 'Khan and I will spend the night in this house. And do not forget to bring two mattresses and two pillows, and a flashlight, Soraya Bachem. As you can see, there is nothing in this house.'

After breakfast, Grandpa took the shovel and started to dig once more. I was pouring the tea from the flask into the teacups, when all of sudden I heard him say, 'Here they are!' Grandpa brought out two long bundles wrapped in plastic. He placed them on the ground one by one, and then Grandpa asked us to bring them into the house. We were sitting in his room; Sharouch and I were excited to see the guns. Grandpa removed the plastic. The guns were wrapped in thick red-coloured fabric. Grandpa unwrapped one of the guns and held it up straight. 'This is the rifle,' he said. Then Grandpa passed a white towel over the surface of the gun. 'It is dry,' he said. 'Even though we applied a great deal of oil, it has dried off.' Then looked at the bullets. He placed a bullet into the rifle. 'This one is fine,' he said. Then he unwrapped the other gun. 'This is a shotgun,' he explained. He cleaned it and loaded it also. 'The one is fine as well,' he said. 'These are hunting guns, but they can hurt humans too.'

Sharouch, and I were exited; we could not keep our eyes off the guns and the bullets. 'Can we use these guns, Grandpa?' Sharouch asked.

'You do not need to use these, but I will use them if I have too,' Grandpa stated. After that Grandpa explained to us why he had the guns. 'Kabul was not dry back in the day. I use to go hunt ducks and deer with your fathers in the field where you kids now play football. It used to be filled with water.' He pointed to the rifle. 'I have hunted deer in Bamyan with this, and the last breed *Tazi* (Afghan hound) was with me. His name was Beem had long fur in white a two years old tall baby dog. The Pashtun took Beem away from us.' Tears came down from grandpa Sharouch said 'a dog', Grandpa wiped the tears by his left sleeve shook his head and calmed down.

Grandpa took the rifle and passed it to me. 'If your father had had this with him, those coward Pashtuns would never have had the courage to get close to your father. This was your grandma's idea, to keep these guns in Kabul,' Grandpa said. Then he put his hands up and asked Allah for forgiveness.

It was afternoon. 'I need to go to the city,' Grandpa announced. 'Sharouch, when dark comes, go to your house.' Then pointed at me. 'Khan Bachem, we will stay over here tonight, and your mother will bring us food.' Before he left, he put the guns aside, then shook his head. 'If anyone knocks on the door, do not let them in,' he warned. 'These Pashtuns and Tajiks are the government officials during the day, then they are thieves throughout the night.' He looked at Sharouch. 'Leave after eight tonight,' he ordered.

After Grandpa left Sharouch said, 'Since my dad has gone missing, I have wanted to kill those Pashtuns.' He was always saying, 'I want this and I want that.' For example, 'I want to go to the USA, use taekwondo, and become a movie star.' 'What are these guns?' he said to me now. 'I will use real American guns.' He got exited and began demonstrating martial arts kicks. 'I know taekwondo,' he said. 'Wrestling is bullshit! Then he landed on the ground with his legs split 'Why do you get the good gun?' he asked. Then he pulled up himself and started to kick in the air again. When he finally stopped he asked, 'Khan, what are you thinking about?'

'I want to see the other side of the page,' I said.

'Oh, yes, it is true,' Sharouch said, laughing. I laughed too. 'It is not a problem,' he said. 'Tonight you are sleeping here. I will show you the other side of the porn page tomorrow.'

It was around 8.00 p.m., and it was dark when Sharouch left for the other house. Soon afterwards, Grandpa knocked the door; he brought cooked potato with some bread, and a flashlight. After we ate, he got into the hiding spot, took the hammer, and placed the light next to him. He started to break the concrete. After he brought out all of the broken concrete, I saw he was holding a small wooden box. 'It is heavy, Bachem. Bring this into the house.' He took the flashlight, and we went into the house. 'Do you know what is in this box, Bachem?'

'No, Grandpa, I don't know,' I replied.

'Think,' he said.

'I don't know,' I replied again.

Then he looked into my eyes, and he pulled the tip of his beard down. 'Think, Bachem,' he said.

'Is it a bomb,' I predicted.

Grandpa started to laugh. 'You have balls, Bachem,' Grandpa stated. He kept on laughing to himself, 'Bomb … No, Bachem, this box is full of gold and ancient jewellery,' he said. The lock was so rusty he couldn't break it; instead he broke the box. There were four little statues of Buddha in gold, and some gold coins inside.

'This belonged to our ancestors,' Grandpa explained. 'I inherited this box from my father, and my father inherited from his grandfather. When the genocide was declared by King Abdul Rahman against the Hazara people in the late eighteen hundreds, many of our family members were put into death by the Pashtuns one by one. They killed every one in the Hazarajat territory, but some of our great ancestors managed to hide themselves in the caves in the Bamyan mountains; therefore, they survived. Unfortunately, our lineage never gave birth to more than one boy in every generation. Therefore, this ancient jewellery was passed from one unique male to another in the family. Eventually I inherited it. There were a few more of these ancient golden statues, and I sold them in Iran. I took the money and used it for business. Because of this jewellery, we have money, Bachem. Please do not tell anyone. The only other person who knows about this is your grandma, and your father knew about this.' Then he sighed.

'We don't have to stay here, Bachem,' Grandpa said a bit later. 'We can wait until around three in the morning, and then we can leave for the other house.' He settled, trying to get comfortable. 'Do you know I wanted Ghulam to emigrate to Iran?' he asked me. I remained quiet. 'I wanted to give one of these to him. I have an address. If he had sold just one of these pieces, he would have been able to buy a business and a house. He would have been able to live comfortably for the rest of his life with his children,' Grandpa said. He wrapped the two guns with pieces of cloth. 'Don't think the wars are because of conflicts between Pashtuns, Tajiks, Uzbeks, and Hazaras. Also, you must not think that wars are because of conflicts between Muslims and communists. Wars are human nature, which is politics. We did have problems with the Pashtuns in the past, but they are the majority, and we are a minority within the minorities. Wherever you go, you will see that the minority always suffers the most, Bachem. Because humans are animals, and they love politics and possessing material wealth. That is why the majority wins most of the time.'

Grandpa took a deep breath and looked at me. 'Bachem, I am thinking of sending you to India,' he said. 'I have a friend in New Delhi, and he is an Afghan Sikh. I could send you to Iran, too, but I like India better. I have never been to India, but I have heard good things about the Indian people,' Grandpa said. It was around two in the morning. Grandpa went out, and then returned after short time. 'We can leave for the other house, Bachem. I see no one on the streets.' He asked me to carry the two wrapped guns. He placed the ancient treasure into a bag and carried it himself. We arrived home safely.

A week later, rockets were launched into our Kabul neighbourhoods at the rate of two to three rockets a week. No one knew who was launching the rockets, but the majority believed that the rockets were being fired from the Pakistan border at the command of the Pashtun leaders.

A month later, Grandpa came to me with my passport with an Indian tourist visa. Along with this he gave me airline tickets for a direct flight from Kabul to New Delhi, my birth certificate, and an address in New Delhi.

Not long after that, I arrived at Indira Gandhi International Airport, New Delhi, India.

Twelve

The Indira Gandhi International Airport was the largest building I had ever been in. I watched thousands of people as they walked around in the terminal. They were all ages. They were of different skin colours and wore different clothing, yet no one disturbed anyone else. I did not speak or understood a word in English or in Hindi. I followed the other Afghans passengers off the airplane and managed to collect my luggage and get through customs and immigration. Finally, I exited the terminal.

In the waiting crowed, I saw my name written in Farsi and in English on a piece of paper that was hanging around the neck of a tall Sikh. As I started to walk towards him, he kept observing me. Then he smiled. I showed him my passport. He took my luggage and spoke to me in the Dari language. We got into a taxi, and he spoke to the driver in different language. After a while, we got out of the taxi in front of a building. The crowds, the humidity, the different noises from every corner, and the new smells in the air made me feel as if I was walking into the another world. This world was made of different people … and it was for different people to live in. I followed the tall Sikh into a building, and we went to the third floor. Then I followed him down a long, narrow hallway. At end of the hallway, he entered a room. Next to the window, an old man was sitting on a red sofa. He had a small book in his hand. Was he reading it? He spoke in the Dari language when he saw me: 'It is you, Bachem. Sit … sit.' He pointed to a chair in front of him. He spoke to the tall man, and the tall man left the room.

'Welcome to India,' he stated. Then started to laugh. 'You don't speak Hindi or English,' he said. Then he laughed again. 'But it is good. You are a very young boy.' Then he laughed some more. A few minutes later, the tall man walked in with a bottle of orange soft drink. He opened it and placed it on the corner of the windowsill. He adjusted his red turban, and then he left the room. 'Drink, Bachem,' the older man said. 'It is for you, and it is cold.' He was still laughing. I had no idea what was so funny! 'My name is Amar Singh.' Then he laughed again. 'Drink, Bachem. It is cold.' He finally stopped laughing long enough to ask, 'How are your Grandpa and your family in Kabul?' I told him everyone was well. 'You will be fine,' he said. Then he pressed a button. 'This man will take you for a walk. We will talk afterwards.'

A few minutes later, a middle-aged man entered the room and started to talk to me, but I did not understand what he was saying. The old man was laughing, and he kept on laughing. His long white hair hung down and covered his shoulders; his beard was spread over his chest and flowed all the way down to his waist. Finally, he stood up, took my hand, and led me to the door. He said my name to the person: 'Aftab.' Then he told me to follow the man.

The middle-aged man started to walk, and I followed him. We exited the building and walked into the crowd. There were so many people and vehicles, it was impossible to see the surface of the road. He made a left turn at an outdoor market. The market was less crowded. He turned and looked at me from head to toe in silence. As we walked through the marketplace, the man made certain clothing purchases. He carried the clothes back to the old man's office, and I followed him. We entered the old man's room, he left the bag, and then he left. The old man was sitting in the same place. He looked closely into my eyes, and then he crossed his legs. 'Bachem, whenever you are hungry, let me know,' he said. The tall man came back and gathered up my luggage and the bag with clothes. Amar Singh told me to leave with the man. 'He will take you to where you will spend the night,' he said.

The tall man waved down a rickshaw and told me to sit in the front seat. The rickshaw driver was a skinny young man with a moustache. He drove through the crowd. The traffic was unbelievable! The exhaust from every vehicle filled the streets. There was such noise! And so many people. Finally, he drove over an overpass, and the crowd thinned out. The rickshaw driver stopped in front of a building, and we got out. The tall Sikh retrieved my luggage and the bag. I followed him as he entered a building and climbed the stairs to the third floor. He unlocked a door. 'This is your room,' he said. 'Don't go too far. Come with me. I'll take you for a walk now,' he said. Then he locked the room. Even the hallways of the building were crowded. People were walking, standing, and sitting on the stairs and in the hallways. Empty pails and pails full of water were placed everywhere in the hallways. I followed him through the crowd, and then followed him on a narrow road. 'Here are the Muslims,' he said. You can find halal meat.' Then took me to a vegetable market. 'Here you can find any type of vegetables,' he said. 'There are Afghans nearby. Later this week I will take you to the park where the Afghans play football,' he said. Skinny cows were walking on the streets among the people. One of the cows was shitting and urinating at the same time as she was walking. There was cow shit everywhere on the streets.

I followed the man back to my room. The room was furnished and had two windows, one of which overlooked the main street. The man wrote something on a piece of paper. 'This is your address,' he said, handing it to me. 'Do not go too far, and keep this with you at all the times.' Then he brought out some cash from his pocket. 'Take this,' he said, 'and we bought you some clothes. Amar Singh will come tomorrow morning to see you.'

When he left, it was in the evening. *It is a dream; it is not real*, I said that to myself. *What a world! Everyone is dressed differently from everyone else, and everyone is happy! This is unbelievable. No wonder the Indian movies are interesting to watch.*

I left my room to search for food. It was very difficult to choose what to eat. And communicating was difficult too. I felt like a speech impaired person, who is able to hear, but not able to talk. And I couldn't understand what I heard anyway. Before the dark, I went back to my room. I found that the food I had chosen was too spicy and greasy. The food affected my thoughts, and I found it difficult to fall asleep that night.

The same tall man returned in the morning, and took me to Amar Sing's house. The minute the old man saw me, once again he started to laugh. 'How are you, Bachem? Do you like India?' he asked. I had nothing to say; I nodded my head. 'Today I am sending you to register for an English language school. Your Grandpa has given me enough money; the amount should cover your expenses for another six months here in New Delhi. The room you are staying in – if you do not like it, tell me and I will find another room for you,' he proposed.

The tall man took me to a district called South Extension and registered me for an English course. In the evening, he took me to a park where the Afghan men and boys played football. There were about twenty to twenty-five Afghan males. He gave me directions for getting back to my room, and then left me there. As I was watching the football players, a middle-aged Afghan man came and sat next to me, and then introduced himself. 'My name is Zahir,' he said. Then he asked, 'Are you new in India?' When I said I was, he asked me about the Afghanistan political situation. He had lived in New Delhi for three and half years with his wife and children, and had been refused permission from the American embassy immigration in New Delhi to emigrate to the United States. A few other Afghan boys and men came to meet to me. I was the only Hazara among them; everyone else was a Tajik or Pashtun. This was interesting; for the first time I was able to tell them my identity. 'My name is Aftab. I am Hazara, and I am a Shia Muslim,' I told them. One of them stood up from the bench, 'Oh, there are some Afghan Shia who live in Malviya Nagar, and Malviya Nagar is not far from here. It is about forty minutes' walking distance from here,' he said. Then the conversation changed to religions. One of them asked me about the Shia Muslim's doctrines and practices. I gave a little information about the Shia faith, which I knew. Almost every one of them started to disagree, saying those were not true Muslim beliefs. I thanked God I was not in Kabul; otherwise, every one of them would have attacked me physically, and hurt me. Every one of them left, except one, who was called Jawed; he wanted to take me to the part of the city where the Shia Hazara people lived.

I attended the English beginner course the next day. It was interesting to learn the English language. I began with the English alphabet. Everything was new to me. A sudden change had dropped me into a different world in which I experienced freedom I never had, and isolation from my family, which I had never experienced. One the other hand, the culture of India and her people was unknown to me, except for what I had learned from the Indian movies I had watched. *India, what a world of creations ... it is interesting*, I said that to myself.

Thirteen

I learned that, in the building where I lived, everyone called me 'Khan Sahib,' and they knew I had come from Afghanistan. Before going to bed that night, I tried to lock the door and the windows, but one of the windows did not close properly. The next morning, I explained my problem with the window to the tall man, and then he tried to shut the window, but was not able. 'It is not cold. Why you want to shut this window?' he asked.

'Security reasons,' I said.

He started to laugh. 'This is India. Don't worry, kid,' he said, and then he laughed again. 'I will take you to Amar Sing today. You need to talk to your family in Kabul.' When we arrived at Amar Singh's house, Amar Sing opened his arms to me, his long hair and beard flowing. 'This is your third day in India, Bachem, so how are you feeling?' he asked.

I nodded my head. 'I am fine,' I said. Then I saw the most beautiful girl with gorgeous eyes. Her thick, long, black hair was hanging down below her waist. She had the most beautiful smile as she walked towards us in the living room.

'This is my granddaughter,' said Amar Singh. 'She was born in Kabul, but she does not speak Dari, and her name is Mona. Let's have breakfast,' he said with a laugh. 'After that we will call your grandpa.' After breakfast the old man walked towards the corner of the room and sat on a chair next to the telephone. He dialled the numbers. While he was holding the telephone to his right ear, he was staring at me, and then he smiled. He stopped smiling, but never stopped staring at me, and then he smiled again. He started to talk on the telephone, and then I stood up from the chair as he waved at me to come closer to him. He was saying, 'Khan Sahib, Khan Sahib,' Then he started to laugh out loud. 'The young Khan is next to me,' he said.

He passed me the phone, and I heard Grandpa. 'Khan Bachem, how are you? Is everything fine?' Grandpa asked. When I replied that I was fine, he continued, 'Everything is fine here in Kabul. I want you to listen to me carefully,' he said. 'Amar Sing is my good friend; therefore, you must respect and trust him. Everything he says, listen to him. I have found you an address where the Afghan Hazara people live. Listen to Amar Singh as you have listened to me,' he said. 'Talk to me. Do you like India?' he asked.' I replied that I liked it there. 'Every time you need money, ask him. There is no problem. I will take care of the amount of money,' he said. 'Learn English. It is very important,' he said.

The telephone line was not good, and finally we were disconnected. Amar Sing took the phone from me, ground his teeth, and breathed out through the gap between his teeth. 'The telephone line is not good, Bachem.' Then he slammed the telephone down. 'I have to call back to get the address for you, Bachem. It is okay, and I will try today, if not tomorrow. Eventually I will get that address for you,' he said. He kept on dialling Grandpa's number, but could not get through, and then he looked into my eyes. 'Little Khan Sahib, do you feel better after talking to your grandpa?' he asked.

It was the first time I had spoken with Grandpa from India. It felt good to hear him confirming that I could trust, and even respect, Amar Singh. I nodded my head and smiled. 'Yes,' I said.

'This is your first smile, Bachem. Don't worry. I will teach you how to laugh too,' he said, and then he stood up. 'Follow me to the other room.'

In that room, I saw the largest book collection I had ever seen. There were probably thousands of books placed on the shelves, one book next to the book. Amar Singh sat on a sofa next to the window. 'Come and sit next to me,' he said. I could not keep my eyes away from those books. 'Bachem, are you literate in the Dari language?' he asked.

'Yes,' I replied.

Then he pointed to the shelves in the corner on the bottom. 'Those books are in Dari,' he said. 'Go and get me a book.' There were more than a hundred books in Dari, and I began looking at them. 'Just chose one,' he said. I saw a book of Hafiz and passed it to him. He started to laugh. 'Hafiz … Hafiz,' he said. He recited a poem from Hafiz. 'Sufi mysticism,' he said. 'Why Hafiz, Bachem?' he asked. 'Maybe you don't know any other books but Hafiz books,' he said. Then he laughed. 'I have promised your grandpa to treat you like my son. I am a Sikh Hindu, and you are a Muslim. What brings us together is that we worship the same God, but we try to approach that God from different angles.' Then he asked me, 'Do you pray?'

'Yes, sometimes,' I replied.

'"Sometimes." I like that,' he said, and then he kept on saying, 'Sometimes … sometimes,' and kept on laughing out loud. He pointed to a chair next to the sofa and asked me to place the chair in front of him and sit down. Because of his nonstop laughing, tears had come out of his eyes and flowed down into his beard. 'I am not crying,' he said. His big, glossy eyes were calm, and as he breathed, his big belly, which was covered by his long beard, moved up and down.

The pretty girl, Mona, came suddenly came into the room. 'Telephone … telephone,' she said. The old man stood up started to walk from the room. 'I need to use a cane,' he said. The pretty girl left and quickly returned. '*Ajaa*, ajaa,' she said (come, come). 'Telephone.' I followed her. Today her hair was in a long ponytail that hung to her waist and swung from left to right as she walked. She looked back. 'Ajaa, ajaa,' she said, and smiled. The old man passed me the telephone. 'Say hello to your grandpa.'

Grandpa had news: 'I gave the address to Amar Sing. He will take you there, and your Uncle Ghulam said *salaam* to you. Next time I call, I will give you his address and telephone numbers in Pakistan so you can keep in touch with your uncle.' The telephone line was much better this time. 'I am using the post office telephone,' he explained, 'and I will call back in a few weeks. We miss you,' Grandpa said, and the telephone connection ended.

Mona came back and served us tea. 'I know you are used to black tea, but Indian tea is better because it has milk,' Amar Singh said. 'This address is in Malviya Nagar, and it is not that far from here. I am sure you will have good time with your new friends.' And then he said, 'Don't miss your English lessons. I am home most of the time. Feel free to come and see me at anytime.' A few minutes later, a man arrived. He had a long black beard and wore a green turban. Amar Singh handed the address to him then gave me a piece of paper. 'This is my address. Follow him. He will take you to your new friends. My telephone number is on that piece of paper too. Don't lose it.'

The humidity, the smoke in the air, and the crowd – the rickshaw passed through it all. The noise from every vehicle, the different music from every corner, and the sticky sweat on my body – it was all different to me. The rickshaw stopped. 'Khan Sahib, ajaa, ajaa,' the man said. I followed him on foot, and he stopped walking in front of a building, '*Rookie*, rookie, (wait, wait)' he said. The man came back in a short time, followed by an Afghan lady. She was wearing a red T-shirt, blue sandals, and a long, chocolate-brown skirt. She was wiping a glass with a white towel. She smiled as if she had known me for very long time. She kept on staring at me. 'Come … come inside,' she said. She took me into an apartment fully furnished with Afghan carpets, a television set, and mattresses to sit on. The man waited at the door. '*Ache hi*, ache hi' (is it good), he said, and left. 'My name is Zenat,' she said.

She sat close to me on the mattress. 'My children will be home soon,' she said. 'They are at school. Are you Ghulam's son?' she asked.

'No. My mother's name is Soraya,' I replied.

She sighed. 'You are Aftab,' she said. 'When did you arrive in India?'

'Two days ago,' I replied. She went to the kitchen. The TV was on; the programme was in English. Some family pictures were framed on the walls.

Zenat returned with a tray that held a glass and a teapot. 'I heard your Uncle Rustam went missing. Any news about him?' she asked.

'No. No one knows where he might be,' I replied. 'How long have you lived in India?' I asked.

'Almost two years. We came a few months before the new policy was instituted. My husband is in Germany, and he sends us money. India is a very good country – very good people ... and it is safe. Where is your other uncle, Ghulam?' she asked.

'He is in Pakistan with his family,' I said.

'Pakistan,' she said. 'When did they go to Pakistan?' she asked.

'They left Kabul for Pakistan about four months ago,' I said. 'They are in Peshawar. I spoke to my grandpa this morning. They are doing fine, and Grandpa gave me your address today.'

'Where do you stay now?'

'I live in Lajpat Nagar, and I have a room there.'

'Who helped you to find the room?'

'My grandpa's friend, who is an Afghan Sikh, picked me up from the airport.'

'There are too many Afghans living in Lajpat Nagar,' she said. 'If you meet them, do not become friends with them.'

I smiled and I told her that I had met a few Afghan boys and men the day before. I said that, once I told them I was Shia, they walked away from me.

She started to laugh and said, 'Yes, in India they cannot do anything. But stay away from them. Some of them are extremist Muslims. Here in Malviya Nagar there are about nine Afghan Shia families, and two or three single homes where young boys like you share rooms,' she said. Then asked, 'Do you speak English?'

'No, I don't. Not even a little,' I said. 'I attended the Amani High School, so I know a little German.'

'Ohhhhhh, German,' she said. 'My husband told me the German language is much more difficult than the English language to learn. My husband studied English, but he went to Germany by a smuggler,' she said.

'Don't be shy with us,' she continued. 'My son is fourteen years old. His name is Nezar, and my girl is twelve years old. Her name is Soman. They should arrive from school soon.' She looked her watch. 'I have to heat the food. When they arrive, then we will eat. My son will show you the neighbourhood,' she said. Then she left for kitchen.

It was not long before Nezar and Soman arrived, both wearing school uniforms in light blue with white shirts. It was so cool to watch them. They took their shoes off and said, 'Salaam.' Nezar came and sat next to me. His mother introduced me to him, and then said to him, 'Go and change your uniform. Take this money and buy bread. Make sure it is fresh,' she said. Nezar smiled and asked me to go with him, but his mother said, 'No, no. Go quickly and come home quickly. Aftab is tired.'

But Nezar put his hand under my arm. 'Let's go,' he said. I followed him as he walked through his neighbourhood. On our way to the bakery, Nezar said hello six or seven people, and every one of them called him Khan Sahib. He spoke in Hindi, and kept pointing his finger towards me, and towards those to whom he was saying was hello. He kept on asking me, 'How are you?' 'There is a park where we play football and volleyball,' he told me. 'I will take you there this evening.' Then he asked, 'So you came alone to India? Where is your family?'

'In Kabul,' I said as we arrived the bakery.

It was crowded both inside and outside the bakery. At least five people were sitting around the tandoor in which they baked the bread. Every few seconds, the bakers removed freshly baked bread from the tandoor. All the bakers were dressed in white. They wore hats and were bearded. Once the man who was in charge of the cash saw Nezar waiting in the line, he said, 'Khan Sahib, ajaa, ajaa.' He immediately gave us the hot bread, so we didn't have to stand in line. The man was chewing on red-coloured tobacco and was spiting on the floor.

As we left, Nezar said, 'Do you like India? It is good. I have many friends here.'

I had the first delicious food in India on that day – vegetables with rice. Nezar asked me to come with him to the market. 'No, no. It is too hot right now. Go later,' his mother said.

'It is hot all the time,' Nezar said. 'It is even so hot at night that I can't sleep.'

'When are you going to buy air-conditioning?' Soman asked her mother.

'Soon,' Zenat said. 'We will buy a fridge first, then air-conditioning.' She sighed.

Nezar invited me to go on the balcony with him, because the room was too humid. 'My mother does not allow me to go to the single boys' home; they are young … about your age and older.

They watch Indian and American movies all the time. They rent the TV and VCR for one night, and they watch six to seven movies in one night. In the evening you will meet them. One of the guys is called Babur. He is seventeen years old, and he has money at all the time. Babur has been in Nepal by himself, and he liked it.' Then asked me, 'How old are you?'

'I am sixteen,'

He laughed, 'I am fifteen, and I am taller than you!' Then he said, 'If you want to learn Hindi, you must watch Indian movies.' He even recommended a list of his favourites. 'They are good to watch,' he said. 'Let's go back to the room. I will show you how to make air-conditioning.' Nezar came to the room with a pot of water and placed it in front of the fan, then he adjusted the head of the fan so it would blow over the pot of water. 'Come … come … feel how it is cooler now? My Indian friend taught me this,' Nezar said. 'You should come and live in Malviya Nagar. I will ask my friend Babur if you can live with them.'

'No, no, no,' said Aunt Zenat. 'Not with him! He is not a good boy. Never call him your friend. He is a bad boy. His uncle sends him American dollars, and he spends all the money here and there,' she explained.

'He receives one hundred dollars at the beginning of every month from his uncle,' Nezar explained. 'Babur told me one hundred dollar is nothing in America, but in India it is a lot of money.' Nezar laughed. Before Nezar and I left for the park, Aunt Zenat – she had asked me to call her that – insisted that I come back for dinner. She said she would cook chicken with rice.

In the early evening, we walked into a very big park. A narrow walking path went through the park. Everything in the park was green, except for the path, which was light brown. Birds were flying everywhere in the park. They sat on the branches of the tall trees and sang. The male peacocks opened their tails wide to show off their pretty, colourful, and detailed feathers, and the female peacocks just hung around the male peacocks. Monkeys jumped around on the branches of the trees and made those funny faces. Insects were everywhere. It seemed as if the humidity had given birth to every creature in that park. 'Snake! Snake!' Nezar shouted. Then he threw a stone in the snake's direction. 'Oh, I missed it,' he said. 'The stone hit the bush.' Suddenly he began to jump around. 'We Afghan named this park Jackie Chan Park,' Nezar said. Then he pointed towards a hill in the park. 'Behind this hill there is the football field. I hope all the boys are there,' he said. When we passed the hill we saw that three boys were playing ball. 'Oh, Babur is not there,' he said. Then he addressed his friends: 'Boys, boys, this is Aftab. He just arrived in India three days ago from Kabul, and he is like my cousin,' he said.

The boys were between the ages of sixteen and nineteen years old. They smiled, and one of them kicked the ball towards me. 'Do you know how to play football?' he asked.

'A little,' I said. Nezar asked them where we could find Babur. They all started to laugh. One of them said, 'Oh Babur … you know where he went – Old Delhi.' Everyone started laughing. We played football, and after a while Nezar said, 'Let's go. Maybe Babur has returned from Old Delhi.' Nezar and I walked back to Malviya Nagar to meet Babur. On the way Nezar said, 'You must meet Babur. His roommates are very different from these guys. I don't like the boys you met today. They are cowards,' he said. 'All they do is to learn English and play football. Babur is cool. He never stays home. At night he watches movies. He speaks very good Hindi and

English.' Then he smiled and shook his head. 'Oh, Aftab, remember not to tell my mother that we went to Babur's house. My mother thinks Babur is a bad boy.' He started to walk faster. 'We will arrive his home in a few minutes.' Then he pointed to a road. 'Babur's home is parallel to that street, and I hope he is home. Babur has one roommate. I will talk to him. If they accept you to live with them, then you will have a lots fun,' Nezar said. He shook his head, looked me in the eyes, and smiled.

Nezar pointed towards a guy who was sitting on the steps. 'That is Akbar, Babur's roommate.' He started to walk faster. 'Akbar! Akbar, how are you? Why didn't you come to the park? Where is Babur?' Nezar asked.

'Babur is not back from Old Delhi. Let's go up to the room,' Akbar said. Nezar introduced me to Akbar, and we sat on the mattresses. Akbar asked me when I had arrived India, then asked about my family. After I told him, he said, 'I know. I know. I use to be in the same school with your cousin Sohrab. He was cool. He saved me from fighting two of my Pashtun classmates in the schoolyard. One of the Pashtuns called me a flat-nosed Hazara and told me I should go to Mongolia. He told me I wasn't even Muslim, and then that Pashtun punched me, and the other Pashtun pushed me on the ground. Sohrab came and took one of them by his neck, and the other Pashtun came and grabbed Sohrab, but Sohrab bent over and grabbed that Pashtun's legs and lifted him up in the air, then threw him down on the ground very hard. The other Pashtun escaped,' Akbar said. Three of us started to laugh. 'Those Pashtuns were jealous, because I was the captain of the class,' Akbar said. 'From then on, every time they saw me hanging with Sohrab they put their heads down and walked away from us. Once Sohrab told me that one of those Pashtuns saw him on the street and he crossed the road so he wouldn't have to face Sohrab,' Akbar said, and we laughed again. 'Where is Sohrab?' Akbar asked.

'He went to Pakistan with his family,' I said.

'Oh, man, I wish he had come to India. I miss him,' he said. 'Sohrab went to Russia a few years ago for a wrestling tournament, and he won the second place … a silver medal!' Akbar said.

Babur arrived. Nezar stood up, called his name out loud, and then asked, 'Where were you?'

'Old Delhi,' Babur said. Babur sat on the mattress, and Nezar sat close to him, pointed at me, and said, 'This is Aftab. He arrived India three days ago.'

Babur looked into my eyes. 'I have seen him before in Kabul; I have seen him in the mosque a few times. I know his cousins Sharouch and Sohrab. I was friends with Sharouch. Where is he now?' Babur asked.

'In Kabul,' I said. 'And Sohrab is in Pakistan.'

Babur seemed nervous. 'I have to wait another two days. The money is not there. My uncle sent the money yesterday,' Babur said. Every time Babur spoke, everyone was quiet.

'It is dark,' Nezar said. 'I have to be home.' He looked at me. 'Aftab, we must go; otherwise, my mother will kill me.' He turned back to Babur. 'Can Aftab live with you guys? He is alone, and he's living in Lajpat Negar.'

Everyone became silent, then Babur looked at his roommate. 'The rent is seven hundred. Can you pay 233 rupees?' Babur asked. I said I could. 'Do you have money right now?' Babur asked. I said I did. 'When do you want to move in?' Babur asked. I said I didn't know. 'I need money, and if you pay me now you can start living with us from tomorrow,' Babur said.

I took the money out of my pocket. The boys looked at me. I counted 233 rupees and gave it to Babur.

Nezar stood up and said, 'Aftab, let's go. It is dark.'

'No. Let Aftab pass the night here, and tomorrow I will go with him to Lajpat Nagar to bring his stuff here,' Babur said.

'Yes, but my mother has cooked chicken with rice for him, and he is our guest for the night.' Babur looked at Nezar and shook his head. 'Okay, okay, but what should I tell my mother?' Nezar asked.

Babur smiled. 'Tell your mother we played football, and I took Aftab to his room, because he did not know how to get home, and Aftab will come and visit this week,' he said.

'Okay,' Nezar said, and then he left.

We left to have dinner. 'Tandoori chicken is good,' Babur suggested. I know this Muslim restaurant where they have the best tandoori chicken. Usually, we cook at home,' Babur said. Akbar and I followed Babur; it was dark, and crowded like usual. Indian music was played on every corner. We reached the restaurant, and there was a line, but Babur walked through the people, and he picked up the food. An employee said, '*Khuda hafiz*, Khan Sahib' (may God protect you). We took our Tandoori chicken back to the room and ate there; it was as tasty as Babur had promised. 'Tomorrow I will take you to the United Nations,' Babur said. 'You must have your passport, and two passport-size photos so that you can register as a refugee in the United Nations. The United Nations will open a file for you. You must explain in writing why you left Afghanistan; I have a friend who can write that for you. The United Nations also will give you an allowance. Once they accept you, then you can apply for a one-year visa to stay in India. The United Nations will also introduce your refugee statues to the Western embassies that are in New Delhi. My uncle, who lives in the United States, lived India for three years, and more. He got very lucky. His interview went fine, and the US embassy paid for everything. Once he arrived in the United States, he started to work in the restaurant. Now he drives a taxi.' Then he started to laugh. 'Once he told me that a hundred dollars is nothing in America, and he promised to send me a hundred dollars a month. Sometimes he forgets, and I have to call him. Every time I call him, he reminds me to learn English and tells me not to worry about anything.' Babur continued, 'I know some families have waited for more than six years before they are invited for an interview. A family that lives not far from us was refused by the Canadian embassy. Trash embassy immigration judge discovered lies in their interviews. The wife said something about her husband's military service, and the husband said something different. Therefore, the family refugee applications were refused, and they were not allowed to emigrate to Canada. They now live on the United Nations allowances, and they are very poor.' I knew nothing about any of this.

Akbar said, 'An Afghan man put gas on himself and burned himself in front if the United States embassy after his application was rejected.'

'Remember that the embassy will question you about whatever you write on your United Nations application. Even if you say different dates from the ones you have written on your UN application, they will reject you,' Babur said. 'It is a long process before you are asked to come for an interview.' And then he said, 'If you have money, smugglers can prepare fake passports and will send you to the Western countries, but my uncle doesn't want to take the risk. Every time I mention smugglers, he tells me to wait, and to learn the English language.'

'I have to go to my English class tomorrow. Can I go to the United Nations the day after that?' I asked. Then I told them about Amar Singh, my grandpa's friend.

They both started to laugh. 'Afghan Sikh – they are good people,' Akbar said. 'We have a Shia centre here, and there are few Hazara Shia who are English teachers. One of them is really good. He can help you fill out your United Nations application. We will do it this on Thursday.'

The three of us slept in the same room. Our bathroom was on the first floor, and we had a very small kitchen. Next morning I went to pick up my clothes from Lajpat Nagar. In the evening I went to see Amar Singh. He said, 'I am very happy to hear that you found your Hazara friends. From now on I want you to come and see me at least once a week. There are many important things I want to teach you. We will start in a few weeks. Keep up with your English course, and also register for the Shia community English class. Whenever you need money, just ask me. Once you get to know your way around the city, use the busses. I know it is unbelievably crowded, and you should walk … walk as much as you can … you are young,' he said.

Fourteen

The same week I moved in with Babur and Akbar, and I met a few more Shia Hazara people in the Shia centre, which was a fifteen-minute walk from my new address. I also registered for refugee status at the United Nations that week. I started to learn a few words in English and in Hindi. I started to learn how to cook and how to wash my clothes. Everything was new to me, and I had no choice but to get accustomed to it all. In the evenings we played football, and sometimes we rented TV and VCR so we could watch Indian and American movies. We split the rental cost amongst five to six people, all between the ages of fifteen and nineteen. We would rent seven or eight movies and watch them all in one night. The duration for an Indian movie was about two to three hours, while the duration for an American movie was an hour and a half. We would aim a fan to blow on the VCR so it would not overheat with nonstop playing. Sometimes the VCR did not function properly, and then we would have to return it to the store. Babur was the leader in our group; he ultimately made most of the decisions. Every now and then, there were disputes among the boys. Babur mediated and solved the problems between us. Most of the time, Babur had made the right decisions to solve issues. I fit easily into the Shia community centre because we shared the same ethnic background and the same Islamic religious beliefs and practices.

A month and half after my last visit to Amar Singh, I needed money. For that reason, I went to see him in his house. 'I was worried about you,' he said to me. 'The last time I saw you I told you to come and see me once a week, because there are things which I need to teach you. Today you came to see me because you need money, but you must listen what I tell you. A week ago your grandpa called and asked me about you. I told him that you were fine, even though I didn't know where you were. The political situation is getting worse in Afghanistan. The Russian troops have left Afghanistan, and if the right regime takes over the Afghanistan government, your grandpa might ask you to return to Kabul.' Then Amar Singh passed his palm over his oily long white moustache. 'I know you are not ready to learn what I want to teach you, because you are still new in India,' he said. 'It is almost two months that you have been here.' Then he brought out a piece of paper. 'This is your Uncle Ghulam's address in Pakistan,' he said. 'You must write him a letter, and also write a later to your grandpa in Kabul. Leave the letters with me, and I will send them when someone leaves for Kabul.'

I wrote a letter for Grandpa, and one for Uncle Ghulam, telling them both that I was safe with Amar Singh. 'I will take care of the letters,' he said, and then asked me to tell him something in the Hindi language.

'Kyā hāla hai?' I asked (how you are?).

He laughed heartily and replied in Hindi, '*Acchā*, acchā … good, good that is good,' he said, and then he laughed. I laughed too; in fact, I was not able to stop laughing! 'You are learning how to laugh,' he said. 'That is good.' After a while, he pointed his index finger in my direction. 'Okay, Bachem,' he said. 'Go to your friends. Be a good boy, and in three weeks come and see me. You should be ready for your first lesson.' Then he asked, 'Are you going to take the bus or walk home?'

'I will take a rickshaw,' I replied.

He laughed, and then held up his hand, showing me three of his fingers. 'In three weeks – not three months – I want you to come and see me,' Amar Singh said.

When I reached the room, no one was there. I washed the dishes in the small kitchen, and then went grocery shopping. I cooked vegetables with rice for dinner. Akbar walked into the room. 'Do you remember Ali, the tall guy?' he asked. 'He was supposed to be smuggled from the airport in Bombay to America, and he had to fly through the Hong Kong airport. Hong Kong immigration discovered that Ali was carrying a forged passport, and they sent him back to Bombay. Officials in Bombay tortured him in order to find out who his smuggler was. His smuggler was an Iranian with German passport. The smuggler took five thousand dollars from Ali's father and then disappeared.' Akbar finished his story by saying, 'Ali's brother told me all of this and said that Ali is in the hospital recovering.'

When Babur arrived, Akbar told him the story too. 'I already heard the story from Ali's father, and I went to see Ali in the hospital that afternoon,' Akbar said.

'His father says, if the Iranian fox does not return half of the money, he will kill him!' Babur said.

At that moment Akbar started to laugh. 'Kill? His father is so skinny, I don't think he has the strength to kill a chicken!' Then everyone laughed.

Babur laughed so hard he choked on his food, and then coughed. 'You are right. I think Ali's father does not have the courage to kill an ant.' Then we laughed. There were many stories about the Afghans being smuggled from India to the Western countries.

There was another interesting story about a different Iranian smuggler who had appropriated $25,000 from an Afghan family – two parents and three children – promising to smuggle them all into Canada. The smuggler acquired Nepal visas on their Afghan passports and had assured the family that, after two days in Nepal, they would fly from Tribhuvan International Airport in Kathmandu to Amsterdam, and after three hours in Amsterdam, they would fly to Canada. They would land in Toronto Pearson International Airport, and the duration of this last flight would be seven hours. The family had trusted the smuggler; consequently, the smuggler flew with them to Nepal, and reserved a nice five-star hotel for the family in Kathmandu. The next day, that Iranian smuggler disappeared from that hotel with the Afghan's wife's jewellery, and the $25,000 in large US bills.

Then there was the story of a young Afghan man who had a brother living in Australia who had paid $6,500 to an Afghan Hindu smuggler in Australia to smuggle his brother from India to Australia. That Afghan Hindu smuggler travelled from Australia to New Delhi because of that deal. The smuggler was supposed to use the passport of the brother who had paid him, and was supposed to change the photo on the passport. After meeting the brother in New Delhi, the Hindu smuggler did not change the original photo, assuming the brothers looked alike, even though the brother in New Delhi was two years younger than his brother in Australia. On the day of his flight from the Indira Gandhi International Airport to Australia, at the airport, the New Delhi immigration personnel discovered that passport did not belong to the passenger. The police at the airport then severely tortured him to find out where he had obtained the passport, and who was behind the illegal procedures.

That young Afghan man did not say a word about his brother in Australia, or about the smuggler in New Delhi. Finally, the police released him after three days of tough torture. On the same day of his release, that young Afghan man found where the Afghan Hindu smugglers were hiding, and he stabbed that Hindu smuggler seven times in his liver with a fourteen-inch flat screwdriver. On approximately the same day, the brother in Australia got drunk with his friends and gang raped the Afghan Hindu smuggler's wife and his seventeen-year-old daughter at their residential address. Both brothers were found guilty. The brother in New Delhi was charged with first-degree murder at the New Delhi courthouse, and the brother was charged with participating in gang raping a daughter and mother.

Yet another story involved a tall, fat Pakistani man who had agreed with a smuggler to carry heroin in his stomach from Chatrapati Shivaji International Airport in Mumbai (Bombay) to New York City. This passenger had a stop at Doha International airport in Qatar, and from there had a direct flight to New York City. Because of the long flight from Doha to New York City, the Pakistani man had not been able to keep the drug in his stomach, so he had gone into the airplane's toilet, delivered the packet into the airplane's toilet, then retrieved it and put it into his pocket. Then he had gone back to his window seat. Because of the bad smell, the passenger sitting next to him complained to the flight attendant. That Pakistani man was travelling with a forged American passport under his name. Because of his terrible English accent and his frustration, which caused him to become confused, he was no longer able to express himself verbally. Therefore, the flight attendant called on security personnel to conduct a body search. From the man's left coat pocket, the security guard pulled out a large condom which had been stuffed with heroin.

However, there were some stories with happy endings. Some smuggled passengers had reached their final destinations. Most of the displaced Afghan families and individuals had close relatives living in the United States, Canada, Germany, England, or other Western countries. These family members were able to afford to pay the living costs of their family members in India. A few other families and individuals were supported financially by family members living in Afghanistan.

Fifteen

For three months, I attended the English language school that Amar Singh had helped me to register for. After that, I attended the Shia centre English courses on a regular basis. I purchased my first bicycle in India after living for two months in New Delhi. Some Afghan Shia Hazara that I met had lived in Iran, some had lived in Pakistan, and some had experienced both countries prior to their arrival in New Delhi. In fact, they favoured their life in India. I questioned those who had lived in Pakistan and Iran about their lives there. I was told that the Pakistani and the Iranian general population were racist towards them. They did not like us because of our physical appearance. We look Mongolian, or Turkish. Everywhere we went, we had problems finding decent jobs or renting places to stay. If we were fortunate enough to find a job, we were always looked down on by our employers and were made to do the hardest jobs for lower salaries than the Tajiks or Pashtuns received. On the other hand, it was said that most of the crimes that took place in Pakistan and Iran were committed by the Pashtuns and the Tajiks. Many were smugglers who dealt in drugs, weapons, and humans. Paedophiles, robbers, and murderers were also common.

After three months in New Delhi, I went to see Amar Singh for the purpose of my first lesson. I was curious about what he had in mind to teach me. I arrived his house in the afternoon. As usual, the minute he saw me, started to laugh. 'Come! Come, Bachem. Oh, you have a bicycle now!' And then I followed him into his library. 'Today is your first lesson, and this lesson will be about yourself and your ancestors,' he said. He passed me a pen and a piece of paper. 'Write me your ancestors' names,' he said. He was sitting on his sofa, and asked me to sit in front of him on the chair. 'Write … write,' he said.

I wrote my father's name – Sachi. And my grandpa's name – Hassan Khan. And my great-grandpa's name – Hussein. Then he asked me to read what I had written. I read it out to him, then he shook his head from left to the right. 'No, no, Bachem. Write me *all* of your ancestors' names.'

'I don't know,' I said. 'This all I know.'

He started to laugh again. 'I know why you don't know,' he said, then ground his teeth. Amar Singh brought his face close to mine. 'Who are you?' he asked. I was silent. Then he tapped my right leg. 'Who are you? Answer the question!'

My name is Aftab. I am from Afghanistan.

Then he said, 'Good. Very good. Tell me more about yourself. You belong to which ethnic group?' he asked.

'I belong to the Hazara ethnic group.'

'Excellent,' he said. 'You are a Muslim, but you belong to which sect of Islam?' he asked.

'I belong to the Shia sect of Islam,' I replied.

Then he laughed and laughed. 'Your first lesson is over. For your next lesson you will learn about your ethnic group, the Hazara people of Afghanistan, Bachem.' And then he said, 'I have received a letter from your Uncle Ghulam. Let's go to the living room. We can have tea and open your letter.' Before we left the room, Amar Singh said, 'What we discussed today – don't forget.

Never forget what I tell you. I taught world history at the University of Delhi for fifteen years, Bachem. You are very lucky to have me.'

I was excited to read Uncle Ghulam's letter. I opened it and read that Uncle Ghulam had written about his own and his family's wellbeing in Pakistan. He was working in a vegetable market with his son, Sohrab, and the rest of the family members attended school – an English course. Lastly, Uncle Ghulam stated in his letter, 'Your uncle Rustam is found! And he is in good health. Everyone is happy because of his appearance.' He also asked me to send him a picture of myself, and he promised that, when he wrote next time, he would send me some family pictures. Before I left Amar Singh's house, he said, 'Think about what we have discussed today, and come back in two months for your second lesson, Bachem.' Then he said, 'The roads are crowded. Be careful where you ride your bike, Bachem.'

I always enjoyed shortcuts rather than using the main roads. If I got lost, I would bike back to the main road in order to find the right direction. The routine of cooking, washing clothes, showering every day, attending English classes, going to the park in the evening, and renting TVs and VCRs was uninteresting.

One evening, Nezar showed up in my room with a huge smile. 'Aftab, I have very good news for you,' he said. 'A big surprise!' he said in English. Then he asked, 'Do you know what the word *surprise* means?'

I had learnt that word a few days earlier. I replied, 'Yes, I think I do.'

'You will not believe this. Come to our house,' he said. I asked him to tell me what he had in mind. 'Then it will not be a surprise!' he said. I started to unlock my bike. 'No, you won't need to bike. Let's walk,' he recommended. I had no idea why wanted me to go to his place late in the evening. The walk from my address to his took us less than four minutes. Nezar didn't stop smiling until we reached his address.

I saw that his mother, Aunt Zenat, was standing in front of the door. 'I am happy to see you,' she stated, and pointed to the next room. 'Go,' she said. 'Someone is waiting for you.' I walked into the room and saw Sharouch sitting in the corner. I couldn't believe what I was seeing! I called his name out loud, then he stood up. He seemed very happy and exited to see me. We hugged and kissed each other on the cheeks. Akbar and Babur knew Sharouch from Kabul. We were all happy to have Sharouch, and asked him about the political situation in Kabul. We already knew that the Russian troops had left Afghanistan. 'More and more rockets are launched in the city. They are fired by the Pashtuns Mujahideen,' Sharouch said.

I asked him about Uncle Rustam and shared my joy that his father was finally back with the family. 'You know my father is smart,' he said. 'He was taken by the soldiers on the street, and then was sent to war in the Wardak Province. Three months later, the Mujahideen attacked their military base and killed nearly everyone. Fortunately my father escaped and walked through the mountains. After four days, he reached Bamyan. He lived there for almost nine months. He never told anyone where he had lived in Kabul. He said that, if he had told them where he had lived in Kabul, the soldiers would have come after you guys. And Grandpa told my father he had done the right thing.'

Sharouch was smiling. He said, 'It's good to see you all. You guys are doing well, I can see. At least you do not have to hide, and there is no war in India!' We all agreed on his comments. 'Can you believe how I passed through the airport?' he said. 'I slept on the airplane overnight. Because I am almost eighteen years old, the government official would not have let me pass through,' he said, 'but Grandpa bribed the pilots. I have an Indian visa. Look – it is on my passport,' he said. Sharouch asked us to take him for a walk and show him the neighbourhood. 'India, let's go!' he said.

I still could not believe Sharouch was in India. The next day we went to see Amar Singh. Then we helped Sharouch register with for the United Nations. He also signed up for the English course in the Shia community centre. Sharouch had studied English in high school; his English level was much higher than mine and that of the rest of the boys who had studied English for a year or more in New Delhi. Our room was too small for four people to live in; therefore, Sharouch and I rented another room, and we became roommates. Sharouch was very sensitive. He liked certain people, and he did not like certain things. For example, he did not like Amar Singh. When I told him about my private lesson with Amar Singh, he started to laugh. 'You want to learn about yourself from a Sikh?' he said, and kept on laughing. Even when we needed money, he never wanted to go with me to Amar Singh's house. I also noticed when Sharouch did visit Amar Singh, that Amar Singh did not laugh, and did not smile at him.

I had promised Amar Sing that I would come for my second lesson, so I went to see him. 'Why didn't you bring Sharouch?' Amar Singh asked.

'He did not want to come,' I replied.

'Okay, okay. I understand why,' he said. 'Are you ready for your second lesson?' he asked.

'I think so.'

'Today I will teach you about your ethnic group, which is Hazara.' Then he asked me, 'Do you know what *Hazara* means?'

'No, I don't know.'

'Do you know what *Hazara* means in Dari?' Then he said, '*Hazar* ... the word *hazar*.'

'Yes,' I said. '*Hazar* means thousand in Dari.'

He laughed. 'Good. Good.' He laughed again. His granddaughter, that pretty girl called Mona, came and served us tea. She smiled and said in Hindi, 'You are my grandpa's friend, and he likes you.' She smiled again, and then she said, 'I heard you understand and speak little bit of Hindi and English. If you need help in English, I can help you,' she said.

Then Amar Singh said in English, 'Thank you for the tea. You may leave now.'

'Grandpa,' she said. That day Mona had dressed in light green. Her beautiful, thick, long hair was loose. As she turned her head towards the door, the ends of her hair touched my face. She turned her head back and looked into my eyes. 'Sorry,' she said.

'The history of Afghanistan is a very tragic one,' began Amar Singh. 'It is a nation that has suffered the pressures of both external and internal upheavals. Among all of the ethnic groups, the Hazara people have suffered the most, particularly the Shia sects of the Hazara,' he said.

He put three fingers in the air. 'There are three different theories about the origin of the Hazara people. First is that the Hazara people of Afghanistan could have Turk-Mongol ancestry, as they could be the descendants of an occupying army left in Afghanistan by Genghis Khan. The second theory is that the Hazara are descendants of the Kushans, the ancient dwellers of Afghanistan who are believed to have constructed the Buddhas of Bamyan, which go back to the sixth century. The last theory is that the Hazara people are mixed race of the Kushan dynasty, and the Genghis Khan dynasty.' Then Amar Singh stopped talking, crossed his legs, and had a sip of tea. Using his right fingers, he pushed his moustache up from his lower lip, and then he sighed. 'I agree that the Hazara people are a mixed race,' he said. 'Certain Mongol tribes did travel to eastern Persia and what is now Afghanistan and integrated with the indigenous community. This group then formed their own community, which became the Hazara, with their distinctive facial features, sometimes termed Mongoloid, which bear the origins of their Central Asian ancestry. I am saying this because of the similarity between the facial structure of the Hazara with those depicted in Buddhist murals and statues in the region. Genghis Khan's grandson, Mutagen, was killed in Bamyan. Historical records mention a particularly bloody battle around Bamyan, which is why Genghis Khan allegedly ordered Bamyan to be destroyed in retribution,' he said. 'Islam was brought to Afghanistan in the eighth and ninth centuries by the Arabs.' Amar Singh smiled. 'What do you think?' he asked.

I was very impressed to hear all of this from an Afghan Sikh. 'I don't know,' I said. 'All I know is that it is almost shameful to be Hazara in Afghanistan. Whenever I had disputes with other boys in school or in my neighbourhood, all I heard from them was that the Hazara people are ugly, flat nosed, and not originally from Afghanistan.'

Then Amar Singh started to laugh. In fact, he was not able to stop laughing, 'That is right, Bachem,' he said. 'It is because the Pashtuns have governed Afghanistan in the last two hundred years, and they do not want to reveal the truth about your ethnic groups,' he said. 'Khan Sahib,' he assured me, 'this is India. Don't worry.' Then he asked me, 'Do you know what the word *khan* means?'

At first I shook my head. Then I said, 'It means elder of the family.'

'That is good. *Khan* means "leader", Bachem, and the first khan was the great Genghis Khan, whose army occupied almost all of Asia from the backs of their horses. They were the true khans; today there are many Khan names in India, in Pakistan, and in Afghanistan, but they have nothing to do with true khans.' He kept on laughing. He had the biggest smile and looked into my eyes. 'You know nothing,' he said. 'That is enough for today. Next time I will teach more.'

I was about to leave his house when I found his granddaughter waiting for us in the living room. She had prepared tea, and had put some cookies on a dish on the table. 'Before you leave, have some refreshment,' she said. Amar Singh asked me to sit and then pointed to the chair. The girl left, and I told Amar Singh, 'The people at the room you rented for me called me "Khan Sahib", and even when I go to the market to buy groceries, they call me and my friends "Khan Sahib".'

He laughed even louder than before, and I started to laugh too. 'That is right, Bachem. This is India. Even local people know who Khans were and who they are. It is good that I have enlightened you.' Then, he asked, 'How is Sharouch's English?'

'He speaks much better than I do because he started to learn English when he was very young,' I replied. 'Unfortunately I attended the German school in Kabul.'

'Okay … there is something I want to tell you. Your grandpa called me last week, and he asked if it would be possible for me to find a smuggler to send one of you to a Western country. There is a long waiting list to go by the United Nations, and even that is not guaranteed. The majority of those poor families that have applied for refugee status in the United Nations are hoping to start new lives in the Western countries, but they are refused over stupid reasons. Anyway, bring Sharouch here this week. I need to discover his English level. If his English is acceptable, I know a few smugglers who are trustworthy.'

I tried to tell him the awful stories I had overheard about smugglers.

'I know, Bachem, don't worry. I am Amar Singh, and I am from here.' Then he pressed his palms together and made fists of both hands. 'And it is possible,' he said. 'Don't tell anyone – not even Sharouch. Just bring him here. Then I will decide.' Then he asked what Sharouch had been doing since he arrived in India.

'He is very selfish' I told him. 'He loves to buy new clothes. He attends the English class level five. He purchased a new bicycle a month ago, and he keeps all the money to himself. He justifies this by telling me that he is older than me. We really don't get along very well. He has his own friends; we live in the same room. Sometimes he goes to Old Delhi with his friends. He thinks he is smarter than everyone else because he speaks better English.'

'Okay,' he said. 'I know what you trying to say. I have seen him only once, but tell him to come and see me. And think about what I taught you today. I wish you understood English. I have some good books that are authentically written about your origin, but it is okay.'

I left soon after that, and biked back to my room. Sharouch was not there. I biked to the park. There were only a few Afghan boys there, and I asked them if they had seen Sharouch. They said 'Old Delhi … Old Delhi,' and giggled. I waited for Sharouch; he arrived very late that night. I mentioned to him that Amar Singh wanted to see him. 'That Hindu! What does he want from me?' he asked.

'I don't know. Just go and see him.'

'I don't like Hindus,' he said. 'Especially the Sikhs. They never shave their hair, and they smell very bad. Last time I was there, I almost vomited in his house.' Then he smiled. 'Look, I bought this T-shirt today. It says, "free and fresh".'

'Don't worry about that T-shirt,' I told him. 'You must go and see him. He wants to tell you something important, and he is Grandpa's friend.'

'Grandpa's friend. Ah … Grandpa also has Pashtun friends, and those Pashtuns killed your father. They almost killed my father too. If Grandpa had allowed us to leave Afghanistan a few years ago, we would be in America, Canada, or in Europe. What does he know? All he says is that the right regime must take over Afghanistan,' Sharouch complained.

'Yes,' I said, 'but Amar Singh has something to tell you that is very important.'

'Why do you insist that I see him?' he asked.

'This is very important,' I said. 'I swear to Allah.'

Then he stopped talking and looked me in the eyes. 'Is everyone okay in Kabul?' he asked.

'Yes, yes … it is not about Afghanistan. Just go and see him. We can bike to his house; it is not far.'

'Okay, okay. I will go and see him this week,' he said.

'If I were you, I would see him tomorrow,' I said, 'and I swear to Allah this is important, and it is good.'

'You, Khan, you and Grandpa always kept secrets from us in Kabul, and you and this old Sikh now …,' he said.

'Okay, okay, don't go!' I said. 'Do you think I gave a shit?' I said.

Then he lay down on his mattress, turned off the light, and covered himself with the bedsheet. 'Khan Sahib,' he said, and then he sniggered.

In the morning, he came out from the ground-floor bathroom, which we shared with our landlord. I prepared tea, and we had jam with bread for breakfast. 'Is it really important to go and see Amar Singh?' he asked.

'It is very important,' I said. 'If you want, I will not go to my English class this morning, which starts at ten. Instead I will bike with you to his house.'

'It's that important? Oh, oh, really,' he said. Finally, I convinced him, and then we biked to Amar Singh's house. I knocked, and his pretty granddaughter opened the door. Once Sharouch saw her, he became amused and spoke English to her.

'You are here,' she said to me. 'Grandpa is taking bath. Ajaa, ajaa (come, come). Is this your cousin?' she asked.

'Yes,' I said.

Then Sharouch asked me in Dari, 'Do you know her?' I said that I did, and we followed her to the living room. Sharouch sat on the sofa. 'Aftab, you must go to your English class,' he said. Then he smiled to the girl. 'Go, go. I know how to find my way back,' Sharouch told me in English.

'Oh, you speak good English,' Mona said. Then she asked me with her soft voice, 'What time does your English class start?'

'Ten o'clock.'

'Ya,' she said. 'You should go. You have twenty minutes to get there.' At that moment I left.

Sharouch came home late that evening from Amar Singh's house. His attitude had totally changed. His mind was somewhere else. 'Oh, man, I am so happy,' he said. 'I can't believe this. Why didn't you tell me this last night?' he asked. But then he said, 'I understand. I understand. Amar Singh told me never to say anything to anyone also.' And then he said, 'Mona spoke to me all day. Amar Singh thinks my English is good enough for me to fly on a forged passport to the Western countries. He has known Grandpa for very long time, and Grandpa has already sent him the money for the smuggler. Grandpa prefers North America – Canada or the United States. I can't believe it, Bachem!' he said. 'Tomorrow I have to go and see Amar Singh again. There are a few words and phrases in English that are used at the airport and on the plane. I have to learn them, and that girl is so pretty! Oh my God!' he said. Then he brought a piece of paper out from his pocket. 'Bachem, I have to learn these words and sentences, and tomorrow I will go to his house again.'

The next morning, Sharouch kept on repeating what he had told me the night before. Before leaving for Amar Singh's house, he pointed his finger at me. 'You don't tell anyone about this,' he warned. 'When you go to your English class, say nothing. I don't want anyone to know about this.' And he left. It was late in the evening when he returned from Amar Singh's house. 'The girl was not there today,' he told me, 'but the smuggler was there. He is Iranian. His name is Ahmed, and he was with us for the whole day. Soon everything should be fine. The smuggler took me to a photo shop where we got passport-size pictures taken. He asked my address. The smuggler told me to stay home and wait for the right time to come. This Iranian is smooth. He has long, curly hair down to his shoulders, and he wears a moustache. He never smiles, and he looks like those American actors in the movies.' Then he said, 'However, he promised that in less than a month everything should be ready – my forged passport and a ticket to North America.' Then Sharouch started to count how long he had been in India. 'For only two months and seven days,' he said.

Sharouch was so excited he was not even able to sleep that night. I went to bed, and he was still awake. I was asleep when I heard someone is calling, 'Khan Sahib, Khan Sahib,' in the middle of the night. The light on the balcony was on. I saw that Sharouch was sleeping. He had covered himself with a bedsheet. I stood up and saw our landlord standing in front of the door. 'There is someone looking for Sharouch,' he told me. 'Go and get him.' I was not even fully awake, but I walked down the stairs. There was a taxi outside with the engine running and the lights on. The driver pointed at me and motioned for me to get close to him. I approached the taxi and looked through the window. I saw a man with long, curly hair and a moustache. He was wearing a black leather jacket. 'Aftab,' he said, 'wake up Sharouch. Ask him to come and see me.' He spoke in Farsi. I had never met that person, but he had spoken to me by name, as if he had known me for a very long time.

I said in Dari, 'What is your name?

'Ahmed the Iranian,' he replied. I knew he was the smuggler. I went up the stairs and tried to wake up Sharouch, but he was in a deep sleep and did not want to wake up. I had to raise my voice. 'Wake up! Wake up! He is here!'

'Who, who, who?' He finally came to consciousness.

'I think your smuggler. He is waiting for you outside.'

'What? What? He said in a month!' Then he put on a T-shirt and walked down the stairs. He approached the taxi. I had followed him, and I was standing right behind him. Sharouch got into the car and sat next to the smuggler in the backseat. A few minutes later, he got out of the taxi and went back to the room. He started to search for his passport. When he found it, he faced me. 'That is him. He wants me to go with him right now. The smuggler just told me not to bring anything but my passport. Then he hugged me. 'Aftab, Bachem, I am going. Amar Singh told me to listen to whatever he had to say.' Soon Sharouch was in the taxi. He left with the smuggler, just like that.

Sixteen

Sharouch disappeared in the blink of an eye. I was not able to sleep that night. I waited until 7.00 a.m. and biked to Amar Singh's house to inquire about Sharouch. I arrived early in the morning and knocked on his door. Amar Singh opened the door himself and shook his head left to right. 'What is going on, Bachem?' he said.

'The smuggler took Sharouch at around three o'clock this morning,' I said.

'I know, so what is wrong? Come inside the house,' he said.

When Sharouch came from your home last night, he said he might be going within a month, but the smuggler took him on the same day,' I said.

'Yes, I know. Sharouch was here all day yesterday, and the smuggler and I trained him properly, and taught him a few words. We thought he was ready,' he said. Then he laughed. 'Look, Bachem, the smugglers are like wolves and foxes. They are unpredictable. We don't know when they will attack, or when they will use their charms. The smuggler has taken him to Bombay. Within two to three days we will have news. Just pray. I have been praying for Sharouch to arrive safely at his final destination.' He smiled and said, 'I have known this smuggler for five years, and he is good. You know why? Because he can be a wolf and a fox,' he said. I have paid him three thousand dollars, which is half of the total amount. I will pay the other half if Sharouch settles in North America,' he said.

'Where? Canada or the United States?' I asked.

'Your Grandpa likes North America,' he said. 'If Sharouch gets caught on the way, we will lose the three thousand.' And then he said, 'You know your Grandpa is stubborn, smart, and tough. I need to go back to my prayers. You have to attend your English course. Come and see me in two days' time, and then I should have information for you.' He scratched his tummy then said, 'I do not like to repeat myself, but I remind you not to say anything to anyone. If any of your friends or Sharouch's friends ask about him, say he went to see the Taj Mahal,' he said.

I biked home and fell asleep. In the evening, I biked to the park to play football with the boys. Almost everyone asked me where Sharouch was. There were about seven or nine boys, and we met up with two boys who were cousins who had arrived from Kabul the day before. Akbar asked me, 'Where is Sharouch, Aftab? Why don't you talk?'

'Sharouch went to see the Taj Mahal,' I said, but everyone started to laugh. They even stopped playing football to laugh. Then Akbar got close to Babur and whispered into his ear. Babur smiled and shook his head. 'No, no,' he said. Then Babur asked me where Sharouch was.

'The Taj Mahal,' I said, and everyone started to laugh again, even louder. I felt humiliated, and I stared at every one of them.

A skinny boy, who did not like to talk much, said, 'Taj Mahal. I'd like to go to the Taj Mahal too.' Everyone laughed again. Finally, I left the football field and walked towards my bicycle to leave. Babur ran after me and put his hand on my shoulder. 'Aftab, tell me, where is Sharouch?'

'I told you,' I said. 'He went to see the Taj Mahal. Then I pushed his hand off my shoulder and grabbed my bike. I could hear everyone chanting, 'Taj Mahal, Taj Mahal.' They were laughing and giggling.

It was not easy to be alone and humiliated. I was not able to sleep, eat, or drink. The next morning I attended the English class. I heard boys still saying 'Taj Mahal' while rolling their eyes and whispering with one another.

Late in the evening, Babur and Akbar came to my room for visit. They sat across me. Akbar was smiling, but Babur seemed much more serious. Then Babur lit a cigarette and sighed. 'Listen,' he said, 'we know he did not go to the Taj Mahal. Maybe he told you that, but what time did he leave last night?'

'Before I went to bed,' I said, 'Sharouch left. He said would be back in three or four days.'

Then Akbar had a smile on his face. 'Three or four days,' he repeated, and he looked at Babur.

Babur turned his face and blew smoke. 'How did he leave? Who did he go with?'

'I don't know,' I said. 'He just left.'

Then Babur looked at Akbar. 'If he is not back tonight, we have to go to Old Delhi and look for him,' he said. I was curious about Old Delhi. Then Babur smiled at Akbar. 'Overnight,' he said, 'but just one night.'

I had no idea what they were talking about, then Babur tapped Akbar's shoulder. 'Let's go,' he said. 'We'll wait until tomorrow.' And they left me with my curiosity. Next morning I did not go to my English class. I knew if I went, everyone would ask me about Sharouch. In the evening I went to the park. The boys were playing football. Everyone stared at me. I sat on the grass next to my bicycle; I did not want to chat with any one. They still were giggling, and were saying 'Taj Mahal, Taj Mahal'. One of them called out and said that Babur and Akbar had gone to the Taj Mahal to look for Sharouch. Then everyone started to laugh again.

I could not believe what was going on with Sharouch, Old Delhi, and the boys. The next morning I left for Amar Singh's house to find out more about Sharouch's travelling. As usual, we sat one on one, and face to face. 'Sharouch left yesterday. He is travelling to New York City,' he told me. 'Just pray, Bachem, for him to arrive his final destination safely. The good news is that he has passed through the airport in Bombay with no problem on an Indonesian passport with a student visa. Now he has a stop in Paris, then a direct flight to New York.' He continued, 'The smuggler told me Sharouch is brave; therefore, he has good chances on passing through his layover in Paris. Just pray, Bachem.' I was smiling; Amar Singh shook his chin, and asked me softly, 'What is it?' When he shook his chin, his long white beard undulated all the way down to his belly button. Than he passed his palm over his white, long beard. 'Are you making fun of my long beard?' he asked.

'No, no,' I replied.

'Then what is it?' Amar Singh asked one more time. I told him how the boys had asked me where Sharouch was and how they had made fun of me when I had told them Sharouch had gone to see the Taj Mahal. I also told him about Old Delhi, and that a couple of his friends went to search for him in Old Delhi, even staying overnight.

He started to laugh. 'Afghan boys,' he said, and then Amar Singh asked me to tell him everything about the Afghan boys. I told him about what had happened on the football field, and about my humiliation when they had made fun of me the day before in English class. I told him about Akbar and Babur's visit the night after Sharouch had left, and about their plans to search for Sharouch in Old Delhi. 'Okay, okay,' he said. 'I know everything now. You do not have to say anything.'

Then I asked him, 'What is it about Old Delhi that I don't know?'

'Bachem, it is okay. There are bad places there where men go to drink alcohol and see women, and things like that.' Then he said, 'Look at me … you don't go there, you understand? I can't believe Sharouch went there. He was in India only for two months, and already discovered those bad places.'

Then he said, 'You stay here tonight. I know your friends will come to you tonight again and ask about Sharouch.' Then started to lecture me about his friendship with Grandpa, and the promises he had made to Grandpa to look after his grandchildren as his own, and so on. He pointed to the hall. 'On the left of that hallway there is my granddaughter Mona's room. Sleep there tonight. Mona will be back in two days.'

Then I asked him, 'Where is your granddaughter?'

'She left to see the Taj Mahal two days ago on a college trip.'

Once he said *Taj Mahal,* it made me laugh. I kept on laughing; I was not able to stop.

He stared at me. 'It is not the Taj Mahal that your friends are thinking about,' he said. 'It is the real Taj Mahal.' The way said it made me laugh again, and then he started to laugh too.

I said, 'Taj Mahal!'

He smiled at me and shook his head. 'You Afghan boys are really a bunch of jokers,' he said. 'Go go and see the room in which you will spend the night. Don't touch anything. Just use the bed. I do not want my granddaughter to find out you have spent a night in her room. Anyway, tomorrow by this time we will know if Sharouch has survived his six-hour layover in Paris and made it to New York. Anyway, that is what the smuggler told me.'

I lay on her bed. What a soft bed. And I could smell the perfume in her room. The way she had placed all her stuff made her room as clean and as pretty as her beautiful thick hair. Late in the evening Amar Singh came into the room and mentioned it again: 'It is good you are spending the night here; otherwise, those Afghan kids would not have left you alone. They would have persisted in asking where Sharouch is.' Then he said, 'Good night,' in English, and left for his room.

It was in the middle of the night that I heard Mona whispering into my ear. 'Aftab, Aftab, wake up. I am back from the Taj Mahal.' Then she passed her soft palm over my face, and she lowered herself against me. Her pretty hair was all over my face. Then she straightened her body. I saw her big eyes and her round, naked breasts as she looked down. 'I know you like me,' she said. 'And I like you, but Grandpa is home.' The tone of her beautiful, soft voice became lower, and lower until she disappeared. I awoke with sweat all over my body. Amar Singh was sitting on an armchair reading a small book he held in his right hand. 'Good morning, Bachem. Open the fridge and eat whatever you like. Boil your own tea. If you want to take a shower, you know where the bathroom is.'

After I washed, I opened the biggest fridge I had ever seen and searched for food. 'You don't have to go to your English class today,' he said as he walked into the kitchen. 'I know those boys will not leave you alone until they know where Sharouch is.'

I spent some hours in Amar Singh's library. Books were everywhere. The phone rang a few times. Every time he answered the phone, he spoke in a different language. There were two air conditioners installed in his house. When I left the house and walked into the yard, I saw a little garden in the corner. There was a broken wooden bench. A tall stool was standing next to the bench. A little bird was singing. The wind came and blew the pretty flowers, and made the flowers and leaves move back and forth. Another bird appeared. It was red with blue dots around its neck. It opened its wings and sang.

'Aftab, Aftab, come here!' Amar Singh called. I went to see him in the living room. 'Keep the door closed when the air conditioning is on,' he said. I went back to see the birds, but they were not there. It was not long after that the phone rang again. I heard Amar Singh speak much louder on the phone. He kept on saying, 'Sharouch, Sharouch, you arrived, Bachem!' When I heard that, I ran from the library to the living room. Amar Singh was all exited, and he waved his hand towards me to come close to the phone. He passed me the phone. 'Here, here,' he said, 'Sharouch is in New York!'

'I am in America at the smuggler's friend's house,' Sharouch said. 'His friend got me at the airport. I cannot believe this!'

I kept on saying, 'Good, good, good.' There was nothing more to say or to ask.

Then Amar Singh took the phone. 'Bachem, be careful in America … Hello, hello, hello?' Amar Singh hung up the phone. 'Disconnected,' he said.

Amar Singh was a lot more excited than I was. He had the biggest smile, yet he kept passing his arm over his eyes to wipe the tears from his face. He put his hands up. 'Thank you, thank you, God,' he prayed. He got up from his armchair, waved both of his hands in the air. 'Yes, yes, yes!' he said. The phone rang again just then. Amar Singh answered it. 'It is you. Good. Thank you. Yes, I am at home,' he said, and then he hung up the phone. He looked into my eyes with his own glassy eyes. 'The fox is coming, Bachem. You should leave. He does not want to see anyone but me; he is coming to take the other half of his money,' he said. 'Now you can tell all of your friends where Sharouch is.'

I took my bike and left. I could not believe that Sharouch was in America, a country where every one of the Afghan displaced wants to be. It was afternoon; still early to go to the park. I arrived at the park, but none of Afghan boys was there. A couple hours later, I saw five of the boys walking towards the football field. One was holding the ball, and every once in a while he bounced it against the ground and caught it. Babur walked tall up front as if leading the boys. Akbar had his left hand on the shoulder of another boy as they walked towards me.

Everyone seemed worried; particularly Babur had his head down. Akbar, with another boy, got close to me. 'Where were you? We have been looking for you everywhere,' he said. 'Any news about Sharouch?' he asked.

'Yes,' I said.

'Why are you smiling then?' Babur got closer to me. 'We are worried, and you are smiling,' he said. 'Where is Sharouch? Why don't you say something?'

'Sharouch is in America,' I said.

'What, what, what?' Everyone repeated the same word over and over, and then I was surrounded by the boys instantly. I heard everyone saying, 'America, America, America.' Then everyone giggled and laughed. No one believed me. Once I finished explaining what had happened over the last four days, and our relationship with Amar Singh, eventually they trusted me. Everyone got exited, especially Babur and Akbar. 'Sharouch is in America … oh my God,' they were saying to each other.

Everyone was happy about Sharouch's arrival in America. They asked me to throw a party for them on the same evening. I had no choice but to accept their request. Our party was, as usual, to rent a TV, VCR, and a bunch of movies to enjoy all night. Babur took my hand and asked me to talk to him in private. 'I swear,' he said. 'Akbar and I were so worried about Sharouch, especially when we came to your room last night. We waited for you for a few hours. You did not show up. I am telling you the truth.' Then he said, 'A few weeks ago, Sharouch asked me to find him women. I was the one who took him to the whorehouses in Old Delhi. At first when he went and didn't come home, I thought he had stayed at the whorehouse overnight with girls. The second night, I assumed Sharouch had gone missing. Then last night we could not find you either. I swear, I was so worried that even I was not able to fall asleep last night. Akbar and I had no idea what to do to find you and Sharouch,' Babur explained. 'We had kept the secret about the prostitutes mainly because Sharouch had asked us not to say anything to you. "Aftab will report everything to Grandpa in Kabul," Sharouch told us. If you do not believe me, why don't you ask Akbar?' he said. 'Now I think you are cool,' he continued. 'If you want, this week I can take you to a prostitute,' Babur proposed; then he smiled.

Akbar, with the other boys, had already selected the movies, except there was argument over one American cowboy movie that some of us had already seen (*The Good, the Bad, and the Ugly*). Akbar took Babur aside in private and whispered into Babur's ear, and gestured for me to join them. Then Babur asked me, 'There is another thing that we need to know – have you ever seen porn movies?' I said I hadn't.

Babur and Akbar giggled, and then Akbar asked me, 'Do you want to watch a porn movie tonight? But the price for the porn movie is higher. It is up to you since you are paying for the whole thing,' Akbar said.

'We cannot watch the porn movie with everyone, because they will talk,' Babur said. 'Do not invite anyone else but us.'

'How about Nezar?' I asked.

'No, no, if you invite Nezar, his mother will get very upset with me. She does not like me,' Babur said. Babur asked everyone to gather around, then he made an announcement: 'Tonight Aftab is inviting us to watch movies. I am sure we will enjoy watching the movies. But under one condition: that we will tell no one – I mean no one.' Everyone agreed.

'Our room is bigger than yours, and we are six people, so let's do it in our room,' Babur said. Then Babur asked the other boys to come to his home at 8.00 p.m. The other three boys, who were roommates, left the park. 'I want to give my uncle's phone number to Sharouch,' said Babur. 'Why should he stay with the Iranians? Why not with my uncle? My uncle drives a taxi in New Jersey. I will give you my uncle's phone number, and the next time you go to that Hindu house, give Amar Singh the phone number, so he can give it to Sharouch. There is a shop next to our house where my uncle calls me sometimes. I should give you that shop's telephone number too,' Babur said.

Then Akbar said, 'How can we watch the porn movie without this crowd knowing?'

Babur started to laugh. 'Like usual,' he said. 'We will watch five regular movies, which we should be finished watching by five or six in the morning. Then we will ask that coward to leave. We'll put the porn movie on, and three of us will watch. We have done this before.' Then Babur asked me, 'Aftab, remember the last time we watched six movies, and then you left, but Sharouch stayed? We watched the porn movie then too. Were you suspicious, Aftab, that we had another movie?' I said I was not. 'Yes, Sharouch was so good at keeping a secret,' Babur said. 'There is another shop, which is a little far away. I like to rent from her. That shopkeeper is a woman. I have seen all the porn movies from the shop where we rent usually, and that guy is an asshole too. Last time I was late only for half an hour, and I had to pay extra. I told him his VCR was not functioning properly and that was the reason we were late, but that Hindu did not believe me. We have seen most of his regular movies too,' Babur explained.

We walked through the crowd, and eventually we reached the shop. Babur and Akbar started to choose movies from her selection. We selected two Indian movies, one Bruce Lee movie, and two American action movies. Babur got close to the shopkeeper and whispered into her ear, and then she turned red. 'No, no, no!' she said.

Then Akbar said, 'Of course she has porn movies. Look at her face.' Then he said, 'Babur, tell her if she does not rent us the porn movie, we will cancel everything, and we will go to another shop.'

Babur said, 'No, no. I am sure she has them. I want you guys to go and wait on that corner. I will speak to her in private. Maybe she will say yes.' Akbar left the six movies on the counter. The lady stared at Akbar. I left with Akbar, and we stood on the corner. Babur was talking to her, and she was shaking her head right to left. Finally Babur came towards us. The lady was staring at the three of us. Babur said, 'This bitch does not want to rent us the porn movie. She thinks we are too young, and she says you have to be over nineteen years of age. She is so smart. She told me we are not even seventeen years old.'

'I can't believe this,' Akbar said. 'Go and tell her we are not asking to have sex with her! It is just the movie that we want to watch!' Three of us started to laugh at Akbar's proposal.

Then, Babur said, 'I can try something else.' She was still looking at us as she was selling groceries to her customers. 'I can tell her that we rent from the other shops all the time. If she doesn't rent to us, we will never come back to her shop ever again. If she rents us the porn movie, then we will rent from her shop two to three times a week.'

'Yes, yes, that is good,' said Akbar. 'And tell her we promise we will never tell anyone that we have rented porn movies from her shop.'

'Okay, okay … you guys stay here,' Babur said. 'I will make this deal with this bitch.' He walked towards her shop. The lady refused again. We could see her shaking her head, and she was looking at us as she was talking with Babur. From far away, Akbar put his palms together and brought his hands close to his jaw and bowed towards her and smiled. Then she looked at us. Babur turned his face towards us and winked. Akbar was about to walk towards the shop, but Babur waved his hand and shook his head as he walked back towards us. We were about fifteen meters away from the shop. Babur came and said, 'I told her all that, but still she says no. Too young, she says.'

Akbar got emotional and said out loud, 'This has taken almost an hour! Fuck her, let's go to Raja's shop.'

Then Babur said, 'Calm down. I will try for the third time, because I asked her how many porn movies she has. She said one.'

'Fuckin' bitch,' Akbar said. 'I know she has more than one.' Finally, the three of us walked towards her shop. We told her that we would never, ever go to her shop ever again. We were about ten meters away from her shop, heading to Raja's shop.

Suddenly, we heard, 'Brothers, brothers!'

Babur turned and told us, 'Wait here.' Then he walked towards her. She bent down and whispered into Babur's ear. Then Babur looked at us and smiled. Akbar put his hand around my neck. 'I knew it! I knew she would accept!' And he started to laugh out loud. 'I can't believe you have never seen a porn movie,' he said. 'The first time I saw a porn movie was in Kabul, with my cousin, and my cousin was killed in the Helmand Province a few years ago, when he was soldier. He was so cool. I miss him.'

Babur came back with the biggest smile. 'We got it!' he said. 'The prices are the same, but her TV is a little smaller than Raja's. It is only seven o'clock. She said come back at eight to pick it up. We must return everything tomorrow morning before nine.'

'Let's go and wait in the park for another hour,' Akbar said. While we were waiting at the park, Akbar and Babur talked about nothing but sex. They made fun of me, saying I was Grandpa's son, I had never seen porn movies, and I was a virgin. Both were looking at me, laughing.

'Let's go! Let's go. It is seven forty-five. We have fifteen minutes,' Babur said.

I paid the money. Babur took the VCR, and Akbar carried the TV. I picked up the movies, and we walked for fifteen minutes to get to the room. Three other boys were waiting in front of the building. 'Look at those cowards,' Akbar said. 'They do not do anything. We carry everything, and they are not going to pay anything. I wish we had not invited them.'

'I know. If they were not here, we could watch porn all night,' Babur said in a funny way. Then we laughed.

'It is good that I have hidden the porn movie under my shirt,' Akbar said. 'That guy, whom I don't like, is so stubborn. He loves porn movies. Last time, I almost had to fight him over which movie to watch first.'

'I know,' Babur said. 'I don't like Jawad either.'

'If these guys argue over which movie to watch first, I swear I will kick the three of them out of my room,' Akbar said.

'Yes, yes,' Babur confirmed.

'They are not paying for anything anyway. Sharouch is our friend, and even Sharouch did not like them!' Akbar said. Once we got close to the boys, Akbar passed the TV set to Jawad. 'Hold this. I need to open the door,' Akbar said. Jawad took the TV set and sighed.

Then Babur passed the VCR to Shams. 'Take this. You boys are dressed as if you've been invited to a wedding,' Babur said, giggling as he walked up the stairs.

The minute we sat around the room, Babur said, 'Look, Aftab has paid for everything, and he will choose which movie to watch first.'

Akbar smiled at me, and then winked. 'I know which movie Aftab wants to watch first,' he said as he plugged in the TV and the VCR. Jawad got up to look through the plastic bag to see which movies we had selected to watch for the night. Akbar pulled the bag from Jawad's hands. 'You don't touch anything,' Akbar said. Jawad did not say anything. He got back on the mattress, leaned his back against the wall, and sighed. Then Shams took a pillow from the corner of the room, put it against the wall, and leaned his back on that. Babur was out on the balcony. He waved at me to go talk with him. Then he whispered into my ear, 'Don't say anything about the porn movie,' he said. As I was passing through the kitchen door to enter the room, Zeya was standing in the kitchen. He looked into my eyes, then smiled.

Six of us were in the room, and we played the first movie. Everything was fine until we were watching the fourth movie, an Indian movie. The lights were turned off. The only light in the room came from the TV screen. The dispute started when Babur wanted to leave the room for a smoke. Babur's right foot touched Jawad's leg, and Babur fell to the carpet. Then Akbar stood up and kicked Jawad's leg. 'If you are sleeping, go to your room! Look, everyone is sitting, and you are lying on your back as if you are watching movies in your mother's house.'

Then Jawad stood up and pushed Akbar. 'Don't mention my mother's name,' Jawad said. Akbar regained his balance and grabbed Jawad by his neck. The two were about to start punching one another.

Babur interfered to prevent the fight. 'Yes, yes,' he said, 'Akbar is right. If you are falling asleep, go to your room.'

Jawad tapped a few times on his chest. 'If you want to fight, let's do it outside. Don't talk about my mother,' Jawad said. This was around five in the morning.

Babur stopped the movie and switched on the light. 'Look, anybody who wants to leave, leave. Otherwise, we watch the American movie after this Indian one,' he said. Every one of us in the room was half asleep. Shams, the skinny guy who did not talk much, said, 'We all have seen this old Indian movie. Of course we are falling asleep. And it is three hours long!'

'Aftab has not seen this movie, Akbar said, 'and he is the one who has paid for everything. If you are tired, go to your room.' He pointed in the direction of the room.

All of a sudden, Jawad stood up. 'Let's go, Shams. This is the last time we'll watch movies with them.' Then he said, 'Zeya, let's go. What are you waiting for?'

'I will wait to watch the American movie after this Indian movie is over,' Zeya said.

'Okay, okay, Jawad, let's go,' Shams said, and finally they left.

Babur and Akbar wanted Zeya to leave too, but Zeya said, 'I always wanted to watch *Rocky II* again. I love that *Rambo* movie, and I am not tired.' He smiled.

Akbar wanted to play the movie, but Babur said, 'No, let's take a break … let the VCR cool down.'

'Ya, ya, let it cool down,' Zeya said, and he kept on smiling.

Akbar started gossiping about Zeya's roommates. He said they were cowards, and that they were aggressive and ignorant, especially Jawad.

Zeya did not want not to say anything, but he said this: 'Ya, ya, but there are only a few Hazara in New Delhi, and we must be united.'

Babur was about to fall asleep. He was tired like every one of us. We had not stopped yawning in that room. Akbar was quiet. He shook his head. 'Let's play the movie,' he said.

Zeya smiled at everyone in the room. 'Put on the movie – the *real* movie,' he said.

'What real movie are you talking about?' Akbar said. 'There are only two more movies we have not seen yet.'

Zeya kept on smiling. 'You know what I mean – the *movie*.' It was so funny the way he said it. Zeya made the three of us laugh, then he said, 'I am talking about the cartoon movie.' And then we laughed again.

'We did not rent a porn movie this time.' Akbar said. 'We asked for it, but the shopkeeper told us that we were too young. Babur started to laugh. I laughed, and when Akbar saw us laughing, he started to laugh too.

'Babur, I heard you whisper into Aftab's ear. I was in the kitchen,' Zeya said. He sat up straight and pressed his palms against his face and laughed.

'No way ... did you hear me for real?' Babur asked, then he sat straight on his mattress and smiled. 'You haramzada (bastard),' he said. Everyone laughed. Babur unfolded his mattress and took the movie out, and we got excited. The movie was wrapped in a piece of white towel. Babur unwrapped it.

Akbar and Zeya were so exited. At the same time, they said, 'Put on the *real* movie ... put it on!' Then Akbar and Zeya looked at each other and started to laugh. 'I don't care,' said Akbar. 'I have seen so many porn movies, and we rented this porn because of Aftab. He has never seen a porn movie in his life!' Then we started to giggle and smiled at each other. 'I hope I have not seen this movie,' Akbar said as he took the movie from Babur and put it into the VCR. When the movie started playing, Akbar and Babur started swearing at the shopkeeper. 'We have seen this movie,' said Akbar. 'This will be our third time watching this movie! Last time we watched it with Sharouch, which was a week ago.' he said. 'Sharouch is in America, and I am sure he has already tried a blond American girl.'

We laughed over and over. It was unbelievable to watch a porn movie for the first time. I saw everything in the first five minutes of the movie. 'Wait, wait, Aftab,' Akbar said. 'There is a blond girl with a black man. She is very hot.'

'No, no,' said Babur. 'I think the girl with black hair, when she makes love with blond girl, is much hotter.' In that one porn movie, I saw men with women, and women with women. I could not believe what my eyes were watching.

Seventeen

My perspectives had changed; so had everything else. A couple days after the movie party, I went to Amar Singh's house to find out more about Sharouch. I had the contact information for Babur's uncle who lived in New Jersey to give Sharouch.

Amar Singh looked at me. 'What has happened to you? Were you sick, Bachem? It seems you have lost weight.'

'No, nothing has happened,' I replied.

'I spoke to your grandpa the day before yesterday' he said. 'Everyone is fine, and they are very happy that Sharouch has arrived in America. The political and economical situations are really bad in Kabul, and thank God your family members are good. And I called your uncle in Pakistan. Everyone is fine. Why don't you say anything?' he asked.

I told Amar Singh about Babur's uncle in New Jersey, and gave him the contact information. 'Oh, good, good. Sharouch asked about that. He is living with an Iranian man, and working for a restaurant. New York is a big city with too many crimes. It would be good for Sharouch to move to New Jersey,' he said. Then he laughed. 'A seventeen-year-old Hazara boy fresh from Kabul in one the biggest cities in the world – New York. I cannot imagine how will he behave!' And then he laughed again. Finally he asked me, 'Why are you so quiet? Come here. Do you have a fever?' he asked, and he put his palm on my forehead. 'No, no, you do not have a fever. Have you been eating properly?'

'Yes, yes, I have. Nothing is wrong. I have not been sleeping that much. In the last two days, the boys made me watch movies to celebrate Sharouch's arrival in America,' I replied.

'Oh, I see. How did the boys react when you told them that Sharouch is in America?' Amar Singh wanted to know.

'Everyone got exited,' I told him. 'No one believed at first. Then I explained everything to them, and finally they believed me.

'That is right,' he advised me. 'Don't tell anyone about this smuggler. And don't give my address to anyone. I do not want to get into trouble with the police here, Bachem.' Then he said, 'Mona returned from her Taj Mahal trip yesterday. She is so smart, she smelled you in her bed, but she didn't mind. She will be back tonight, and next week she will start her first year at the university in Bombay, and I will be lonely again. Please don't be shy. Whenever you need money, ask. The money I give you is your grandpa's money. Your Grandpa and I have unfinished business to take care of,' he said. Then he laughed and laughed. As usual, every few minutes or so, he pushed his moustache up from his lower lip. Then he passed his palm over his long white beard, which covered almost all of his upper body. Sometimes he would put his hand under his beard and tap a few times on his big belly. 'Your grandpa … what a stubborn man! He wants to teach me, but sometime he has reasons,' Amar Singh said.

The air pollution, crowds, humidity, evening football, English class, and general noise were tiring. On the other hand, the free animals, colourful environment, pretty birds, and hearing different stories from the boys kept me entertained. A few weeks after my talk with Amar Singh, I went back to see him and pick up some money in order to pay my rent. He wrinkled his forehead when he saw me. 'Come, come, we need to talk. Where were you? Ah, ah … I was worried about you. What is wrong with you?' he asked. 'Since Sharouch left for America, you have changed, and you don't talk much. You look at me and I feel that I don't know you anymore. Why don't you say something?' he asked.

'Nothing is wrong, Uncle,' I said. 'The weather is very hot. I am busy studying English, and I stay at home most of the time.'

Then he asked me about my room – how big it was, and if I had an air conditioner. I told him I did not have an air conditioner. Then he sighed and shook his head. 'I understand. Let's go see your room. I want to know how you live. Leave your bike; we'll take a rickshaw.'

After a short journey, we entered my room. Then he asked where my kitchen and bathroom were. 'I cook on the balcony,' I said, 'and I share the bathroom with the landlord. It is on the first floor.'

'No, no, Bachem,' he said. 'This is not how you should live. I will find you another room. Sorry, this is my fault. I should have checked on you when Sharouch left.' Then he said, 'Let's go. Lock your door.'

We went back to his house, and he called a few people. In the evening, Amar Singh asked me to pass the night at his house. 'Whenever you are ready for your private lesson, let me know, Bachem,' he said. Because of the heat and humidity, I stayed indoors. I was in his library lying on the sofa. Amar Singh entered into the room. I started to get up, but he said, 'Relax, relax! It is cool here.' Then he laughed. I pulled up my legs, and he sat next to me and pointed to the bookshelves. 'Go and get me that book,' he said. I approached the bookshelves and put my hand on a book. 'No, two books to your right,' he said. The minute I gave him the book, he asked me to go and get his comb from the living room. I left to search for his comb, and when I came back, he said, 'Finally, you found it.' Then he pointed his finger at the chair. 'Sit down,' he said.

He opened the book to a page on which the world map was printed, and then he stretched his index finger to point to the map. 'Here are India, Iran, Armenia, Georgia, Kazakhstan, Kyrgyzstan, Mongolia, Tajikistan, Turkmenistan, Uzbekistan, Iraq, Pakistan, the west of China, Russia, and Afghanistan. Genghis Khan conquered all of those nations. His empire covered about thirteen million square kilometres. The Mongol Empire reached its greatest extent under Kublai Khan, his grandson, at almost twenty one million square kilometres. The Mongol Empire of Genghis Khan was much bigger than Alexander the Great's territory. It stretched across Asia to Central Europe. It was the largest empire in world history …Genghis Khan had the largest empire of the world, even it was larger than the empire of Alexander the Great, needless to say the Empire of Persian, Roman, Arab and Macedonian.

He ended the circle with his finger and sighed. 'Genghis Khan was a true king, Bachem. Then Amar Singh said, 'So figure about thirteen million square kilometres. I exclude the successors of Genghis Khan, since they just built on what Genghis Khan had already conquered. The name of Genghis Khan often raises the image of a harsh, brutal empire which destroyed the civilized world with no mercy.

This is all written by their enemies, Bachem.' He scratched on his belly, then pushed back his moustache, and said, 'The surprising truth is that Genghis Khan was a visionary leader whose conquests combined Europe with the flourishing cultures of Asia to trigger global advancement … an unprecedented explosion of skills, trade, and philosophies. Genghis Khan's era was the making of the modern world, and it was astonishing to the world's history. He and his descendants led the world into modernity and gave it a rapid start towards technology. Genghis Khan was an innovative leader, and the emperor of all the emperors. He was the first ruler in many conquered countries to put the power of law above his own power. He encouraged religious freedom, created public schools, granted diplomatic immunity, abolished torture, and instituted a free-trade economy between nations. Genghis Khan was the true leader, Bachem.' Amar Singh passed me the book to put back on the shelf. 'Genghis Khan …' He repeated the name a few times, and then sighed and said, 'Khan, Khan …'

Before long, he continued his lesson: 'Genghis Khan made a business trade agreement with Khwarazm-Shah, the king of Persia, who was Turk. Khwarazm-Shah had not taken Genghis Khan seriously. Khwarazm-Shah seized Genghis Khan's caravan and then killed all the fifty of the Mongolian traders, except one, who returned to Genghis Khan and explained what had happened. Genghis Khan sent another three ambassadors – two Mongolians and one Muslim – to rescue the caravan. Khwarazm-Shah beheaded the Muslim and shaved the two Mongolian ambassadors and sent them to Genghis khan. Genghis Khan could not accept such intolerable behaviour from a king. Neither could he tolerate a human population being ruled by such a corrupted leader, Bachem,' he said. Then Amar Singh flipped to the back of the book. 'Genghis Khan equipped over two thousand soldiers and left Mongolia for Iran where he arrested Khwarazm-Shah. Genghis Khan melted silver and poured it into Khwarazm-Shah's eyes, ears, and nose, and into his mouth. "Do you want money, or you want to keep your promises?" Genghis Khan asked Khwarazm-Shah. And that is how Genghis Khan killed the king of Persia, Bachem.'

'You are ignorant, Bachem,' Amar Singh said not unkindly. 'It is good you are young.' Then he stretched his legs out on the sofa and asked me to turn on the air conditioning in the living room. By the time I returned to the library, Amar Singh was snoring.

I went out into the yard and saw a bird sitting on the bench singing. A few hours later, Mona came to the house wearing a green-and-white striped skirt and a white top. She was carrying her book bag. She smiled at me; she was as clean and as and pretty as the bird. 'How is Grandpa?' she asked.

'He is sleeping,' I said.

'And how are you?' she asked.

'I am good, thank you.'

'How about your cousin in New York?' she said, and then smiled. 'Ajaa, ajaa,' she said. I followed her to the kitchen. She opened the fridge and took out the pitcher of water, then sliced a lemon in two. She squeezed the lemon into the water, and then poured the water into to two glasses. 'Drink this; it is good,' she said. 'It is hot outside.' She passed her palm on her forehead, 'How is your English class is going?' she asked.

'It is fine,' I said. 'I am trying to learn the English language,' I replied.

'Is your grandpa still in the archaeology business?' she asked.

'I don't know what you are talking about,' I said.

'Okay, okay … I am going to show you some pictures,' she said. She left the room briefly and returned with a photo album. She sat next to me. 'Look at these pictures,' she said as she flipped through the album's page. 'This is what your grandpa has.'

'This is the statue I saw in Kabul,' I said. 'Grandpa has three of them.

She smiled. 'I study archaeology, and I am in love with the Afghan ancient statues. This is about us,' she said. Her perfume and her pretty eyes never let me think of anything but her. She then took out another book and showed me pictures of the statues of Bamyan Buddha. 'This is the biggest Buddha,' she said. 'Look, it is in Bamyan where you come from.' She flipped the pages. 'This is another statue in the province of Bamyan.' And then she crossed her legs. She smiled again. 'I have just started at the university in Bombay,' she said, and then she left for her room.

Later, when I was watching TV, Amar Singh walked into the living room and sat next to me. 'This is all trash,' he said. He took the remote control from the table and changed the channel to some Indian songs. 'This is good,' he said. 'Mona, Mona!' Amar Singh called her out loud. Mona came to the living room. Amar Singh said something in Gujarati to her, and then she said 'Acchā, acchā' (good). She prepared dinner for us, and then she went back to her room. 'Bachem, you must go to your room, but come back this week,' he said.

A few days later when I came out from English class a man stopped me and said, 'Anā, ānā' (come, come). I followed him to a restaurant on the same street where I lived. Amar Singh was sitting at a back table alone. The minute he saw me he smiled the biggest smile ever. I was very surprised to see him outside of his house. I sat across him. 'Where are you, Bachem?' he asked.

'I am here, and I am good.'

'Sharouch called last night. He is in New Jersey now, and he lives close to Babur's uncle's home,' he said. Then Amar Singh poured some beer from a bottle into a glass and sipped it. 'Ohm, yes,' he said. 'Mona has started her first year of university in Bombay, and she likes it there,' he said. Amar Singh eyeballed me. 'I feel lonely, and I want you to live with me,' he said. And then he said, 'Your grandpa is fine. I spoke to him a few weeks ago, and I know you are lonely too.' He looked around. 'Let's eat something, Bachem. Do you want to eat chicken tandoori?' he asked.

'I am fine. I will eat later,' I replied.

Amar Singh pushed his moustache up then pulled the glass of beer close to him on the table. 'Listen,' he said, 'you are going to die in that room. I am responsible for your safety as I have promised your Grandpa.'

'Okay, I agreed.

'Okay … this is good,' he said. 'Think of me as your grandpa. I will take care of you, and there is no one in the house. I will teach you English, and I will educate you as I have promised your grandpa.' He filled his glass with beer once more and sipped it. 'You know I am doing your grandpa a favour; your grandpa is a good friend of mine,' he said. 'Let's eat, Bachem,' he said.

After lunch, one of his friends helped me to get my clothes and other belongings from my room.

We took a rickshaw, and we arrived at Amar Singh's house in the afternoon.

Eighteen

While I lived with Amar Singh, I attended the Afghan Shia community English courses as usual, and went to the park and played football with the Afghan boys. Amar Singh had two ladies working for him. One lady came once a week to wash our clothes; the other lady came every morning to cook and clean the house for us. Every night after dinner Amar Singh and I had conversations on different topics, but he emphasized learning English and the importance of his private lessons on my origin.

Lately, Babur and Zeya had been after me to tell them who the smuggler was, but I had promised Amar Singh I would not mention anything about the smuggler to anyone. All that I would say to the boys was that I had never met the smuggler. They wanted to know where I lived and wanted to come and visit me at my new address. According to Amar Singh, I was not allowed to give any information about him or to invite any of my friends to the house.

I noticed that my Hindi and English languages started to improve while I lived with Amar Singh. Every morning the lady who came to cook and clean would start a conversation with me, but the lady who came once a week to wash our clothes did not like to talk at all. She washed the clothes, and she left the house without saying a word.

After I had been staying at Amar Singh's house for about a month, he told me one morning, 'Tonight after dinner you will have another two hours of private lesson.' Then he smiled and pushed back his moustache with his fingers. 'It is all good,' he said in English. In the evening he was sitting on the sofa, and called me out loud, 'Khan, Khan, Khan!' I left my room for the library to find out what he had to tell me. 'Sit down,' he said. I sat down on the chair, and then he sipped the liquid from the glass. 'You are Mongol,' he said. Then pulled out a bottle of alcohol and filled up his glass. 'You are Mongol … I wished you were one,' he said. 'Now you know a little about Genghis Khan. And I will tell you more. Genghis Khan's two sons divided his empire into two after Genghis Khan died in 1227. His two sons were Ogedei Khan and Chagatai Khan. Both of whom ruled the Mongol Empires, and Central Asia. Central Asia eventually converted to Islam and became the centre of Islamic scholarship.

Then Amar Singh finished the rest of the drink. 'Do you follow me?' he asked.

I nodded. 'Yes, sir.'

'Listen to me,' he insisted. 'What I tell you is an important part of world history.' He rearranged his cushions and continued: 'Chagatai Khan ruled the non-urbanised communities, therefore protecting the traditional and the nomadic ways of the Mongols. It is mostly agreed that Chagatai Khan's empire was the weakest of all the Mongol-controlled empires, because it was small, and thus it was easily influenced by more powerful neighbouring territories, which were ruled by the other Mongolian khans. After Chagatai Khan died in 1242, his territory became part of Ogedei Khan's kingdom under the control of his grandson, Kaidu Khan, who died in 1301. The majority of the Mongol rulers, soldiers of the Chagatai Khan, were Muslims. Chagatai Khan's territories became an official Muslim state. All khans after him were Muslim, and Central Asia has remained Islamic ever since. With the conversion of Chagatai Khan, all the other three western Mongol empires converted in to Islam also. Chagatai Khan's kingdom fell to Amir Timur, who was a native of Samarqand in Uzbekistan, and a descendent of Genghis Khan's from his mother side. Timur's successors later called themselves the Uzbeks, the name by which they are still known today. The other two main Central Asian Islamic ethnic groups are mixed races of

Mongol and Turk. They are the Kazakhs and the Kyrgyz, and they became known during the same period. Central Asia became part of the Soviet Union in 1917. Today, Turkmenistan, Uzbekistan, Kyrgyzstan, and Kazakhstan are independent countries, living remnants of the Chagatai Mongol legacy in Central Asia.' Amar Singh paused for a moment. 'Are you listening, Bachem?' he asked. 'It is not important who came in to power, but it is necessary to know how they treated the people who lived in their territories.'

After I assured him I was listening, he continued: 'Amir Timur was another gifted man, a born leader. His family was Muslim. He had memorized the holy book of Quran by the age of sixteen. His ambition was to bring justice to his people. Like his Mongolian ancestors, Amir Timur hated to see unjust rulers ruling human populations. Amir Timur was a great commander and a brilliant scholar. On the other hand, he had tremendous respect for men with dignity, and for skilful men like scientists and scholars. He was never defeated in any of his wars. Amir Timur was a man who was able to invent great political strategies and military tactics. He occupied Afghanistan, Iran, India, part of Turkey, and East Europe. Basically, the Genghis Khan's dynasty ended with the 'Great Game' when the borderlines were drawn by the Britain and Russia. The technology, machines, and scientific research that developed during the reigns of these great emperors were real works of art. The Western countries stole their civilization; specifically, the British made weapons out innovations from the Mongol's era and started colonization. I am telling you, kid, believe what I say. Every magnificent example of architecture ever built was built by the Mongol emperors in Central Asia, Pakistan, Iran, and in India. Just look at the Taj Mahal, the Agra building, Lall Qalla. There are also beautiful parks for the public, and mosques. Now, I am going to talk about the genocide that was ordered by King Abdul Rahman Khan against the Hazara people of Afghanistan.' But then and then Amar Singh said, 'Anyway, it is getting late. I am going to finish my drink. Go to your room, Khan.' He pointed to some books on the shelf. 'Take those books with you, and look at the Mongol architecture,' he said. I took two heavy books off the library shelf. Just as I was about to leave the library he said, 'I will take you to the Taj Mahal sometimes next month. In two days the month of *Barsat* will start. It will rain for the whole month of July.'

A few days later, the rain started. It rained during the day and night. It was unbelievable. I was not able to attend the English course, and it was difficult to ride my bike in the heavy rain. I stayed home and practiced my English. I received letters from Kabul and from Pakistan. I wrote answers to the letters, and several times Sharouch called from New Jersey.

On one of the heaviest rainy days, Amar Singh asked me to shut all the windows and the doors in the house, and then he said. 'Tonight I will talk about the genocide which Abdul Rahman declared against the Hazara people in Afghanistan in the late nineteenth century.' Amar Singh did not drink that much alcohol, but every time he wanted to teach me, he drank a few glasses. In the evening, Amar Singh put his finger up in the air. 'In one hour your private class will start,' he said. I was in the library practicing my English. Amar Singh walked in. He had a glass of wine with him. 'Sit, sit, Bachem,' he said. And then he tapped me on my shoulder. 'Sit on the chair across me.' The lesson began: 'The history of Afghanistan is a very tragic one in so many ways.

Afghanistan has been a battlefield among superpowers of its time. Starting from Alexander the Great until today's superpowers which are the USSR and the USA. Wars were spread throughout the nations, which has made Afghanistan one of the poorest nations in the world.

The territory in which the Hazara people have lived for centuries is called the Hazarajat. This area consists of valleys and towering, rugged mountains. There are cold winters, beautiful scenery, and raging rivers,' he said. Then he sipped his wine. 'You are from Bamyan, Bachem,' he said. 'The Hazara see themselves as the indigenous people of the region. They carved the Buddha statues of Bamyan, which are the biggest Buddhas in the world, Bachem. I have been in Bamyan. The statues are huge and very pretty –fifty five and thirty five meters tall !'

He took another sip of wine. 'The Hazara people worshiped Buddha before Islam came. The Arabs introduced Islam to the Afghans, and the Hazara people adopted the Shia sect of Islam. It was around seven twenty-four in the current era, I think. Islam had changed some cultural and traditional aspects of the Hazara's social stratification; however, traditionally they kept their political and social networking structures. The Hazara's political, social, and economical network was unique in the way in which they settled disputes among themselves. Every village in the Hazarajat's territory consisted of multiple families, and these families were related to one another by the roots of their paternal ancestors. These family groups were called *tols*. Each tol had a chief, which was called a *malik*. A malik was responsible for settling disputes among the members of his tol. Every village had one leader, which was called a khan. The khan was responsible for settling disputes between maliks from different villages. The khan was also responsible for the foreign affairs of a specified territory within the Hazarajat territory. The khan also collected taxes from the maliks. The khan was an affluent figure who determined the outcome of any critical issues that arose within the Hazarajat territories.' Amar Singh finished the last of the wine in the glass. 'It is finished, Bachem,' he said. 'Go and bring the bottle. It is in my room under my bed.' And then Amar Singh smiled and pointed at me. 'You must never drink alcohol,' he said. I came back with the bottle and passed it to him. '*Afareen*, Bachem' (good job), he said.

After pouring a bit more into his glass, he continued: 'The Hazarajat territory was a semi-independent enclave of the country of Afghanistan. Political and military influences remained under the exclusive control of the Hazara landed gentry. By 1830, the Hazara maliks and khans had had their own military to protect their people and land. The military consisted of more than a thousand soldiers. The Hazara ruling class and the Pashtun monarchies were based on the principle of ordinary cooperation. The khans of the Hazarajat were expected to pay annual taxes to the king to assure the security of trade routes within the territory. The Hazara lost their sovereignty during the reign of King Abdur Rahman from 1880 to 1901. King Abdur Rahman was supported by the British Imperialist Colonial Movement of the time. During that era, sixty-two percent of the Hazara population vanished from their own native lands. Back then the Hazara inhabited every province of Afghanistan, including Kandahar, Helmand, Nimruz, Farah, Herat, Zabol, and Ghazni. Basically, the majority of the population in Afghanistan were the Hazara people. The British supported King Abdur Rahman to protect its interests in the Indian sub-continent. The British motivation was to create a strong central government in Kabul. For this main reason, they supported Abdur Rahman in the subjugation of the national societies throughout the country, especially the Hazara. To rally public opinion in support of his war against the Hazara, Abdur Rahman encouraged religious leaders to travel to villages and lure people into a religious war against Hazara people. Abdur Rahman vindicated his vicious war on the Hazara by calling it a religious crusade on the grounds that the Shia were godless infidels. In order to propagate his crusade, Abdur Rahman called upon his Pashtun people, saying they must annihilate all those who had rebelled against him. He promised that the Pashtun could have the fortunes and the children of the Hazara people.'

And then Amar Singh filled up his glass with wine, sighed, and continued: 'Nevertheless, the Hazaras fought valiantly in an effort to not become an easy target of King Abdur Rahman's military might. They fought till the bitter end. Their defeat was severe. From 1893 onwards, the Hazara people were victims of enslavement and were subjected to horrible discrimination and human oppression. King Abdur Rahman's main objective was to abolish once and for all the Hazara's sense of unity and sovereignty and to create a division within the Hazara society. By restraining Hazara people, Abdur Rahman's intention was to teach a lesson to other ethnic societies. He wanted them to see that they could experience a similar doom if they attempted to become insurgents against his decree. King Abdur Rahman transferred a large population of Pashtuns from Pakistan and granted them the Hazarajat territory. He was inhuman; Hazara folklore abounds with tales of towers he erected built of Hazara skulls. The genocide of the Hazara people continued until 1970 on the same principle on which it had begun in the 1880s. Killing the Hazara Shia was considered by some Sunni Pashtun teachers a guarantee to Paradise. When the Russian communists entered Afghanistan in 1979, the war started between Muslims and communists; therefore, the Hazara were better off, as they were no longer menaced by the Pashtuns.' Amar Singh laughed, 'This is why you have been able to escape your native land. Like you, in the last two centuries, your ancestors migrated to avoid the Pashtuns atrocities. Bachem, it is political, and it is part of human nature. Minority ethnic groups are always targeted by the majority. You must keep in mind that the Turkmen, Uzbek, Kazakh, Kyrgyz, Tatar, and Hazaras have common ancestors. Your ancestors have ruled most of Asia, and even part of Europe, and in their era the concepts of multiculturalism and meritocracy were well respected.'

Then he sipped his wine. 'You should never forget, Bachem, that your people are very talented, and just as important, they have mercy. Your people have built Central Asia, South Asia, and parts of Europe. They have left beautiful architecture. Your handmade carpets are well known around the world today. Even your music and your food and other customs are good. On the other hand, the Tajik people have given the world great scholars, thinkers, philosophers, and scientists. Then he started to laugh and laughed out loud. 'I tell you something, though, these Pashtuns have nothing. Nothing! Zero talent, zero contribution to the country's economy and civilization. I am telling you they love to kill. The deal in human trafficking, paedophiliac activities, drugs, and arms. They have nothing. Half of the Pashtuns live in Pakistan, and the other half live in Afghanistan,' he said.

Nineteen

Early in the morning I got up and opened the front door. It was raining. I walked outside, closed the door behind me, and sheltered myself on a chair on the balcony. I saw the rain came down as if it was the end of time, yet the land was thirsty and kept on absorbing the rain. The pretty roses, the black-eyed Susans, the jasmine blossoms, the lilies, and the other gorgeous flowers were expecting more rain. The wind spread the drops of the rain into tiny rivulets that splashed into the plants, gently blowing them from side to side. All of a sudden, a powerful wind splashed me with a large amount of water. It even wet the sheet of the paper and the pen I was about to use to write an English sentence. The pen rolled away, and the paper blew out of my hand. Both paper and pen were removed from the balcony to the yard below within a second.

The lady who cooked for us walked into the yard. From the main door, while standing under a black umbrella, she shouted up at me, 'Khan Sahib, *teek ho*?' (are you well?). Then she asked, 'What do you want to have for breakfast?' After Amar Singh got up, we ate eggs and drank tea. 'Another two weeks of rain, then the weather will calm down, Bachem,' he informed me. 'Work on your English language. Use the English dictionary to learn the words you don't understand.' Then he asked, 'Do you know why you should use the English dictionary?' he asked. I told him I didn't. 'Because the English words are defined in the English language from the English perspective. To learn another language, it is essential to learn their native way of thinking so you will be able to understand the actual meaning of the words. This method of learning helps you to learn the English culture. On the other hand, as you read a word's definition, you learn many other words at the same time, plus a few synonyms for the word you are searching for. There is an Oxford English dictionary in the library,' he said. 'Use that dictionary.' Then he giggled to himself. 'English culture,' he repeated. 'English culture. I will take you to the Taj Mahal after the month of Barsat is over. Just focus on learning the English language. Whenever you are ready, I will smuggle you to America to be with your cousin,' he said. Then he stood up.

Amar Singh spoke to me as he walked around the room. 'I am two years younger than your grandpa, and I have known him for the last forty-five years. We were young just like you. Time passes so fast. I remember those days as if they happened yesterday,' he said. Then he sat down and sipped from his glass of tea. He pulled the coffee table forward and rested his legs on it. 'I knew your grandpa before he got married. He was so much in love,' he said. 'If you want to know, I can tell you how he met your grandma.'

'Yes,' I said. 'Sure. That would be interesting.'

'Listen, Bachem, and do not talk,' he said. 'That old house in which your grandpa lives in Kabul was built by your great-grandpa. Your great-grandpa had only one son, who is your grandfather. Your great-grandpa had green eyes. He was tall and had light skin. He was a very nice-looking man. He married a second wife in order to have more children, but it never happened. Your great-grandpa's name was Azamat Khan. The Hazara people had great respect for him. I am sure the Hazara people of your tribe still respect your grandpa. You are a descendent of the Khan family, Bachem; there is no doubt about that. Your grandpa was a young man when he was married to your grandma,' he said. 'I am not sure how old he was, but I remember the day your grandma gave birth to your grandfather's first son – your Uncle Ghulam. Your great-grandfather owned a shop next to my father's shop in Kabul and was very good friend of my father. The soldiers took your grandpa from his shop because he had to serve military service. A year later, I would have had to serve my military service, but I left Kabul for India where I continued my university education in New Delhi. I returned to Kabul after four years and saw that your grandpa was setting in his shop. He had three sons at that time. That week, your great-grandpa went missing. Your grandfather searched everywhere in Kabul, but we never ever heard from him. I was the only friend your Grandpa trusted back then.' He paused in the story to ask the lady to make more tea, then he continued, 'Two months after your great-grandpa went missing, your grandpa came to me and said, "You know that you are my good friend." And then your grandpa said, "I have something that my father told me could be valuable. I need to know what you think." Then he brought out a little gold statue of Buddha from his pocket. There was a fifteenth-century date on the bottom. I was shocked I could not believe it! I asked him how many more of these he had, and he said he had four more and some gold coins. That treasure has kept our friendship until today, Bachem. I had no idea how rich your grandpa was at that time. I was not able to estimate the price. All I said to him was that he should keep those things and never talk about them. I believed they were priceless. I promised him that I would sell them, and then he got excited and asked me again about their value.'

The lady brought the tea, and after we poured ourselves some, Amar Singh continued. 'Your Grandpa turned his face towards his shop and looked at my shop. "I want to have a big business like yours," he told me. "I have children." He smiled happily when he said, "Three sons." Then your grandpa looked at his own shop and put the treasure back into his pocket. "Oh, there is a customer waiting," he said. He put three of his fingers in the air. "Three boys," he said again, and he smiled again.'

I was enjoying this story. 'Bachem,' he said, 'I love your grandpa. He is honest. I recommended that he go to Iran to sell one of those pieces. He did travel to Iran, and sold one piece, but that little ancient statue was worth much more than he received for it. But he used that money to begin his wholesale business. I wanted to take one of those pieces to India, and not to just for my own pleasure. I spoke to him a few years ago. He still has them. I am not sure …' he said, 'It is difficult to pass that sort of thing through the airport customs, because they will confiscate it.'

I smiled at Amar Singh, and he asked, 'Why you are laughing?'

I stated, 'Your granddaughter showed me the picture a day before she left for university.'

Amar Singh got all excited. 'Which photo?' he asked. I got up and went into the library. I returned with the photo album and showed him the photo. 'This is it, yes. But why did Mona …' Then he then smiled. 'Ohhh, yes. She knows about it.' Then he asked me, 'Do you know about this treasure?' I told Amar Singh about how Grandpa and I had taken the treasure out of the hiding spot. After that, he asked, 'How many pieces are there now? How about the coins?' I told him everything. Then he calmed down and seemed satisfied. 'Oh, God, he has them! That Haramzada still has them, so he was not deceitful!' he said. 'Don't worry,' he said to me, 'your grandpa is my friend. I can call him Haramzada – or anything. He is my good friend.' Then he clapped his hands together, pulled his legs off the coffee table, and stood up. 'He has them!' And then he walked out onto the balcony with the biggest smile I had ever seen him with. I followed him. 'He has them!' This time he said it very loudly.

'From now on speak English to me,' he said. 'Forget the Dari and Hindi languages, and you will see the improvement of your English language yourself.' For another two weeks, because of the rain, I remained indoors. I did go out a few times just to the market, and I went for walk in the park that was close to the house. After the month of Barsat was over, I went to the big park to see the boys and to play football. The boys were excited to see me; every one of them questioned me about how Sharouch was doing in America. They also wanted to know where I was living. Akbar and Babur that evening told me that we should rent VCR and watch movies. There were a few newly released American and Indian movies we had not seen. Babur said, 'There is also a good porn movie that has just come out.' Then they started to laugh. I told them that I was not interested, because where I lived we had a VCR and a TV, and I could watch movies anytime I wanted.

Babur said, 'I spoke to my uncle in New Jersey three days ago. Sharouch works in a restaurant, and he makes good money. You must ask him to send money to you.' After a few months staying with Amar Singh, however, I had changed a little. What they were saying and dealing with seemed like nonsense to me.

My English teacher at the Afghan English community centre noticed that my oral English had improved, and he congratulated me. When I told this to Amar Singh, he said, 'Good job, Bachem. If you listen to me, within a few months, you will be standing by to be smuggled.'

A few weeks later in the evening, Amar Singh said, 'Tomorrow I will take you to the Taj Mahal.' The following day we took the bus to Agra, Uttar Pradesh. After a seven-hour journey, we arrived at the Taj Mahal early in the morning. Amar Singh rented a hotel room, and we had late breakfast. In the afternoon we went to see the Taj Mahal.

We took a taxi from the hotel to the Taj Mahal. The minute we got into taxi, Amar Singh began talking: 'The Taj Mahal is a significant masterpiece of the world's architecture. Among all infrastructures the Mongol emperors have built in Asia and east Europe. The Taj Mahal is an extraordinary work of art. In 1631, Emperor Shah Jahan's 3rd wife Mumtaz Mahal died when she was giving birth to their 14th child. Therefore Emperor Shah Jahan built Taj Mahal as the tomb for remembering Mumtaz Mahal. On the other hand, it is believed that Taj Mahal is an obsession for "LOVE", Amar Singh said.

Amar Singh then gave a brief introduction of the Taj Mahal in Dari. When we got out of the taxi, he continued in English: 'Here it is. Sheer beauty. From now on I will talk to you in English, Bachem.' As we walked through the crowd towards the Taj Mahal, Amar Singh was not able to walk as fast; therefore, he asked me to walk slowly with him and listen to what he had to say about the Taj Mahal.

The city of Agra was fascinating to me. It was the first time I had seen so many Caucasians, Chinese, and other foreigners.

Amar Singh continued his lesson: 'The Taj Mahal was constructed over a period of twenty-two years. It sounded as he had lived in that era. Amar Singh pulled on my arm. 'Here, Bachem, let's sit on this bench for a few minutes. I am old,' he said.

He pointed towards the main building and said, 'The Taj Mahal stands on a raised square platform that is one hundred eighty-six on each side. The four corners are truncated, forming an unequal octagon. The architectural design has used the interlocking arabesque concept, in which each element stands on its own and perfectly integrates with the core structure. He has used the principles of self-replicating geometry and equilibrium of architectural elements.' Amar Singh coughed, then asked me to get a bottle of water from the canteen. It was unbelievable, the amazing architecture of the Taj Mahal impressed every visitor. I got back with two bottles of water, and Amar Singh pointed to biggest dome of the building and said, 'Its central dome is around eighteen meters in diameter and rises to a height of about sixty five meters. It is flanked by four subsidiary domed chambers. The four graceful slender minarets are fifty meters each. The entire mausoleum in the inside as well as outside is decorated with inlaid designs of flowers and calligraphy using precious gems such as agate and jasper. The main archways are chiselled with passages from the Holy Quran, and the bold scrollwork in a flowery pattern gives a captivating charm to its beauty. The central domed chamber and four adjoining chambers include many walls and panels of Islamic decoration,' he said, and then he got up. 'Let's visit the inside.' What a work of art! I felt it was so beautiful my eyes even doubted its existence. When we walked towards the other side of Taj Mahal, Amar Singh and I could not find any empty bench to sit on; therefore, we sat on the grass right in the middle of the yard in the midst of the crowd to take a break from walking.

'The mausoleum is a part of a vast complex comprising a main gateway, an elaborate garden, a mosque to the left, a guest house to the right, and several other palatial buildings. The Taj Mahal is at the uttermost end of this complex, with the river Jamuna behind it. The large garden contains four reflecting pools dividing it at the centre. Each of these four sections is further subdivided into four sections and then each into yet another four sections. Like the Taj Mahal the garden elements serve as an arabesque, standing on their own and also constituting the whole,' said Amar Singh. Then he told me to go walk around. 'But don't go too far,' he said. 'I will be waiting for you right here.'

After visiting the Taj Mahal in Agra, we returned New Delhi. Two days later I noticed that Amar Singh was starting to teach me new words that were all about airports and travel – *departure, flight numbers, customs, immigration, visa, duty-free shop, food area, terminal, pilot, flight attendant, seatbelt, boarding pass, departing, landing, layover,* and many more words, and phrases.

Twenty

It was dark one evening as I arrived Amar Singh's house. The minute I entered the house, Amar Singh took my backpack and threw it on the sofa. 'Where were you? You disappear when there is something urgent,' he said.

'I was with the boys at the park,' I explained. 'There will be football match between our team and the Indian football team.'

I saw that Ahmad, the smuggler had both hands against the library doorframe and had extended only his head into the hallway. He smiled. 'Ah, football match,' he said, and then he started to laugh. 'Come, Bachem, come sit with us in the library,' he said, 'but first go take a shower. You are all sweaty.'

When I came out of shower, Ahmad Singh and Ahmad were sitting in the sofa in the living room. 'Sit, sit,' Amar Singh said. 'This is my friend Ahmad.' Both were drinking, and an old Indian song was played in background.

Ahmad took a small plastic bag from the side pocket of his black leather jacket, put it on the table, and opened it. Then he took out something small and chocolate-coloured and started to cut it into smaller pieces. 'This is Afghan hashish,' he said. Then he took a cigarette and emptied out the tobacco. He mixed it with the smaller pieces of hashish and put it back into the cigarette paper. Then he looked at Amar Singh and nodded his head towards the front door. 'Let's go,' he said. They went out and got comfortable on the seats. As they smoked, I noticed that the white parts of their eyes turned red and seemed to shrink. Their smiles, and the way they had laughed ten minutes ago had changed.

'The combination of alcohol and hashish makes me honest, generous, and creative,' Ahmad said, and then both started to laugh. After that Ahmad took a bunch of passports in different colours from his pocket. 'Look, this is a British passport,' he said. 'I purchased it for five hundred dollars, and it is valid for another two years.' He held up another one. 'And this is a Canadian passport. I purchased this for four hundred, and it is valid for another fourteen months. And this is a Swedish passport … very special, because it is valid for another three and half years. I paid seven hundred for this one,' he said. Ahmed reached out and laid the passports on the edge of the sofa. 'All these passports need are new photos,' he said. 'And I am good at changing passport photos.'

Amar Singh and his friend Ahmad both laughed, and then the smuggler put his hands together, leaned towards me, and looked right into my eyes. 'I smuggled your cousin on a Malaysian passport with a US student visa,' he said. 'Unfortunately, the airports have become very strict these days. It is very risky for me, and most of the time the airport immigration officers detect forged passports.' After saying that, the smuggler looked at Amar Singh and asked a question, 'Why am I saying all this to you?'

Amar Singh giggled. 'Honest, creative, and generous,' he repeated, then as one, they started to laugh. Ahmad took an envelope from his pocket and put it on the table. Then he took my own passport from that envelope. 'You are going to London on your own passport,' he said. After had another sip of his drink, he said. 'Today is Tuesday. On Wednesday morning – which is tomorrow – you are leaving for Calcutta by train. In thirty-six hours you will reach Calcutta. You have a flight from Calcutta airport to Dubai. And after a two-hour stop at the Dubai airport, you have a flight to Bucharest, Romania. You will have a six-hour layover, and then you will fly to Rome, Italy. Then you will fly from Rome to Logos, Nigeria.' Then he opened to the page of my passport that displayed a Nigeria tourist visa for one month. 'There will be somebody to pick you up at the airport in Nigeria. You will stay there for a week. Use your return ticket from Logos to Calcutta, and you will have a stop in London at Heathrow Airport. Once your plane lands at Heathrow, you will find a toilet, rip up your passport, and flush it down the toilet. You will return to the airport terminal and find a chair. You will sit down and not speak to anyone. You will not speak English. When the airport officials approach you, they will provide you with a translator. You will tell them that you are from Afghanistan, and you are seeking asylum as a refugee. They will ask you where you have come from. You must tell them you have flown from Islamabad, Pakistan. Everything will be fine,' he said. I was in shock, but I continued to listen to him. 'Everything you hear from me, never tell anyone. Just keep it for yourself,' he said.

'Forget the football match,' Amar Singh said, and then giggled.

'An Afghan football team playing against an Indian football team,' Ahmad said. 'That would be a very interesting football match to watch.' There was more laughter between the men. 'Hazara people are brave,' Ahmad said. I had nothing to say. 'Remember that nothing is illegal,' he said. 'You will have a long journey. As you travel, do not talk to anyone, and don't look at anyone. You will be in London within two weeks,' the smuggler said. 'In addition,' Ahmad said, 'Afghans speak pure Farsi, Dari. Farsi is the same language, but the fuckin' Arabs have diluted our Farsi language with the Arab language. More than sixty percent of Iranian Farsi is made of Arabic words. Keep your language; it is very important.' He took out another envelope from his pocket. 'These are your plane tickets.' Then looked at Amar Singh. 'I have to go.' And the smuggler was gone.

Amar Singh looked at his watch. 'In four hours you are leaving for Calcutta,' he said. 'Go to your room and rest. You have long journey ahead of you.' I went to my room, but I could not believe what I had heard and seen. A few hours later, I was half asleep and in deep thought, when Amar Singh turned the light on in my room. 'Wake up, Bachem. It is time,' I heard.

There was a backpack on the coffee table in the living room. He opened it. 'Take these with you,' he said. 'This is the suit that you will wear in Calcutta before your flight. There are a few T-shirts and shirts, two pairs of pants, and some underwear and socks. Your toothbrush, toothpaste, and two bars of soap are in the side pockets. This is all you need, Bachem. Memorize my phone numbers, and once you arrive in London call me.' He stood up. 'Hurry up, someone is waiting for us at the train terminal.'

As usual, we took a rickshaw to the train station. We went into the restaurant next to the train station where a man was waiting for us. 'This is the boy,' said Amar Singh. 'His name is Aftab.' And then Amar Singh introduced the man to me. 'This is Abdul. He will take you to the airport in Calcutta. From there you are on your own until you reach Africa,' he said. Then Amar Singh hugged me. 'Don't forget what I told you. Listen to Abdul and do whatever he says.' Then Amar Singh left.

Abdul spoke in Hindi to me; we got on the train. There was a bed for me, and the train was packed full of people. All the windows were open, and almost every passenger smoked. I fell asleep. When I woke up, I saw that Abdul was awake. He was a middle-aged man, very skinny;

most of his teeth were rotten, and he had red lips from chewing the red tobacco. Every time I looked at him, he shook his head and said, 'Teek hoo, Khan Sahib?' (Are you good, Khan?). Abdul looked at his watch constantly, and every time he gave me an estimation of the remaining time before we arrived in Calcutta. It was over thirteen hundred kilometres from New Delhi to Calcutta. Abdul would pass his half-missing upper teeth over his red lower red lip, and he would spit out the side of his mouth. Then he would smile at me and repeat himself: 'Teek hoo, Khan Sahib.' The train stopped for every station. Some passengers would get off, and some new passengers would get on. On the both sides of the train, I viewed small agricultural villages – farms, goats, cows, beautiful hills, and green landscape. Every now and then I left my bed to use the toilet. Other than that, I sat, lay, or slept on my train bed.

I was asleep. I heard Abdul talking to me: 'Teek hoo, Khan Sahib. Wake up.' He spit, and then he smiled. Then Abdul zipped up my backpack and put it on his shoulder. When the train stopped, we got out. Abdul looked at his watch. 'Your flight is in three hours.' He put his hands in the air and flapped them. 'Flight! Flight!' he said.

Calcutta was even more crowded than New Delhi. We took taxi to the airport and found a restaurant. Abdul opened the bag and took the dark blue suit out. He pointed to the washroom and told me to change into the suit. Then Abdul took my passport out of his pocket and gave it to me. He took my airplane tickets from his bag and showed them to me. 'This is your ticket from this airport to Rome, with Air India. This ticket is from Rome to Nigeria, with Alitalia, an Italian airline. And this is your return ticket from Nigeria to Calcutta, with British Airways. On your return ticket, you will have a stop in London,' Abdul explained, and then he blinked his eyes and passed his half-missing teeth over his red lower lips. He smiled at me. 'Finish your soda,' he said, and then he pointed towards the big digital departures board. 'Go, go, Khan Sahib. Insha'Allah, everything will be fine,' Abdul said. All that time I'd had no idea that Abdul spoke English.

I went through the gate with my tickets and my passport. I had no idea what the date and time were. I kept the smuggler's advice – I smiled but I did not look at anyone. It was not long before the plane landed Dubai. We took off again and landed in Bucharest. From there, after a few hours, we flew to Rome. I was questioned at the Rome airport about the purpose of my visit to Nigeria. I told them I was a tourist. The Rome airport was much larger and more modern than the last three airports I had passed through. Finally, I travelled on Alitalia from Rome to Logos, Nigeria. When we landed, it was the first time I had seen large numbers of black human beings.

Twenty-One

The female Nigerian immigration officer looked through my passport and then asked, 'Have you booked a hotel?' I replied that I hadn't. Then she asked me, 'Where are you going to stay?' I told her a friend was supposed to pick me up. 'What is your friend's name?' she asked. I told her his name was Reza. She sighed and left the counter. When she came back after a short time, she said, 'I went out there and could find no one by the name of Reza.' She smiled and asked me again, 'So, where are you going to stay?' I told her I would go to a hotel. She said, 'No, this is Africa. It does not work that way.' She pointed towards a person to her right. 'He is the police officer,' she said. 'You must fill out an entry form. Only after he stamps it can I let you go.' I went to see him, but he was busy filling out forms for the other passengers. I waited and waited … for more than forty minutes. I noticed that some of the passengers were holding Pakistani passports.

Finally it was my turn. The officer asked me the same questions, 'Where are you going to stay? Do you know anyone in Nigeria?'

'Yes, I have a friend in Lagos,' I replied.

'Do you have his telephone number?' the officer asked. I answered no. He said, 'Sorry, it does not work like that. You need to go and see the immigration officer.'

I went back to the immigration counter. The lady picked up my luggage and locked me in a room. 'We will send you back where you came from on the next flight to Rome, which is tomorrow morning,' she said.

I was locked in a dirty, dark room. There were two beds, two toilets, and a shower. I had no idea what to do. I kept on banging on the door and asking them to please let me out of this room. I said I was very tired, and it was hard to breathe in there. No one replied; they were laughing in front of the door. The immigration officers came to use the toilet every thirty to forty minutes I asked them to please let me go to the city, but they ignored me every time. I asked them please, but the only thing they said was, 'Stop banging on the door. Our boss has left for the day, and he will talk to you tomorrow morning.' I was getting hungry. Through the door I asked them, 'Please, I need to eat.'

Then a lady opened the door. 'Do you have money?'

I said, 'Yes, of course I have money.'

'Okay, wait for another thirty minutes. A police officer will accompany you to the airport cafeteria.'

I waited for a long time. Finally a police officer came and took me to the departure section, which was on the second floor. 'This is business class,' he said. After eating my dinner, I asked the officer to please wait with me a little longer there. He said, 'No, I need to go, unless you pay me.'

'How much do you want?' I asked him.

'How much can you give?'

'I can give you ten dollars.'

'Ten dollars!' He laughed out loud. 'No, my friend. What is ten dollars?' And then he said, 'If you give me twenty, I can keep you here for another thirty minutes.' I gave him $20, and I went to use the clean washroom. Soon the thirty minutes were over. Before retuning for the detention hall, I purchased a soft drink. It was around 10.00 p.m. local time.

The officer locked me in that room again. It was not easy to fall asleep in that room. Everything smelled really bad. There were cockroaches and other insects creeping and flying around. I was not able to stop scratching my body. The last time I had showered was five days ago at Amar Singh's house. I probably did not sleep more than two hours that night. In the morning, I asked them, 'I need to have breakfast, please.'

A lady whispered through the closed door, 'A police officer will accompany you, in half hour.'

I waited and waited in the dark room; finally a police officer showed up and accompanied me to the second floor to have breakfast. Before I got my food, the officer said, 'I want to eat too.'

I said, 'Sure, let's eat, and I will pay for it.'

'No, I do not like the food here,' he said. 'Please give me cash. I will eat outside.' I paid about $6 for him to have breakfast, but he asked me to pay him $20. And he said, 'Since you like to stay here longer, let's make a deal.' I paid him, and then I went to look around the departure terminal. I saw a souvenir shop. After I used the clean washroom, the officer accompanied me back to the dark room.

I kept on knocking on the door and asking them to let me out of the room. An officer asked through the door, 'What do you need?'

I was frustrated, all I wanted was to get out of that room. I kept on saying through the door, 'I am here to see Lagos and a friend. Please let me out of here!' I heard nothing but giggling and laughing through the locked door. By afternoon I was not even hungry, but I wanted to get out from that dark room at least for a few minutes. After saying the same thing for more than ten times, an officer opened the door and said, 'Wait. A police officer will come to accompany you to have lunch.'

'I want to speak to your superior,' I yelled. Unfortunately, no one listened. My eyes were tired; it seemed as if the sun had stopped shining permanently. There was no hope. I looked around at the walls of my prison. I was not the only one who had been locked in there. People had written notes on the walls. For example, one had written, 'I love Somalia, and I hate Nigeria.' Another had stated, 'This is not a prison, but free lodging.' Yet another person had left a note: 'God is great.' Another had written, 'You stupid people have made fun of your government, but all you want is money!' There were many statements even in the Chinese language. Some people had written paragraphs, and I saw even two short essays on that wall. I knew that, if I asked to go for lunch, I would have to pay $20 to the police. I waited and asked through the doors, 'Can I please talk to your boss?' No answer. I waited and waited. I told them I was hungry and wanted to eat.

Finally, a black lady opened the door and said, 'Wait for half hour. A police officer will accompany you.'

An hour later, a policeman opened the door. 'Do you want to have lunch? Let's go.' I followed him to the second floor – 'business class' as they called it. I paid for a small meal and a soda.

As I was eating, a lady in a red uniform stood above me and asked, 'Are you still here?' I said I was. 'My name is Diana,' she said. 'And I work for the airport.' She turned to the officer. 'How much longer do you want this lovely boy to suffer in that dark room?' she said to him. 'He has been in that nasty room for more than twenty-six hours! When are you going to release him?' And then she looked at me. 'I am a mother. I have feelings. I don't know what is wrong with people!' I thanked her for her concern. She said, 'You are welcome. Can you buy me lunch, please?'

I said, 'Sure, what do you want to eat?'

She said, 'No, I do not like to eat here. I love to eat out. Just give me twenty dollars. It is enough.' I had just bought lunch and a soda at the airport for $10. I gave her $20, and she gave me a very good smile in return and walked away.

The police officer sitting across from me kept on smiling. I tried to finish my soda as slowly as possible so I could stay longer. The policeman said, 'Kid, finish your soda. It must be warm by now. Finish it. Let's go.' I had to leave, or I had to pay $20. I finished my soda, and the officer asked, 'Do you want another soda?'

I said, 'No, Let's go.' The policeman was laughing, and kept on laughing. At this point all I could do was hope there was someone by the name of Reza waiting for me. They locked me in again. I tried to take a nap, but I was not able to sleep. I tried to use the shower, but there was no running water.

About two hours later, a lady opened the door, and said, 'Your friend is here.' I thought I was released, and was very happy, but then she said, 'We are not letting you go. We are sending you to Rome tomorrow.'

I said, 'No, I want to see Lagos, and a friend of mine.'

She said, 'No, you do not have a place to stay.' Subsequently she brought me to her office. A black man was sitting across her desk. 'This man is your friend's friend, and his name is Nathan,' she said.

Nathan said, 'Reza has sent me to bring you to his house. Reza is out of city. He will come back into town tonight.'

The lady officer said, 'Okay, you both need to go see the police and fill out the release form. When the police officer stamps the release form, only then I will allow you to enter Logos.'

Nathan and I reported to the police officer, and the officer confiscated Nathan's identification, saying, 'We will keep your identification card.'

Nathan said, 'Sure. That is not a problem.'

Another officer asked me to follow him. Once we entered his office, he asked me to have a seat. I sat on the chair in front of his desk, and he said, 'I will help you. So, how much are you going to give me?'

'I will give you forty dollars and thank you for your help.'

He stared at me. 'Forty dollars? You must be joking, kid. At least two hundred!'

'I have already have given the police officers and immigration officers almost a hundred dollars in the last twenty-eight hours,' I told him.

'I am talking about myself,' he said. 'I can help you to get out of here, kid.'

Amar Singh had given me $400 before I left New Delhi. I brought all the remaining money out of my pocket. It was only $160. 'I have only this much,' I said.

He said, 'Yes, if you travel, you must have money.' The police officer took the $160 and put it into his pocket without thanking me, and then he pointed towards the door. 'Go see your friend,' he said.

When I got close to Nathan, I whispered into his ear, 'Do not give money. I have already given them all I had.' He shook his head and said nothing.

Nathan took the release form to the officer finally. The officer stamped the form and said to Nathan, 'In two days, if you have not come and brought his friend, Reza, I will come and arrest you at your address.'

Nathan said, 'Sure. And thank you, sir.'

The officer gave me back my passport and pointed towards the immigration counter. 'Go and get your entry.' I walked towards the counter and gave my passport to the immigration officer. She said, 'Give me fifty dollars.' I looked at Nathan. Without saying a word, he gave the lady $50. With that, we were finally allowed to exit the airport.

Nathan had smile on his face, and said, 'Let's go, kid.' I picked up my luggage. When we arrived at the airport parking lot, another man approached us and said, 'My name is Jimmy. I have been working for Reza for more than twenty years. I will drive you to his house.'

Nathan said, 'See you tonight, kid,' and he left. As we drove through the city of Lagos, I saw many people. They were walking on both sides of the street. There were traffic jams with cars, bicycles, and many motorcycles. Jimmy drove to the top of a hill and stopped the car in front of a big, black gate. He honked the horn several times. The gate opened, and he drove through. I got out of the car and followed Jimmy from the yard to the house. There was Reza. I said, 'Salam,' and we shook hands.

Reza said, 'Welcome to Lagos. I cannot believe they detained you.' I was very tired, and I felt sick. On the other hand, I was very happy to be out of that nasty, dark room. Reza passed me a white towel. There were two black ladies in the house. One was sitting in the sofa and the other was in the kitchen cooking. Reza asked the lady who was sitting on the sofa to show me where the bathroom was.

Twenty-Two

Reza woke me up me in the morning to have breakfast. In the kitchen he asked me, 'How long do you want to stay in Nigeria?'

'I am only here until it is time to go London,' I said. 'That is all I care about.'

'I know that, but how long you want to stay? I can book your return ticket tomorrow if you want,' he said. A lady opened the door and called Reza. Through the window I could see that the big gate had opened and a few young black men had driven into the walled yard on motorcycles. There were two additional doors in the yard walls, and Reza opened them. He went into one of the rooms. The young men had parked their motorcycles and had formed a straight queue in front of the door. Out of curiosity, I went to see what was going on. I entered one of the rooms and saw a man standing in front of a tall desk. There were two small furnaces in the first room; I could see the fires were burning very hot. The young men were holding small paper bags, or small plastic bags. The man standing at the desk had a scale. One by one, he took every young man's paper or plastic bag, dumped out the contents, then weighed it as the man watched. The material he was weighing looked like mixture of earth and sand. After the man weighed the stuff, he wrote down what I assumed was the amount. Then he poured the stuff into a cup and gave it back to the man to whom it belonged. Each man then moved on to another queue, which started right in front of the two fires. The young man who was in charge of the fires had two long pieces of metal, one in each hand. When a man approached, he used these pieces of metal to pull a metal cup about the size of a coffee cup from the middle of the fire. He took the substance from the man and poured it into metal cup, then he placed it back into the middle of the fire. After a short time, he pulled out the metal cup from the fire and dropped it into a small tank of water.

There was a second man who was in charge of the water tank. He waited for two or three minutes and then pulled the cup out of the water. He tipped something out and passed a brush over it. He had seen me standing there watching. He turned to me and said, 'Open your hand.' Then placed the warm piece in my hand. It was heavy. 'Gold! Gold!' he said, and then laughed out loud. He asked me to give to the person to whom it belonged. The boy pressed that piece in his hand a few times with biggest smile. He went to see Reza in the other room, and I followed him.

In the second room, which was Reza's office, there was another scale. Reza weighed the refined gold and gave US dollars in return to that man. Reza was the only Iranian; everyone else besides me was black. Reza had set up a very simple and small gold refinery system. After everyone left Reza told me, 'I bought four kilograms of gold today.' In the evening, while we were having dinner, Reza asked me again, 'Do you want to stay for another day? Or you want to fly to London tomorrow?'

I said, 'The sooner the better.'

'I have lived in this country for the last nine years,' he said, 'and I love it here. These black people are very good people. I buy gold from them and send it to Iran and Dubai. I sell the gold for a reasonable price.' Then he laughed. 'I send the gold over the land with truck drivers, and over the sea with people who travel on ships.' Then he laughed again. 'I have done business with your smuggler Ahmad for more than ten years. In this country the local population are very good people. Unfortunately, the government is corrupt. I was at the airport yesterday when you arrived, but they asked for a lot more money than they are supposed to.' Reza smiled and said,

'Sorry they kept you in that dark room. I have been detained in that room twice in the last nine years.'

The next day, I got up early in the morning and walked around in the yard. I saw the beautiful blue sky, with thousands of birds flying in it. I saw a gorgeous eagle come down from the sky and sit on a branch of a tree in the yard. The eagle looked into my eyes with his brown eyes. It was a baby and had dark chocolate-coloured feathers and a black tail. Its beak was yellow, and there were white feathers on its face around its dark, glassy eyes. The baby eagle flew off the branch and then sat on the corner of the roof. It stared right at me again. It said something, then it flew away … far away until it vanished in the clear sky.

I heard Reza's voice through the window calling me to breakfast. Reza was around fifty years old, with dark skin and almond eyes. 'I am an Iranian Turk,' he said, 'and you are an Afghan Hazara. We have some common ancestors. Yesterday I purchased four kilograms of refined gold, and today I may buy even more. I have booked your returned ticket. Your flight is at around two o'clock this afternoon. You must be at the airport two hours before your flight,' he said. Reza leaned his upper body towards me as we sat at the dinning table, and whispered. 'Once you land at Heathrow in London, destroy your passport and your return ticket in the washroom and then flush everything. Tell them you have flown from Pakistan. Also tell them you do not speak or understand the English language, and you do not know anyone in London. You are young. You must educate yourself. England has a good education system,' he said.

A few hours later, a black man drove into the yard, picked me up, and took me to the airport. After a few hours of waiting at the terminal, I got on the plane, and a few hours later the British Airlines flight landed at Heathrow Airport. I followed Reza's instructions. I destroyed and flushed my passport and return ticket, then I went into the terminal and sat on a bench. Within a short time, an officer came and asked me something in his weird English accent. I said, 'Afghan refugee.' The minute he heard that eyeballed me, and then asked me to follow him.

He took me into a room where I waited. After some time, I was escorted into an office. A lady officer was waiting for me. Once they found that I was an Afghan asking for refugee status, the lady provided me with an Afghan interpreter. The interpreter asked me questions: Where had I come from? How old was I? And many other questions. The lady filled out an application form, and then I was taken to a hotel room in London. I stayed in that hotel for a few days. A government social worker took care of my bills. After that I was sent to a furnished room in a house. The lady social worker gave me a cheque book and explained to me that I was entitled to get paid twenty-eight pounds per week from the closest post office, by showing my cheque book, which had my name printed on every page.

I had called Amar Singh during the first few days of my arrival in London. Because of the high cost of telephone calls, I was not able to talk more than a few minutes. I made phone calls to Sharouch in New Jersey and to Uncle Ghulam in Pakistan in the first month of my stay in London also.

The English people spoke with funny accent; I felt as if I didn't speak English at all! It was not easy to understand them. A couple months later, I met an Afghan Hazara in London. He introduced me to an Iranian pizza place called US Pizza. The owner of the pizzeria provided me with a Honda scooter with a box on the back in which to carry hot pizza. He also gave me a small map of the city. I started delivering pizza to different address. The first time I ate pizza was in London. Everything was new. I worked three to four nights a week, and I was paid in cash. I kept the government allowance in order to save money. In the morning, I attended the English-as-a-second language class, which was provided by the government. I noticed that there were various English dialects as I got to know some people in the city. London was diverse in terms of culture. It was a multicultural city, and each nation and ethnic group had something special to offer. People of different nationalities lived together in different neighbourhoods. I lived in Ealing Broadway with a few young housemates. We each had a private bedroom, but we shared the kitchen and bathroom facilities. I was fascinated at meeting different people from different parts of the world. It was also my first time using the underground; it was impressive how fast the subways moved.

I took the underground to my English class. After a month or so, I found there was a red double-decker bus that went in the same direction to the language school. I met an Afghan Hazara man, and we became friends. His name was Ramazan. He was from the Wardak Province of Afghanistan. Ramazan had lived London for five years, and he was a few years older than I. I drank my first beer with Ramazan in a pub close to where I lived, on the same night we went out with a few English girls. The young, blond girl English girl to whom I made love called herself Kelly. I never saw her again. Ramazan could not believe that I had never drunk alcohol and had never had made love. It was on the weekend, around one in the morning. I had delivered the last pizza. Ramazan was waiting for me at the pizzeria. I deposited the amount of money I had collected with the boss. As usual, I kept my tips. Ramazan asked me to go clubbing and to pick up girls. We arrived at a club and danced for a while. That night we were not lucky to meet girls. Ramazan invited me to his house that morning; we continued drinking beer at his flat. He was concerned about his fiancée in Pakistan. 'I spoke to her once when I was seven years old,' he told me. 'She is my cousin.' Then he showed me her picture. 'If I was not already committed in this arranged marriage, I would have chosen my future wife by myself,' he said. 'My parents and siblings are in Kabul. My fiancée lives with her family in Pakistan. In the last three years, I have been supporting them so they can live there. Her father is my uncle from my father's side. I am not ashamed to send them money, anyway,' he said. He was drunker than I was. 'America is good,' he told me. 'People can make more money … and the freedom … man …' he said.

I noticed that majority of people in London dressed in black, and they interacted with one another very rapidly. The people looked at their watches constantly. Living in London meant no escape; delay was not accepted by employers or even friends. London was serious, and this was accentuated by the height and power of the architecture. Speed was the essence of living in London, and every day passed just like every other one.

By around 8.30 in the morning in London, on every street, bridge, office building, newspaper stand, clothes store, underground station, bus station, and coffee shop, people all moved at once. Daylight and sunshine were rare, and their charms were felt for only short periods of time. The rain and the foggy sky kept people off the street most of the days. Everything about living in London, including the pigeons at Piccadilly and Trafalgar, represented the age of modernity. London life ran like clockwork, and the people either flourished or were crushed under the pressure of high security alert. As the evening arrived, a different London evolved. The city lights came on; the river appeared as the only clear patch of darkness amongst an accumulation of sparkle. The surface of the river reflected the streetlights with grey ripples, as if there was an underground living city. Theatres, restaurants, clubs, and pubs in Market Place, Hoxton Square, and Carnaby Street were full to overflowing. London nightlife was like life in another city.

I received a letter from Uncle Ghulam. After the greeting, Uncle Ghulam asked me to send him money. 'Everything in Pakistan is getting expensive, especially the home rent and food. The fruit market in which Sohrab and I have worked was burned down to ashes, and we no longer have jobs.' After six months staying in London I had saved around 1,500 pounds, and I sent Uncle Ghulam 450 pounds. He confirmed the receipt of the amount by telephone.

My boss liked the way I worked. I was fast in delivering the pizzas and showed up for work on time. Therefore, my boss gave me few extra shifts. I worked six days a week delivering pizza. Once I had an accident. It was January, and I had three orders to deliver to three different addresses. Because I did not want to be late, I used a one-way street as a shortcut. All of a sudden, a car turned left onto that tiny street. I was speeding. I pressed the brake, but the scooter skidded on the thin film ice that covered the surface of the street. The scooter hit the front bumper of the car, and I flipped over the roof of the car. The car stopped, and the scooter fell into the right side of the vehicle with the light still on. The driver came out to see if I was okay. I got up, and he seemed concerned about my physical wellbeing. The driver saw I was able to walk and to speak. I took my helmet off. I was wearing a long, black-and-red leather jacket. To keep warm, I was wearing winter pyjamas over my jeans. 'I have to call the police,' the driver protested. 'This is a one-way street, and you have damaged my car.' We were not far away from the pizza place. I asked him to come with me to the pizzeria and discuss the situation with my boss. Once I explained to the boss what had happened, he started yelling at the driver, and told me to get back to work. 'Make sure the pizzas are delivered on time!' A few minutes later the driver left without saying another word.

I received a letter from British immigration, which had stated that I had been accepted as a refugee in England. I called Sharouch in New Jersey, and he told me, 'You are very lucky. I have been in the America for more two years now, but I have not received my green card. I have given a lot of money to my immigration lawyer, yet it is pending. I live on my work authorization.' Sharouch called me a few weeks later and asked me to come to America. I was alone in London; on the other hand, everyone I spoke to said, 'Oh, America is the land of opportunity. The quality of life is much better than it is in London.' Even two of my housemates who were from Somalia, and one Iranian and two Pakistani said the same about America.

I applied for British travel document, which I received after a week. Then I went to the US embassy in London and applied for a visa. But the US embassy rejected my tourist visa application since I was holding a British travel document, not a British Passport. I called Sharouch, and he recommended that I apply for Mexican tourist visa. From Mexico is easy to enter US soil. I went to the Mexican embassy in London and applied for tourist visa. They issued me tourist visa after a few days.

I purchased my plane ticket from London to Mexico City from Aeroflot, Russian Airlines. The aircraft flew from Heathrow Airport to Moscow. After a short layover, it flew to Ireland where we had another layover. Then it flew to Miami for another short layover before flying to Mexico City. Finally we landed on Mexican soil. I left the airport, went into the city, and checked into a hotel. I called Sharouch, and he told me to travel closer to the US border. I found communicating very difficult, as no one spoke English. Finally, I managed to find the Greyhound bus terminal, and I purchased a bus ticket to Matamoras. After a sixteen-hour bus ride, I arrived at the final bus stop and booked into the Grand Hotel in Matamoras, which was ten minutes away from the

Texas border. In the evening I took a taxi to see the US border. I noticed that there were four counters and thousands of people entering Mexico from Texas, and leaving Mexico for Texas. There were men women and children. Some were pedestrians; others were riding bicycles, motorcycles, cars, and trucks of all sizes. There were traffic jams and long lines of people lined up to get approval from the officials at the counters. The officials and guards inspected the trunks and all other areas of every vehicle travelling from one country to the other. There was a bridge in Mexico right before the US boarder began. The territories were divided by a tall wall built out of barbed wire. It was getting dark. I watched as a young Mexican man climbed the barbed wire wall. After jumping down and landing on the US soil, he ran under the bridge and disappeared. A few other young men followed his footsteps.

I returned to my hotel room and called Sharouch. I told him that I had arrived close to the US border in Texas. I gave him the address of my hotel. He said, 'Wait there for a few more days. I will start searching for a smuggler to get you through the US border. Probably in the trunk of a car, or in the back of a truck. Or the smuggler may use fake identification to bring you the America.'

As I was on hold, the following day in the evening, I went back to the US border. That evening many young men were climbing the barbed wire wall. One after the other, they went under the bridge and vanished. I thought, *I can do the same thing! Why should I wait for something that I don't know?* I went back to my hotel room and got my luggage, which was a small backpack with some clothes in it. I had my passport and my plane ticket. I took a taxi and waited right on the spot where the kids were climbing the barbed wire. One of the kids said, 'No bag … no bag!' I had no idea why he was saying that, so I did not listen to him. Instead I waited until a big truck came and blocked the American Security guards' view. First, I threw my bag over, and then I climbed the barbed wire. I climbed up to the top line of the barber wire wall. I jumped onto the US territory. The minute my shoes touched the US soil, I heard a whistle, and heard a loud shout: 'Man with a bag! Man with a bag!' At that point, I took out my British travel document and my plane ticket and buried them in the soil under the bridge. I saw a black American policeman coming towards me from the other side of the bridge. 'Stop! Stop! Police!' he shouted. I dropped my luggage and then kept my hands up in the air. The policeman pushed me onto my knees on the ground and put one of his hand on the top of my head and then pulled back both of arms and handcuffed me. He took me to the station and started to speak in Spanish. Then he tried English. 'No English. Afghan refugee,' I replied.

Twenty-Three

I was taken to the police station in handcuffs. One of the police officers emptied my bag on the table and searched everything in detail. He could not find anything illegal … just my clothes. He looked at me and shouted, 'Where have you come from?' I had Reza's advice in mind, and I repeated, 'No English. Afghan refuge.'

He stared at me as he slumped on the desk. 'Where are you from?'

I said again, 'Afghan refugee.' The black police officer left, and I was left alone in a locked room. He came back after a while and provided an Afghan interpreter over the phone. I said to the Afghan interpreter, 'I have come from Pakistan. The smuggler told me to climb the barbed wire. My grandpa paid the smuggler ten thousand dollars. I have a cousin who lives in New Jersey.' And I gave him Sharouch's phone number. Speaking over the phone with the interpreter, the police officer filled out a form on my behalf. It was getting late in the night, so two of the police officers drove me to a building where I spent the night.

In the morning I got up. There was a place where we could get breakfast. I met many young boys there. I was able to speak poor English at the time, but I never said a word in English to anyone. There must have been between thirty and forty kids in that large building, and four of us shared a room with separate beds. Most of the kids were from Mexico, and the rest were from the other South American countries. After breakfast, we attended English language class. On Sundays a priest came and provided religious education.

The US immigration contacted Sharouch. After ten days at the boarding house, I was sent to New Jersey. This was in April 1991. Sharouch picked me up from the airport and took me to his apartment. I had around £1,700 in cash, and I gave it all to Sharouch. He exchanged it to US dollars that evening. 'Pounds are good currency,' he said, 'It became a lot of US dollars.' Sharouch was working forty hours a week for Roy Rogers's fast food as a cook. In two weeks we moved into a bigger apartment, and I had my own bedroom. I started my first job in New Jersey in a landscaping company. I was paid $10 per hour, and worked five to six days a week. The money I earned each day I left on the kitchen table for Sharouch. I expected Sharouch to pay for the rent, the immigration lawyer, and our other expenses.

Sharouch was very happy to have me in New Jersey, and I was happy to be there in the beginning. Unlike London, New Jersey was big – the streets, the cars, the buildings, and even the people. Once we called Uncle Ghulam, and Sharouch spoke to him and the family. I asked Sharouch to give me the phone so I talk to Sohrab, but he hung up the phone. 'It is very expensive,' he said. Then I punched the wall and brook the telephone. 'How can you do that? I need to speak! He is my friend,' I said

'Listen,' he said to me, 'Sohrab is my cousin too. Do not forget that I am older than you are. Remember what Grandpa said. I make decisions.' I went out to the gas station and purchased beer and got drunk. Unlike London, there were no bars close by. Everything was far from our apartment building. The closest shopping centre was a twenty-minute walk. I did have not have a work authorization or a driver's licence.

Sharouch worked until late at night, and I worked during the day. By the time I came home, he had already left for work. I kept buying beer from the gas station, and a few months later I started smoking cigarettes. Although I was making good money, Sharouch kept complaining about money, saying the rent and my immigration lawyer were very expensive, and he sent the rest of the money to Pakistan and to Grandpa.

In the late fall of 1992, I went to New York for my first immigration interview. I received my work authorization. I started my first legal job as a dishwasher at a Friendly's restaurant. I was washing dishes at night and working for the landscaping company during the day. It was a small landscaping company; we use to cut down and trim trees and bushes. My boss's name was Mark. He was married to a French lady, and they had a little boy. Mark climbed the trees and started chopping the tree from the top. In order to protect the roofs of the houses and the fences from the falling branches, Mark tied a long rope to the branches he was going to chop off. I was on the ground holding and pulling the other end of the rope to lower the branches carefully and prevent them from doing any damage. Before climbing the tree, Mark put on a safety harness and boots with spikes coming out of the sides. He put a rope around the trunk of the tree and attached the rope to his harness. He put his weight against the rope and dug the spikes into the tree in order to climb. He carried a big chain saw as he climbed the tree. Once Mark reached the top of the tree, he started to chop the tree into pieces. I was on the ground collecting the branches and pieces of the trunk and putting them into the back of his truck. I used a smaller chain saw to cut the bigger pieces into more manageable sizes before I loaded them onto the truck. Sometimes we cut down four to five trees a day and unloaded the truck into Dumpsters. Mark drank at least twelve bottles of beer a day and smoked marijuana while he was working. He was a white man. He grew moustache and had slim body, all muscle. He did not like to talk much. He was around forty-two years old. Mark picked me up in the morning and dropped me off at my address in the evening.

Twenty-Four

Sharouch some nights did not come home, especially those nights when he was off from work. Once I asked where he went. 'I have a girlfriend,' he said. In the winter of 1993 he put on my winter jacket so he could go out to warm up his car. When he came back to the apartment, he discovered a pack of cigarette in my jacket pocket. He placed the cigarettes on the coffee table. I was watching TV at that moment. 'Are these your cigarettes?' he asked.

'Yes,' I said.

He dragged the coffee table aside, and stood tall in front of me. Then he pushed me hard on my shoulders. 'Why do you smoke?' he shouted.

'I smoke,' I said. I was about to stand up, but he pushed me back onto the sofa and punched me hard on my nose. The blood gushed out. I covered my face with both hands to stop the blood from pouring onto the carpet as I walked towards the bathroom. I shouted at him, 'Why did you punch me?' When I returned to the living room, Sharouch had already gone.

After that incident, Sharouch disappeared for a couple of days. Early one morning the phone rang. It was Aunt Zeynab from Pakistan. After greeting me she asked where Sharouch was. I said he must be at work. 'Why didn't he send us the money for this month?' she asked. I was giving all the money I was making to Sharouch. I was keeping just little pocket money out of my pay cheque, and Sharouch was taking care of the expenses such as our rent, electricity, phone bill, and our immigration lawyer fees. And he was sending $500 per month to Uncle Ghulam's family in Pakistan.

Sharouch came home that evening. He seemed very tired, and he went to his bedroom. I went out and returned home late at night, yet he was asleep. In the morning I told him about Aunt Zeynab's phone call, and the money she had asked for. He got all upset. 'Why don't you find another job? All the money we are making we send to them,' he said. And then he asked me, 'How much money do you have?'

'I have only a couple hundred in my bank account I said.

'Withdraw that money today and give it to me. I will send to Pakistan,' he said.

I found a morning job at the Marriott Hotel as a room service person. In the late fall, the weather had got cold and my landscaping employer, Mark, stopped working. 'There are no trees to cut,' he told me. At night I was a dishwasher. I worked between fifty to sixty hours a week at two jobs.

A couple months later, during the Christmas holidays in 1994, a few Afghan men gathered in our apartment to eat and to drink beer. After dinner they decided to go to a casino in Atlantic City. There were five us. It was my first time in a casino. Babur's Uncle Zaman, the taxi driver, was one of the group.

They all gambled, but I did not know how. A few hours later we gathered together, as we had planned, at a certain place in the Taj Mahal casino. Thousands of people under the same ceiling were busy gambling. As we were descending on the escalator one of the Afghan men pointed at a chandelier. 'Look,' he said, 'that chandelier is worth more than half a million dollars, and there are hundreds of them on this ceiling alone!' Everyone started to laugh.

As we were walking towards our vehicle in the parking lot, they started asking each other how much they had lost. Zaman asked Sharouch, 'How much did you lose?'

Sharouch said, 'Only two hundred.'

Then Zaman and the other two men started to laugh at how Sharouch had responded. Zaman said, 'No, you always say that. I am sure you have lost more.'

Then Sharouch got frustrated. 'Shut up. I do not want to talk about it!' he said, and then everyone laughed out loud.

One morning when I was at work at the Marriott Hotel, my manager said, 'After work, go see the human resources department.'

I went to see the lady at the human resources office where I had my first interview to get the job. 'Your work authorization will expire in two weeks,' she said. 'You must provide us with a valid work authorization as soon as possible.'

That was the first thing I mentioned to Sharouch when I got home. Sharouch contacted my immigration lawyer and made an appointment for the same week. We went to New York City, and my immigration lawyer said, 'I have appealed the last decision in which immigration refused to give you a green card. I have gathered all the valid proof that the Hazara ethnic group has been discriminated against in the last few centuries in Afghanistan, so I am hoping this time we will win your case.' A week later, the immigration lawyer, who was called Marguerite, called to give me my immigration court date in New York City.

I presented myself in the morning on that date at the US Immigration courtroom. Finally, the court procedure was over. Marguerite asked us to wait at the coffee shop on the first floor. After a short while, she joined us. 'I have convinced the judge that the Hazara ethnic group of Afghanistan has been victimized by the majority ethnic groups, but you do not have any authentic evidence to prove to the judge that you have come from Pakistan, such as an airplane ticket, a passport, or even a boarding pass. Only with such documents would there have been a strong case.' Sharouch left to get Marguerite a coffee. 'Medium black,' she said. She eyeballed me. 'Where are your documents? You have no identification papers?' she asked.

'Before I climbed over the barbed wire fence, the smuggler took away my identification,' I responded to her.

Sharouch returned with a cup of coffee and a piece of carrot cake. He placed the plate of the cake right in front of Marguerite then put the coffee on the table. 'No, no. I do not want cake. Just coffee,' she said, then she looked at her watch. 'Anyway, as I was saying, at this point the judge has not made any decision. I did ask the judge to allow you another twelve months' work authorization for the third time. The judge said he will send the decision by mail within a few days to my address, and a copy to your home address,' Marguerite said.

The following week, I received the US Immigration decision letter. I was to be deported; I had to leave the country within six months. I contacted my immigration lawyer. 'This is the US Immigration Department's final decision,' Marguerite said, 'and I cannot help it. I am sorry.'

I showed my deportation letter to Sharouch and told him my lawyer had given up on my case. Sharouch called an Afghan who had lived in the States for more than twenty years. 'Maybe Nabi can find a lawyer,' he said. Nabi invited us to his house. He was a family man, and a taxi driver. He had two gorgeous daughters who were born in the States. They were between seventeen and nineteen years old. That evening his wife was at work. We sat in his living room. Nabi looked at my deportation letter and shook his head. 'This is serious,' he said.

One of his girls sat next to me in the sofa, and she touched my hair. 'You have beautiful hair.' She said it in English, and then she smiled.

Nabi looked at me. 'My girls do not speak Dari, and their mother is white American,' he said.

My name is Laila, and I am an artist,' she said. Then she stood up and pulled my hand. 'Let's go to the basement. I will show you my artwork.'

Nabi started to laugh out loud. 'Aftab, you are a very shy young man. You have turned red,' he said. Then he stopped laughing. 'Go, go, Bachem. It is okay.' She pulled my hand and took me to her basement and showed me a few canvases she had painted that were hanging on the wall. She started talking about her paintings, and her friends.

Not much later I heard Sharouch calling from the first floor, 'Aftab, let's go.' I was about to step up the stairs when she pulled my hand. 'Give me your phone number,' she said. She wrote my telephone number on a piece of paper, and we went up on the first floor.

'Sit down, Bachem' Nabi said. 'Aftab, Bachem, once the US Immigration places you on deportation, it is very serious. I know you have come from London, England. Your real name is Aftab, and you have used different name here, which is Jawed Hassani, and I like that. Honestly, I can help you to make fake green card, and you can live in the States, but the question is for how long? Your cousin Sharouch has lived in the States for more than five years yet has not received his green card.' He picked up a teacup and sipped his tea. 'Listen to me very carefully' he said. 'You are young, and if I were you I would go and start a new life in Canada.'

I was shocked. 'Canada?' I said.

'Yes, Bachem, Canada,' he said. Canada is a very good country. It is a cold country, but they accept Afghan refugees very easily.' He continued to explain: 'About seven years ago, a young man like you had trouble in getting his green card, and I helped him to pass across the border from the United States to Canada. Now he is Canadian citizen and lives in Toronto. He is very happy,' he said.

'How can I get across the border? I asked.

'I know a Mexican man who makes fake green cards. I will ask him to make you one, and then you can use it to cross the border. Once you arrive in Canada, turn yourself in to the police and tell them you have been smuggled from Pakistan. Use a different name and date of birth. I am sure you will be accepted in a year. Do not hire another lawyer, Bachem. They are a bunch of thieves. All they want is your money,' he said. Then he drank the last of his tea. 'This Mexican will charge three hundred dollars,' he explained. 'Bring me two passport-size photos, and in a week you will have your green card.'

Sharouch and I were about to leave Nabi's house when his daughter Laila came and shook our hands. Then we left.

That night I dreamed of a white falcon. It had a light and shiny yellow beak and blue eyes. At first, it sat on my right shoulder, and then it flew away. I watched it until it disappeared. In the morning, without saying anything to Sharouch, I got my passport-size pictures and took $300 to Nabi's house. Nabi was at work. I left the money and pictures with his American wife to give Nabi.

That afternoon, Laila called me and asked if I could go and watch a movie with her at the movie theatre. In the evening went to watch the movie *Far and Away* with Tom Cruise, and Nicole Kidman. 'What a beautiful movie,' Laila said.

I dropped her at her house late at night, and her father was at home. He saw us together and smiled. 'Aftab, Bachem, in a week you will have your green card,' he said.

When I arrived home, Sharouch was with one of his Afghan friends, Rahim, drinking beer. I opened a bottle of beer, then Sharouch asked, 'Where were you?' I told him about giving my photos and money to Nabi's wife that morning. Then I told him about watching the movie with Laila. Rahim was a college student. He started to laugh out loud. 'You went out with Laila? I cannot believe this!' Sharouch started to get mad, and turned red. Then Rahim laughed out loud again. 'Laila … she is so hot … oh my God.' I opened another beer, and still Rahim was laughing.

Then Sharouch's lower lip started to shake. 'You went to his house without my permission, and now you want to go to Canada? Why didn't you ask me first?' Sharouch said.

Rahim must have had a buzz from drinking beer, because he mentioned it again: 'You and Laila … I cannot believe it!' Sharouch and Rahim were sitting in the sofa, and I was sitting across them on a chair. Rahim kept on laughing and saying Laila's name. He even described her face and her body and said how sexy she was.

All of a sudden Sharouch stood up and walked towards me. He slapped me hard on my face. 'Why didn't you ask me?' he asked.

I pushed him back. 'It is not your business! This is *my* life!' I replied. Rahim stood up to stop Sharouch, but all of a sudden Sharouch punched me hard on my lips, and then quickly punched my forehead. I fell off the chair. Everything became blurry and dark, and I passed out.

When I woke, I found myself on the sofa. Rahim was next to me. He had a towel and was cleaning the blood off my face. My face was covered with blood, and one of my front teeth was broken. Rahim helped me to the washroom to wash off the blood. 'Sharouch is crazy,' he said to me. 'He could have killed you. What is wrong with your cousin?' And then he said, 'Sharouch likes Laila. So do I, but she likes to go out with you; therefore, it is not your fault.'

I was hurt, and I was crying. 'Why did he have to punch me? Where is Sharouch? I need to talk to him.'

'Sharouch left right after beating you,' Rahim said.

I did not go out of the apartment for three days. The only thing I wanted was to go Canada. I was sick and tired. The manager from my dishwashing job called me and yelled at me over the phone, 'Why don't come to work, Amigo?' I told him that I was sick, but he did not believe me. The next day the manager from the Marriott Hotel called. I told him that my work authorization has expired, and my immigration lawyer could not help; therefore, I had to quit, which he understood. I sold my car for $2,200 to my neighbour, and later on that day picked up my last two pay cheques from my jobs. Then I waited for my fake green card so I could cross the border into Canada. That was the only option I had at that point.

Three days after Sharouch had beaten me came home with smile. I did not want to see his face or talk to him. He kept on saying, 'Khan sahib, how are you?' Then he got close to me. 'It is okay. We are like brothers, and brothers always fight.' Then he left and came back with twelve Heinekens and opened one for me and one for himself. He started to laugh. 'I was drunk when I broke your teeth. I will pay for it.' I had nothing to tell him. The only thing I wanted was for him to touch me again so I could kick his ass.

After a few days, Nabi called and came to see me. Sharouch was out, but Rahim was there. Nabi had my fake green card with him, and then he asked, 'When do you want to leave for Canada?' I told him as soon as possible. 'How about tomorrow morning?' I agreed. 'Pack your clothes in a small bag, and I will take you to the Greyhound bus terminal to purchase a round-trip ticket.'

I asked, 'Why do I buy a round-trip ticket?'

Nabi responded, 'If you have a round-trip ticket from New Jersey to Montreal and back, the Canadian border guards will not ask too many questions, because they will think that you will be returning home. At the border, all passengers must get off the bus. Everyone will have to pass through the Canadian Immigration counter with valid travelling documents. After you pass the border, the same bus will take you to Montreal,' Nabi explained. 'In addition,' he said, 'tell the Canadian guards you would love to spend one week in Montreal. Furthermore, Montreal is a French city. It is very different from the rest of the North American cities. I hope you like it.' Rahim told Nabi about Sharouch beating me. 'He is immature,' said Nabi. 'Don't take it personally.'

In the evening, Sharouch came home with his friends and beer. They already knew I was supposed to leave the States for Canada in the morning. As usual we chatted, cooked, watched TV, listened to music, and of course, drank beer. After Sharouch's friends left, first question he asked me was, 'How much did you sell your car for?'

'Twenty-two hundred,' I said. I counted $1,500 in large bills, put it on the coffee table, and asked him to send the money to Pakistan. I had no interest in talking to him. In the morning Sharouch drove to Rahim's house, and then he drove us to the Greyhound bus terminal. I purchased my round-trip ticket, made sure I had my fake green card and my driver's license, said goodbye to them, and got on the bus.

It was the month of February, so it was cold. When the bus reached the Canadian border, everyone got off the bus and passed through the Canadian border. I showed my fake green card and my return ticket, and I told the Canadian security guard I planned to stay in Montreal for one week, just to visit the city. The security guard asked me, 'How much cash are you carrying?'

I replied, 'Around a thousand dollars.' All the passengers passed through the Canadian border checkpoint without any trouble, and we all boarded the buss again. Just then the bus driver announced, 'Ladies and gentlemen, welcome to Quebec.' He said it twice, once in French, and once in English. The bus reached the city of Montreal in the evening. When I stepped out onto the street I realized how very cold it was. Almost everything was covered in snow. I walked into a coffee shop and destroyed my fake American green card, American driver's license, and the return ticket.

While I was drinking a coffee, I saw a police car outside the coffee shop, so I went to speak to the officer. He spoke in French, and then pointed at his partner in the vehicle. His partner was a lady officer, and she stepped out of the vehicle. I tried to introduce myself to her. When I said I was an Afghan seeking refugee status, she started to laugh. The lady officer interpreted what I had said to her partner, and they both laughed out loud hard.

Twenty-Five

The police officers took me to the station. The lady took my fingerprints, my picture, and asked, 'What is your name?' At that moment I realized that I had to use a different name and date of birth. 'What is your name?' she asked again.

'My name is Ali.'

She wrote it down. Then she move her pen to the next box on the application form. 'What is your family name?' she asked. I had no idea what to say. She stared at me and asked again, 'What is your last name?'

I remained quiet. All of sudden the name *Mehdi* popped out, and I said, 'Mehdi.'

'Do you speak English?' she asked.

'Little bit,' I responded.

'I do not have time for this,' she said, and left the room.

I waited another hour or so. Then a policeman walked into the room and emptied my bag onto the table. He went through my clothes, and then asked me to empty my pockets. I had $1,007 in US currency. The policeman counted it and asked. 'Where is your passport?'

'I don't have one. I am an Afghan refugee. I came from Pakistan,' I said.

'I contacted an Afghan interpreter. He will be here soon,' the officer said, then he left the room and locked the door. Late at night, a police officer entered the room with an Afghan middle-aged man in tow.

'My name is Sabour. It is my responsibility to help the Afghan newcomers to Quebec.' He spoke to me in the Dari language. He opened a folder and took out a blank sheet, and placed it on the table. 'Your name is Ali, and your last name is Mehdi.' I nodded. Then he asked me, 'When did you arrive in Canada, and how?'

I arrived in Canada today from Pakistan. Grandpa gave ten thousand dollars to a smuggler. The smuggler was with me in the coffee shop. Once the smuggler saw the police vehicle, he took my documents away, and told me to turn myself to the police.'

The interpreter asked, 'When was the last time you were at the airport?'

I said, 'This morning.'

The interpreter kept on taking notes. He wanted to know how long my journey had taken from Pakistan to Canada. I did not understand the question clearly, so I asked him to repeat it. The interpreter saw my hand wide open while I asked him to repeat the question. He said, 'Five days, okay.' He looked at the police officer next to him, and then took more notes. 'Did you use an airplane, a ship, a bus, a train, or a taxi in your journey?' the interpreter asked.

I said, 'Yes."

The interpreter glanced quickly at the police officer, and asked, 'But which kind of transportation did you use?'

I replied, "All that you just mentioned.'

Sabour looked at the police officer, and then turned his face to me. He fiddled with his pen in his right hand, and said, 'Okay, last question. Which countries did you pass through in order to get Canada?' He fiddled with the pen again.

'I don't know,' I said. 'I just followed the smuggler.' The interpreter spoke in French to the police officer, then said, 'I will see you this week. *Khuda hafiz*' (God protect you). A police officer drove me to another building. 'This is the Salvation Army,' he said, and then he introduced me to the man who was sitting at the front desk.

I followed the man into a large, dark room full of bunk beds. 'This is your bed,' the man said. In the morning I followed everyone else to the basement where breakfast was served. Everything was in French.

In the afternoon, the Afghan interpreter came with a French lady who was social worker. The Afghan interpreter kept on speaking in French to the social worker, then told me that she would find a legal aid immigration lawyer for me. 'On this application form is stated that you have one thousand seven US dollars,' he said. 'If you want, this lady can find you an apartment to rent, or you can stay here at the Salvation Army until you get your legal immigration papers completed.' Lastly Sabour told me, 'I have told your social worker that you can not speak English. I will write your case and give it to your lawyer.' Sabour pulled out his personal business card and handed it to me. 'Call me at anytime,' he said, and then he left us.

I followed the social worker to a Metro station in the cold and the snow. We rode the train for a few stops, and then I followed her into a building where the lawyer's office was. After I signed some official papers, the social worker took me back to the Salvation Army. I stayed there for another two days.

There were around fifty or sixty males and females living at the Salvation Army. Everyone communicated in French, except for a man with a long beard who spoke English. While we were sitting in the cafeteria having lunch, I asked him, 'Are you from India?'

He looked at me with his glassy eyes and smiled. 'No, Pakistan,' he said.

'How long you have been in Canada?' I asked.

'For twenty years,' he said. 'Where are you from?'

'I am an Afghan.'

He eyeballed me head to toe. 'Are you a Hazara?'

I said, 'Yes.'

He smiled and shook his head. 'I know,' he said.

'Do you have family in Canada?' I asked

Then he got all frustrated. 'Fuck family,' he said. 'I have four children, and my wife fucked me up.'

'Why?'

He stood up and slapped on the table. The tray flipped. An empty soup bowl, a spoon, a fork, a knife, half a plate of spaghetti, and a piece of bread all fell onto the floor. The plate broke in pieces. He shouted at me, 'Why don't you understand my wife fucked me?' Then he kept on saying, 'Why, why? I don't know why ...' Finally he smiled.

A cafeteria security guard appeared and asked me to stay away from the man. 'He is a sick person,' the guard explained.

The next day, I went to a shopping mall in downtown Montreal and purchased myself a winter coat, a pair of gloves, and a pair of winter boots. In the evening, I called Sabour and made an appointment with him. Sabour told me to meet him in the coffee shop across from the Salvation Army. At our meeting I asked him to help me find an apartment with decent rent.

On the same day, after visiting a few places for rent, we found a basement apartment downtown, for $250. It was furnished with a bed and some dishes. 'I am from Herat and I am a Shia Muslim,' Sabour said. 'I know what the Pashtun have done to Hazara people. Don't worry. I will help you to the best of my ability. In a month or so you will start receiving money from the government, and the government will provide you with a French course. If you want to live in Quebec, you must learn French,' Sabour advised. Then he said, 'You are only twenty-one years old. You must learn French.' I asked him to help me call my family in Pakistan. Next morning

Sabour took me to a post office. 'Calling Pakistan is expensive,' he said. 'I will give your new address to your social worker. Stay home in the morning. She may come and visit you this week.' Then he left.

After calling Pakistan a few times, I finally got in touch with Uncle Ghulam. He sounded happy to hear I had arrived in Canada safely. I could hear Aunt Zeynab saying, 'Pass the phone to me! Pass the phone to me!' Without greeting me, she said, 'Send money. We need money.' I tried to explain to her that I had left $1,500 with Sharouch to send to them, but all she kept saying was, 'No, not Sharouch. I am asking you.' Then she said, 'We have an interview at the Canadian embassy next week. We have to go to Islamabad. We need money.' All of a sudden, the phone was disconnected. The time I had paid for was up.

Later that week, my social worker came to my apartment one morning. She invited me to a coffee shop and asked how much rent I was paying. She said, 'At the beginning of next month, which is March, you will receive your first welfare check.' She took a copy of my apartment lease, and I followed her to the welfare office. 'You will receive $537 a month after you are accepted as refugee in Quebec. Then you will start your French course,' she said. Every Monday morning she came to see me, and we had coffee together. On our second appointment, she brought my photo identification. 'This is your temporary identification,' she said. 'Today I will take you to open a bank account so you can cash your welfare check.' She was a skinny lady. Every time we had coffee, she kept both hands around the coffee cup, sat straight, and smiled at me all the time.

I was concerned about Uncle Ghulam's family; therefore, I called Sharouch to find out about the money. Sharouch was mad at me and yelled at me over the phone, 'Why didn't you call? I was concerned about you!' I asked him whether had he sent the $1,500 to Uncle Ghulam's family in Pakistan. Sharouch giggled over the phone. 'Yes, yes, of course, and Uncle Ghulam's family has been accepted by the Canadian embassy in Islamabad. They will migrate to Quebec. Presently, they are waiting for their Canadian permanent residency,' Sharouch said. I was so happy to hear that. 'Within a few months they will be in Canada. Find a job and save money,' Sharouch said. I was about to tell him that everything was in the French language and I couldn't find a job, but the phone was disconnected.

I called Sabour and asked him to help me to find job. Next morning, he arrived at my apartment. 'I know an Iranian who owns a pizza shop that is a few Metro stations away,' he said, and then he lit a cigarette. 'If you want, we will go and see him today. Because you do not have a social insurance number, I will speak to him and ask him to pay you in cash. This way you can keep your welfare money, and at the same keep your job,' Sabour recommended.

On that same day, he introduced me to Kamal, the owner of the pizza place. The name of the pizzeria was Pizza 2 for 1. Kamal trained me how to 'toss' different sizes of pizza dough and add the toppings. He also taught me to make club sandwiches, hamburgers, and submarine sandwiches. After three days of training, he said, 'I will pay you five dollars in hour cash. You will start at eleven in the morning and leave at five. Your schedule is Monday to Saturday. You may take Sundays off.' I worked six days a week, six hours each day. I made $30 a day, $180 a week. Between noon and one o'clock, many school kids came for pizza slices. At 11.30 I had to throw six extra-large pizzas. They were twenty inches diameter. I had to make two plain cheese, two with pepperoni, and two with everything. Every morning before I began to toss the pizza dough, the boss would emphasize, 'Be careful with the cheese!' We baked the pizza in a large stone oven and used a flat pizza shovel with a short handle to place the pizza inside the oven and pull it out when it was done. Depending on the oven temperature, we baked a pizza from between seven to eight minutes. We sliced the extra-large pizzas into eight slices and served the slices on paper plates. The students were between the ages of nine and twelve, and every weekday we received around thirty to forty students at lunchtime. Some of them liked poutine, which was simple to serve: French fries in a small bowl sprinkled with mozzarella cheese then topped with gravy sauce.

A sixty-year-old man came to the restaurant every morning at around 11.30. He carried a big bag and sat next to the window on the same chair every day. He left the restaurant at around three in the afternoon. I asked my boss who the guy was. 'He comes here every day,' I said. 'He does not eat, does not speak, but only drinks coffee.'

My boss looked at me and smiled. 'His wife fucked him over,' Kamal said. I did not understand. I asked Kamal to tell me who the guy was and what did it mean that his wife fucked him over. Then Kamal laughed out loud. 'I have known this guy for more than fifteen years. He used to be an engineer. His name is Roberto … a very nice man. Something happened between him and his wife, and they ended up divorced. By law, his wife took everything from him – house, car, even the family savings in the bank. Since then he lives in the hospital's mental institution,' Kamal said. Then Kamal pointed through the restaurant window. 'That red building is the hospital.' I asked Kamal why the man carried the big bag with him if he lived that close. Kamal started to laugh out loud. 'He keeps his clothes in that bag. That is all the man has to his name, and he thinks everyone is thief, even though he is on medication,' Kamal said.

Twenty-Six

After two months staying in Canada I received a letter from the Canadian immigration department, requesting that I show up for an interview in three months' time. I informed Sabour about the letter, and he came to see me that week. Sabour called my legal aid immigration lawyer, and from then on, Sabour represented me himself.

I was busy working at the pizza restaurant. One morning, Uncle Ghulam called me. He sounded very happy. Aunt Zeynab must have been standing next to Uncle Ghulam, because I could hear her: 'Give me the phone! Give me the phone. I must talk to him!' She repeated this over and over until she succeeded. The minute she got on the phone said this. 'You have never sent us money! Could you send us money at least for once? Only then we can tell your mother in Kabul that you have a sense of honour.

'I can send you a thousand Canadian dollars, which is equal to seven hundred US dollars,' I told her.

'No, no! What is seven hundred? Send us more!' Then she said, 'We have been accepted by the Canadian embassy in Islamabad as refugees. We will migrate to the province of Quebec and will live together again.' Then she gave me a business address where I should send the money.

From the allowance and my job I had saved around $1,500. I managed to send the money on the same day. In two days' time, Uncle Ghulam called and confirmed that he had received it. I asked Uncle Ghulam about the family situation in Kabul. 'Everyone is fine, except a few months ago

Grandma passed away,' he said. That was shocking to me. Then he said, 'This is Allah's wish, Bachem. Just take care of yourself.' With that, the phone line was disconnected.

At first, I could not understand why I had not been told about Grandma. I called Sharouch in New Jersey and asked, 'Why was I not informed about Grandma's death?'

'It was Grandpa's idea not to inform you,' Sharouch said. That night I purchased a bottle of whisky and drank it alone. I was not able to stop crying. I cried until dawn.

By the end of April, the weather became warmer. Finally, the spring came along. The light green grass and the beautiful landscape of Montreal began to come alive. The city reminded me of London – the nightlife, the architecture, and the diversity of the people. Indeed, Montreal's blue sky was much clearer than London's sky. People seemed much more open minded, and calmer. I walked on the busy street of Saint Catherine until late at night every weekend. I knew no one, and out of loneliness, beer and cigarettes became my close acquaintances.

On one of my days off from work, I stopped for coffee in a coffee shop. Two men sitting close to my table were speaking in Pashto. I asked, 'Are you guys Afghan?'

One of the men replied in Dari: '*Bali*' (yes). The other man asked me to join them at their table. I got excited tomeet Afghans in Montreal for the first time. After we introduced ourselves, the older man asked, 'Are you Hazara, Uzbek, or Turk?'

'Hazara,' I said. That man faced the other man and spoke to him in the Pashto language, and then they both laughed. I felt uncomfortable.

Then the other man asked me, 'Do you smoke cigarettes?' As we were smoking and having coffee, the older Pashtun man said, 'Do you know that you are a descendant of Genghis Khan, and that Afghanistan belongs to the Pashtun people?' he said.

That was the last thing I expected to hear. I tried to explain to them the little bit of history I had learnt from Amar Singh about the origin of the Hazara people in Afghanistan. It was difficult because they were both giggling and continuing to speak to one another in Pashto. I had no other option but to leave the table.

A few weeks later, Sharouch called. 'Uncle Ghulam and his family have received their Canadian permanent visa in Pakistan and will arrive Canada within a few weeks,' he said. This was stimulating news; I celebrated that sunset with beer. A few days later, Uncle Ghulam called from Pakistan and gave me the exact date and time of their arrival at the Montreal international airport. 'Rent us a nice house … at least do that for us.' Aunt Zeynab was already on the phone. It was the happiest of evenings. As I was off from work, I headed for downtown Montreal, had a few cold beers, and played billiards in a neighbourhood bar.

On the following day, the first thing after work, I called Sabour and told him about my uncle and his family coming to Canada. I asked his assistance in locating a family house to rent. In two days, Sabour came and drove me outside of Montreal. After crossing a bridge, he said, 'This bridge is called Champlain Bridge. This area is called South Shore. It is a nice district for families to live.' We met a real estate agent; the man took us into three different empty houses. At the end of the day, I liked the one that was furnished and had three floors – three bedrooms on the top floor with a full bathroom, a kitchen, a half bathroom, and a living room on the first floor. It also had two bedrooms, a salon, and a full bathroom in the basement. *This is fantastic*, I said to myself. *Uncle Ghulam and his wife will get the biggest room on the second floor. The second room is for Timur, and the third room is for Murad. Sohrab and I will live in the basement. This is awesome.* I was not able to picture how clean and nice the neighbourhood was; indeed, it was all overwhelming. The rent was $750 per month. Hot water and electricity were not included. Sabour said, 'You should pay the first month's rent. As soon as your uncle's family arrives, they will receive money from the government of Quebec. There ought not to be a problem in affording the rent.'

I signed the rental lease for twelve months. The house was owned by a divorced Irishman. Seven days after I signed the rental lease, I got the house keys from the owner. After making arrangements with my landlord in Montreal, I moved to the house in Brossard. It had taken me twenty minutes to go work from my Montreal apartment. From Brossard to the pizza place took an hour and half. I had to walk for ten minutes to the nearest bus stop in order to take the bus to the Brossard bus terminal. From there I had to take another bus to Montreal. From the bus stop in Montreal, I had to take the orange Metro line, and then switch to the blue Metro line, which would finally take me to the pizza place.

All I cared about was seeing my family after such a long time. From time to time, I even prayed for them to reach Canada safely. At night I cleaned the house, especially the kitchen and the bathrooms. I become cleaning addict because of their arrival. The date of their arrival was approaching. I was excited, but I found it difficult to wait. It was not easy to stop watching the clock and the calendar. The house was fully furnished, except for a room in the basement that had no bed. I discovered a second-hand store next to the Brossard bus terminal and purchased a bed. I went grocery shopping two days before the family's arrival in Canada.

I was at the Montreal airport three hours before their arrival time on Sunday evening. I waited at the arrival terminal watching the board for their flight number from Amsterdam with KLM Airlines. Finally, the plane landed. I walked to the second floor and observed hundreds of arriving passengers all searching for their luggage on the baggage belt. From that distance, I became anxious that I wouldn't be able to spot Uncle Ghulam in that crowd. I saw a lady dressed in red. She was speaking to a young man. That young man wore a chocolate-coloured suit, white shirt, and a dark-blue tie. A boy in a white suit with a red tie was holding a large case. He was standing next to the lady. Right at that moment I told myself, *It is them!* I became agitated, and then descended onto the first floor.

Some people were holding flowers, and a few older people were in wheelchairs. Some people were very excited and others seemed less emotional. The passengers walking through the arrival gate represented many cultures. I noticed diverse skin colours, and clothing. I was not aware of the fact at the time, but Uncle Ghulam's family was the only Asian family on that flight. After I waited for a long time, I saw Aunt Zeynab walk though the gate side by side with Murad and Timur. Then I recognized Uncle Ghulam. Finally, I saw a very skinny man with a moustache walking next to Uncle Ghulam. That was Sohrab, the wrestler.

Twenty-Seven

I was super exited to see them. I kissed Aunt Zeynab's hand, and she kissed me on my cheek. Murad hugged me. We shook hands and then kissed each other on the cheeks. Timur smiled and repeated my name several times, 'Khan, Khan.' We hugged each other. Sohrab had tears in his eyes and hugged me really tight. Finally, Uncle Ghulam walked forward. I kissed his hand, then he hugged me and kissed me on my cheeks. That moment seemed as if it was a dream.

Once we collected all their luggage, we hired a taxi van. After a forty-minute journey, we arrived at our address. Every one of them asked me questions about Canada – the city, the people, the security, the food, and the jobs. They liked the house very much. Timur wanted to watch TV, but every TV channel was in French. After a while he found an English Channel, then he said in Urdu, 'Acchā, acchā' (good). Everyone laughed. I was not able to stop looking at them. While they looked around, I prepared chicken sandwiches for them. After we ate, we drank tea and we laughed more than we spoke. It was the happiest moment I had experienced since leaving Kabul. After a while, I showed them their rooms. After their long flight, every one of them was tired. One after another they stretched their legs and arms, and yawned.

Uncle Ghulam's family had left Kabul for Pakistan about seven years before they finally arrived in Canada. I asked Timur, 'How old are you?'

I am fifteen years old,' he said.

'How old are you, Khan,' Sohrab asked.

'I am twenty-two years old,' I said. I asked Sohrab, 'How old are you?'

He slapped me on the back of my head. 'I am four years older than you!'

And Timur said, 'Sohrab is twenty-six years old.' And then everyone laughed.

Murad said, 'I am twenty-eight years old,' and we laughed.

And then Aunt Zeynab asked Ghulam, 'And you, Ghulam?'

Uncle Ghulam ground his teeth and then passed his palm across his face and opened his mouth. 'I am fifty-three years old,' he said, and everyone laughed.

Aunt Zeynab put her hand in the air. 'Up, up!' she said

'Fifty-three. That is right,' argued Uncle Ghulam.

'No,' she said.

You are three years younger than I,' Uncle Ghulam said. 'How old are you, woman?'

Aunt Zeynab just scratched around her neck and looked around the room. Then everyone laughed.

I asked, 'How is Shreen doing?'

'She has three children,' Aunt Zeynab said. 'Two boys and a girl. We married her off to a Hazara man in Quetta, Pakistan, five years ago. She is doing well. Her husband is a locksmith; he is a good man. Before leaving Pakistan for Canada she came with her children to Islamabad and stayed with us for a couple of nights. The Taliban do not leave the Hazara people to live in peace even in Quetta.'

'The Hazara people left the Hazarajat when Abdur Rahman declared genocide on the Hazara ethnic group in the late 1800s,' Uncle Ghulam said. 'Today there are about half a million Hazara people living in Quetta, but the Taliban send suicide bombers to the Shia mosques in Quetta, and they explode themselves in the bazaars and crowded areas. These Pashtuns are animals!' Uncle Ghulam put both hands in the air and recited a few verses from the Holy Koran. When he was finished, he prayed. 'Oh, Allah, thank you for getting us out of Pakistan.'

'Khan, when are you going to get married?' Aunt Zeynab asked.

I had nothing to say. I pointed at Murad, and then at Sohrab. 'They are older than I am. When they are getting married?' I asked.

Timur started to laugh. 'Khan does not know, Mother,' he said.

Everyone laughed, and Aunt Zeynab smiled. 'They already have,' she said.

'Who? Who are they?' I asked.

Everyone was quiet, but Timur giggled, and then he said, 'Tell him, mother. Khan does not know.'

'Your Uncle Rustam's eldest daughter, Ziba, is Murad's fiancée,' she said. 'And your sister Mina is Sohrab's fiancée,' she said. I could not believe it. I was shocked.

Then Murad said, 'Who is Khan's fiancée?' Everyone started to laugh.

'Mother tell him. He doesn't know,' Sohrab said.

'Do you remember your Uncle Rustam's twin daughters Paree, and Negar?' Aunt Zeynab asked me. Then she lay back on the sofa. 'Negar is your fiancée,' she said. Everyone laughed out loud and stared at me. Again, I was shocked. And I was silent.

Sohrab put his hand on my leg and tapped it a few times. 'Congratulations,' he said.

'Bachem, arranged marriage is part of our culture,' Uncle Ghulam said. 'The arrangements were made when you guys were kids, and your Grandpa choose Negar instead of Paree for you. They are identical, but Negar is a lot more talented than Paree.' Then he looked at Aunt Zeynab, 'Isn't that right?' he said.

'Negar, Negar … she is too young for me!' I said.

'No, no! She is fourteen years old now,' Uncle Ghulam advised, 'and in a few years she will be eighteen. Work hard, save your money, and go to Mazar-i-Sharif and marry her!'

Aunt Zeynab agreed. 'She is only six or seven years younger than you are,' she said. 'That is fine. Girls should be younger than boys when they marry.'

I did not believe that I was engaged to my cousin already. After hearing that, I was not able to smile any more, and then Aunt Zeynab said, 'I have her photo in my album. You want to see it?'

I shook my head and said no. I said I was tired and needed to sleep.

I took off from work for a few days to assist the family with their government paperwork, such as Social Insurance cards, medical cards, and French course registration. I found the nearest high school for Timur. A day before I was supposed to go back to work, my boss called me. 'I have hired someone else to replace you, so you do not have to come to work,' he said. Two weeks later every one of my newly arrive relatives received his or her first pay check from the welfare office, and a few days after that they started their French language course.

Uncle Ghulam, Aunt Zeynab, Murad, and Sohrab left the house after breakfast for their French language courses and returned in the afternoon, Monday to Friday. I called Sabour to find me job. 'I don't know anyone on the South Shore,' he said. 'Wait for your immigration interview. Once you are accepted by Immigration Canada as refugee, you will receive your landed visa, then you will get your Social Insurance card. Only then you will be eligible to work in Canada.'

One evening Sohrab, and I went for long walk in a park along the riverside. When we returned we joined the family who were sitting around in the living room having tea. Aunt Zeynab asked, 'Why don't you find a job, Khan?'

'I don't have the legal documents yet to work or to attend French class,' I told her. 'Within a couple of weeks, I will have an interview with Immigration Canada. If I am accepted as refugee, then I will get my legal documents to work.'

'You have been telling us this since we have come to Canada,' she argued. 'You have been in Canada for more than seven months, and you do not have a job. You have no money, no car, and you do not even go to school.'

I told her again about my job at the pizza restaurant, but she denied everything I was saying as if I was liar. 'No, you are just a lazy person,' she said. 'When we were in Pakistan, it was Sharouch who sent us all the money, and you were drinking, smoking, and sleeping, Khan Sahib!' she said, and then giggled.

I protested. 'No! That is not true! I was making more money than Sharouch in America. All the money I made in America, I gave to Sharouch and asked him to send to you guys!'

'No, it is not true,' she said. 'You are lying. You probably have never worked even one day in your life,' she said.

'I was working for a pizza restaurant before you guys came,' I explained. 'I took off for one week so I could take you to all the government offices in order to get your paperwork done. Therefore, I lost my job. My boss found another cook to replace me.'

She repeated herself. 'You are lying! You have never worked.'

I tried to convince Aunt Zeynab that I had sent a great deal of money from the States. 'Even from Canada I sent you seven hundred US dollars!' I said.

Uncle Ghulam was smiling. Murad was always on his mother's side. Only Sohrab believed me.

Aunt Zeynab continued her criticism: 'Your grandpa loved you the most among all his grandsons. He gave you everything you needed. To save you from war, he sent you to India. Then from India he spent a lot of money and smuggled you to London, and you drank alcohol, smoked cigarettes, found some friends, and enjoyed the white girls.'

I was not able to bear what she was saying, and had no idea why she was blaming me. Finally, she made me cry. I got emotional and stood up. 'Sharouch was lying to you!' I said. 'Everything he has said are lies about me. I have worked very hard in London and in America, and I have sent you money.'

She kept on rejecting. 'Sharouch is not liar,' she said. 'You are a liar! Don't call Sharouch a liar. He was the one who sent us the money to Pakistan.'

Uncle Ghulam saw me crying, and he wanted to calm me down. 'Khan, it is okay. Don't cry. A man should not cry.'

Aunt Zeynab faced Uncle Ghulam. 'You shut up! What do you know? Khan is a liar, not Sharouch. Khan never called us when we were in Pakistan, but Sharouch did.'

I was still crying, and I tried to reply to what she was saying. 'Sharouch never allowed me to speak to you guys on the phone, because of the cost,' I pleaded.

Aunt Zeynab sneered at me. Murad stared at me as if I was a liar. So did Timur. But Sohrab kept quiet. I got up to leave the house. Sohrab got up to follow me. 'You sit down, Sohrab,' Aunt Zeynab shouted. 'Khan is an alcoholic. You stay away from him.'

I left the house crying. I walked to the store and purchased beers and my first pack of cigarettes since Uncle Ghulam's family arrived in Canada. I went to the park.

I went home late at night. Everyone was asleep. When I got up in the morning, they were all having breakfast. I sat at the table next to Uncle Ghulam. As Aunt Zeynab poured tea in my cup, she asked, 'Where were you last night?' I did not say anything. Then she looked at Uncle Ghulam. 'I told you he drinks alcohol,' she said.

Uncle Ghulam did not say anything. He got up. 'Our bus is coming in fifteen minutes,' he said. Murad got up from his chair and walked behind my chair and smelled me. Aunt Zeynab was sitting across the table and looked at Murad's face. 'I am not going to French class today,' Sohrab said. 'I hate the French language. It is very hard to learn.'

Aunt Zeynab said, 'Get up, you idiot. If you miss one day of your French class, the government will deduct twenty dollars from your pay check at end of the month.

'Get up, and let's go. You are stupid,' Murad said.

Twenty-Eight

This misunderstanding of who had sent money while they were in Pakistan was the foundation of our dispute between me and Aunt Zeynab. Every time I wanted to speak about the jobs I had worked at while I lived in New Jersey, Aunt Zeynab would change the subject. If I wanted to talk more about my job experience in the States, she would yell at me, 'Shut up! You have never worked in your life! And it was Sharouch who sent us the money.' If told her that I had given my money to Sharouch, and had Sharouch sent it to them, she would roll her eyes at Uncle Ghulam and Murad. I even did not want to talk about the money, but she always brought the subject to everyone's attention, and then everyone looked down on me.

Finally, my interview date with Immigration Canada approached. I made an appointment with Sabour. He had already written a case story for me: 'You left Kabul with your mother, sister, and grandfather in 1993 for Islamabad, Pakistan, because of the war,' he told me. 'You lived in Islamabad from December 1993 until January 1995, then your grandfather found an smuggler who promised your grandfather to take you to Canada for ten thousand US dollars. You left Islamabad by bus, then you were taken to Greece by ship with many Afghan, Pakistani, and Iranian emigrants. From Greece, your smuggler transported you to Spain in a bus and then in a big truck. Then your smuggler made a forged passport for you, and you had direct flight from Spain to Montreal.' He took a deep breath. 'What do you think?' he asked. I said it was really interesting. He shook his head. 'Why are you smiling?' he asked. ' I am doing all this for you. This is a common way for smugglers to smuggle the Afghans,' he said. Then he tapped me on my shoulder and started to count the pages. 'Look, I have written almost seven pages! It took me almost a month to complete! We are going to give this to your lawyer this afternoon, and your court date is next week,' he said, and then he lit a cigarette. He seemed relaxed. 'Don't forget, if your lawyer asks you, just tell him you do not speak English,' Sabour mentioned.

In the afternoon we went to see my immigration lawyer, and Sabour handed my case to him. My court date was to be one day in the following week in the morning. On that day, I met with Sabour, then we went to the court of justice in Old Montreal on the seventh floor. The court session was conducted in the French language, and Sabour was my interpreter. After an hour or so, I saw that Sabour had a big smile on his face, and so did my immigration lawyer. 'Congratulations,' my lawyer said. 'You have been accepted as a permanent residence in Canada.' I was very happy to hear that.

Then they gave me a Social Insurance number. With that I could get my medical card and register for the French course. After that, I would be eligible to work. I came home and told the news to everyone. They all congratulated me, except Aunt Zeynab, who did not want to come out from the kitchen even though she was listening to everything I was saying.

I was so happy to register for the French course and then find a job. Aunt Zeynab had been constantly complaining about money. 'Food is expensive,' she would say. 'The phone bill, the rent, and electricity …' I was receiving around $550 a month, and I was giving $400 to Aunt Zeynab at the beginning of every month, and so did everyone else, yet she was still complaining. Once she asked everyone to pay fifty dollars extra per month, because, she explained, what she had been receiving was not enough. Then Uncle Ghulam took a pen and a piece of paper and started to do some calculations. 'No,' he said. 'It is even more than enough.' Aunt Zeynab went back to the kitchen and asked Timur to help her wash the dishes. Then she came back into the living room and pointed her finger at Uncle Ghulam. 'You are not old,' she said to him. 'You know that. You can work!' Every time Aunt Zeynab spoke everyone kept quite.

One evening Aunt Zeynab invited an Afghan family for dinner. She had met them in her French class. The family had been sponsored by their relatives from India; the relatives had lived in Canada for many years. They owned a house, and they knew many Afghan families who lived on the South Shore. We were having dinner when Aunt Zeynab pointed me by saying, 'Khan was very young when he left Kabul. Grandpa spent a lot of money to bring him out of Kabul; unfortunately he has turned to an alcoholic.' Everyone at dinner table stared at me. I lost my appetite and went to the basement. A few minutes later I heard her voice calling my name to come up to the kitchen and wash dishes. From the kitchen I overheard her saying to the guests, 'Alcohol is very bad. Look at him. He is young and he speaks English, but he cannot find a job. He lived in the America for three years with his cousin Sharouch. All Khan did was drink alcohol. Not only that, he had relied on his cousin. Poor Sharouch worked very hard and sent us money to Pakistan, besides supporting Aftab.' I had no idea why she was saying these lies in front of her guests; neither did I have the courage to argue with her. I had no other option but to leave the house, go to the park, and drink beer.

I had to wait for another four months to start my French course. Every newcomer to Quebec was eligible to take the French course programme for seven months. In the evening, as Aunt Zeynab, Murad, Uncle Ghulam, and Sohrab went through their French language exercises, they complained about how difficult it was. Sometimes because of the French language, they wanted to move to Toronto, because they were already familiar with English. But it was the Quebec

Immigration policy not to allow new immigrants to leave Quebec before a one-year stay in Quebec territory.

Every time I wanted to speak about the importance of education in today's civilized country, Aunt Zeynab made fun of me by saying, 'You are too old.' Or she would get frustrated and yell at me, 'You are old! Forget about school. Work hard and make money. Your fiancée is waiting for you.' I had no other option but to accept. Money was everything for Aunt Zeynab and Murad, but Uncle Ghulam and Sohrab were different. They believed that money is not everything. Good health and happiness are more important. We do not have to be rich in order to be healthy; neither does money bring absolute happiness to a family. Aunt Zeynab was getting more and more frustrated at hearing these authentic ideas from them. However, I had no major role in that family. I had been lonely before their arrival to Canada, but I was not unhappy about leaving them. Especially, when I was about to start eating food, Aunt Zeynab would ask me all sorts of unnecessary questions: 'Where were you last night? Who did you speak on the phone? Why don't you wash your hands before you eat?' She watched every move I made, and because of her criticism, most of the time I just walked down to the basement.

I found a job at the Mega Bloks toy factory in Montreal; it was about an hour and a half away from Brossard. I started work at 8.00 a.m. and ended at 4.30 p.m. I got home around 6.00 in the evening. I worked Monday through Friday and weekends were my days off. Minimum wage was $6.50, so my weekly pay cheque came to $250. Hundreds and hundreds of employees worked at Mega Bloks in three different shifts. The first shift started at 8.00 a.m.; the second shift began at 4.30 p.m.; and the third shift started around midnight. Everyone rested, but the machines worked nonstop. We were producing toys for kids. My job was to place three specific pieces of a toy into the boxes which were passing in front of me on a running belt. There were six to seven other assembly workers on my line who placed the other parts of the same toy in every box. At end of that running belt, the packaging of the toy was completed, and another employee sealed the boxes. From there they were shipped to the warehouse. Each of us had big boxes of toy parts to our left and right. The line feeder kept on taking the empty boxes away and replacing them with full boxes of parts. Without much of a break, we did the same physical movements more than a thousand times per shift. Every three hours the bell rang for a fifteen-minute break, and our lunch break was thirty minutes. Some smoked cigarettes and had coffee. Others purchased soda, cake, and candies from the vending machines which were installed around the cafeteria. Most of us brought our lunchboxes from home. Men and women from every corner of the earth worked for Mega Bloks.

There was not ever a day in which Aunt Zeynab did not complain about money or criticize me. She doubted every opinion I expressed. If I tried to defend myself, she would yell, 'Shut up, you alcoholic and cigarette smoker!' I had no idea why she hated me so much. Every time she got mad, it was for no reason, and she had charismatic way of adjusting her tone of voice or crying to get what she wanted. So, I dealt with my depression with beer and cigarettes, the only friends I had.

Aunt Zeynab attacked me verbally, especially when I was eating. She questioned me about things I did not like; for example, 'What are going to do with your fiancée, Negar? When are you going to buy a car? Why do you drink alcohol and smoke cigarettes?' This was her common strategy, and most of the time I left my plate without finishing my food. Then she would get even more upset and say, 'Why don't you finish your food? No one is going to eat your leftovers.'

Then I would put the leftover food in the in the kitchen garbage can, and she would roll her eyes at Murad, Uncle Ghulam, Sohrab, and even at Timur. As a consequence, everyone looked down on me. Eventually I noticed that everyone started to hate me. When I was not in the house, she would criticize Sohrab, and sometimes criticize Uncle Ghulam. I was able to hear her charming voice from the basement. Aunt Zeynab suggested that I should leave my extra money with Uncle Ghulam so he could save it for my marriage, which I did.

One night, after dinner, we were sitting in the living room as usual. Aunt Zeynab asked Ghulam, 'Why you don't you look for night job? There is only one more month left for our French course.'

Uncle Ghulam said, 'Let me complete my French course, then of course I will find a job.' And then Uncle Ghulam giggled. 'I will tell you a joke: 'A five-year-old child was at a party with his mother. The kid needed to piss, so he called out loud, "Mommy, Mommy, I need to piss! I need to piss!" He said it loudly several times to get his mother's attention at the crowded party. The mother got closer to the boy. "Never say that again!" she said. "You are not a baby anymore. Say something else. For example, say, 'I want to sing!'" The boy said, "I do not want to sing. I want to piss." The mother said, "I know you do not want to sing. Just say that, and I will lead you to the washroom." The boy and the mother practiced the password a few times on different occasions. A few weeks later, the boy had fallen asleep between his parents in their bed. Early in the morning, the boy had to piss. He found his mother on the right side of the bed snoring. He saw his father on the left side. He was lying on his side. The boy pushed his father's arm. "I want to sing," he said. His father replied, "It is too early to sing, Bachem, sing tomorrow." "But I want to sing now," the kid said. "Come and sing in my ear, then," said the father. "Not too loud, though, because your mother is asleep." The boy moved forward and sang into his fathers' ear.'

Everyone laughed, except Aunt Zeynab. She rolled her eyes at Murad, and then Murad stopped laughing. But Sohrab and I kept on laughing. There was not even one day that Aunt Zeynab did not argue with and criticize Uncle Ghulam, Sohrab, and me. Every argument she made was over money, and she was never satisfied. She denied every good thing I had done for the family. Although I was working between forty and fifty hours each week, she said it was not enough. She said I must find another job on the weekend. After Uncle Ghulam and his family completed their French courses, Uncle Ghulam and Murad got their driver's licenses, and purchased their first car in Canada.

For whatever reason, it was Aunt Zeynab who never liked me. Every time I entered the house, she stared at me as if I was a criminal and questioned me: 'Why are you late? Why don't you dress properly? Who are your friends?' Then she kept on saying bad things about me, even about my mother. 'Your father was killed because of your mother. Your father should never have moved to Bamyan.' If Uncle Ghulam or Sohrab wanted to defend me, Aunt Zeynab would yell at them. For that reason they usually remained quiet. She made me cry two to three times a week. The only thing that did calm me down was drinking beer, smoking cigarettes, looking at the free birds, and listening to their awesome songs at the park. Only then I was able to rest.

Aunt Zeynab, Uncle Ghulam, Murad, and Timur went to Toronto for a weekend to visit some of their friends whom they had known from Pakistan. Sohrab and I decided to go downtown to a nightclub that Saturday night.

Twenty-Nine

'I will buy beer. First we drink, and then we go to downtown,' Sohrab said. Sohrab went up the stairs and searched for Murad's car keys. 'I found his car keys,' he said.

'It is not safe, man. You should not drive,' I said.

'I know how to drive,' he argued. 'I drove his car last weekend. It is so easy to drive automatic cars.'

I said, 'No. Let me drive. I have had a car in the past.'

But he insisted. 'Just wait for me,' he said. Then he opened the freezer and brought out some frozen meat. 'Put this in the sink to defrost. While you are waiting cut up some onions and garlic. I will be back with twelve beers. The weather is very cold. I have to drive to the store.'

Sohrab came back with twelve beers. He opened a bottle for me and one for him. I had the pan on the stove and I had added some cooking oil and the sliced onion. Sharouch started to cut the garlic. 'Put the garlic in after,' he said. 'Then when the onion and garlic turn to a golden colour, put in some tomato paste, and then put the meat. When he opened the fourth beer for us to drink, he said, 'I know my mother does not like you. She does not like me either. She loves Timur and Murad. When we were in Pakistan, she always criticized me as she criticises you here.' And then he started to laugh. 'Khan, I know you have sent us a lot of money. Do you know that Afghan who came from New Jersey to Islamabad to marry his cousin? He told me everything. He told me, "Aftab works very hard, and he makes more money than Sharouch." I told this to my mother, father, and Murad. They know everything. Why my mother denies that, I don't know,' Sohrab said.

I felt released once I heard that from Sohrab. I asked him, 'Why you don't tell that to your parents again?'

'I told them,' he said. 'They know, but for whatever reason my mother does not like you. This I don't understand.' Then he added the garlic and opened another two beers.

We laughed and played music. That was the first time that I actually felt that the Sohrab I knew in Canada was the same Sohrab that I had known in Kabul. We finished the beers, and then we had dinner. At around nine o'clock, Sohrab stood up. 'I will go and buy more beer, and then we will go downtown,' he said.

'You should not drive,' I said. 'It is very risky. Police are everywhere.'

He smiled at me. 'You don't know me, man. In Pakistan I learned how drive. I even know how to ride motorcycles. I had friends in Pakistan. I rode their motorcycles and drove their cars all the time.'

The phone rang, and he answered it. It was Grandpa calling us from Mazar-i-Sharif. Sohrab was talking to Grandpa, and in a few minutes, my mother wanted to speak to me. Sohrab passed the phone to me. 'Bachem, how are you?' she asked.

'I am doing fine, Mother,' I said.

'Now you know that Negar is your fiancée,' she said, 'work hard and save your money. In a few years, come to Mazar-i-Sharif and marry her. Respect Aunt Zeynab, Uncle Ghulam, and your cousins. They are your family. Whatever they say, just listen to them,' she advised. The phone was disconnected. I hung up the phone and called Sohrab's name a few times out loud, but he had already left the house. I stepped outside to see if the car was in the garage, but Sohrab had taken it to get more beer.

I waited for more than an hour for Sohrab; however, he never returned. At that point I was very concerned. I waited for another half hour. Finally, I decided to walk to the convenience store to look for Sohrab. The lady cashier did not speak a word of English. After a while, a customer interpreted from English to French to the lady. 'Many customers come and go, I have no idea who are you talking about,' the cashier said.

I went back home. It was already midnight. I waited for Sohrab impatiently, but he never came home. At around 3.30 a.m., the phone rang. It was the hospital. I left the house immediately and was very concerned to find out if Sohrab was all right. I found Sohrab's room. The nurse said he had been unconscious, but he was awake now. 'I did not see the red light, and I drove through it. A car hit me in the intersection where the store is. When I opened my eyes, I was in the hospital,' he said.

The nurse gave me the police report, and then I went to the police station. A police officer who spoke English said, 'Your cousin is very lucky. He was drunk and went through the red light. He does not have a driver's licence, and the vehicle he was driving was not insured.' And then he said, 'Today is Sunday. On Tuesday you must take your cousin to the courthouse early in the morning.'

I could not believe this tragedy, and I had no idea how to explain this to Aunt Zeynab and Uncle Ghulam. Especially I had no idea how to explain to Murad that his car was a total loss. Yet I was thankful to God that Sohrab was alive.

I went back to the hospital to see Sohrab. I explained everything to him. The nurse came in and said, 'There is no serious injury. Just wait for another couple of hours. The doctor will examine him, and this afternoon you can take him home.'

Sohrab and I had no idea how to explain this to the family. We were smiling at each other, yet we were very concerned. After the doctor had examined him, we left the hospital. The family already had returned from Toronto. It was shocking for them to see Sohrab all bandaged. I was holding his hand and helping him out of the Taxi. When Aunt Zeynab saw us through the window, she rushed out of the house. Uncle Ghulam and Murad followed close behind. She screamed, 'What did you do to my son?' All off a sudden, as she ran down the stairs, she slipped and fell on the ice. Uncle Ghulam laughed and then picked her up, and then everyone entered the house. Aunt Zeynab had hurt her elbow. Sohrab had his head down and tried to explain what had happened. Aunt Zeynab eyeballed me as if everything was my fault.

Murad asked where his car was. 'Your car was towed, and the police have it,' I said. Murad loved his car very much. At that moment, he almost had attacked me and said, 'Why are you doing this to us?'

I knew they would not stop accusing me. Before leaving for the basement, I said, 'On Tuesday Sohrab has to go to the courthouse to hear the judge's decision. I have to get up early in the morning.' Then I stood. Aunt Zeynab rolled her eyes at Murad, and then Murad pushed me down really hard. 'Khan, sit down,' he yelled. 'What about my car?' he screamed.

'It is not my fault,' I said. 'I warned Sohrab not to drive, but he said the weather was really cold. I was on the phone with my mother when Sohrab left.'

Aunt Zeynab said, 'Your mother, that widow, what did she say?'

I had no idea why she had to call my mother a widow at all the time. I was very tired, especially because I had not slept the night before. At around midnight, Timur woke me up. 'Khan, come upstairs. My mother wants to talk to you,' he said.

I went up on the living room. 'Listen to me, you fatherless Haramzada' (bastard). Murad purchased his car for fifteen hundred dollars, and you must pay that amount,' she shouted at me. 'Right now you have saved around eighteen hundred with your uncle. We just want to let you know that we will take fifteen hundred of it and give it to Murad so he can buy another car.' Every time I tried to tell her it was not my fault, she said, 'Shut up, you fatherless Haramzada!' I had no other choice but to be quiet.

The next day after work, I called Sabour and explained the car accident to him. 'It is serious … very serious,' he told me. 'Is the other person injured?' he asked. I had no idea. Finally Sabour said, 'I will come to the courthouse as interpreter. If the other person is injured, Sohrab may go to jail.' When I heard the word *jail*, I was shocked. Sabour asked me to come to court also. Sohrab, Murad, Aunt Zeynab, and I were at the courthouse early in the morning; Sabour was already waiting for us.

Sohrab was still tired from the accident, and he seemed very concerned. 'Is this Sohrab?' Sabour pointed at him. 'Come with me,' Sabour said. They went to an office in the courthouse; we waited outside the courtroom where Sohrab's court procedure was to be held. When we heard his name called, we entered that courtroom. The judge asked Sohrab to come forward. The proceedings were conducted in French. Sabour interpreted what the judge was saying to Sohrab, and what Sohrab was saying to the judge. After a couple of hours, the court ended it.

'The lady's car is damaged, and she is not hurt,' Sabour told us. 'If she had been injured, Sohrab could have been imprisoned today. Sohrab has to pay four thousand dollars to the lady for the damage to her car. Furthermore, Sohrab does not have a driver's license; therefore, he has to pay the police a fine of fifteen hundred dollars. Not only that, but because he was drunk and operated a motor vehicle that caused the accident, he is also fined twelve hundred dollars.'

We could not believe how much money Sohrab had to pay. 'Where is my car? Where is my car?' Murad asked Sabour.

'I don't know,' Sabour replied. 'You must ask at the police station where your car is.'

Aunt Zeynab never took her eyes away from me. Sohrab sat in the front seat of Uncle Ghulam's car, because was still sore from the accident. Murad sat in the middle of the backseat. Aunt Zeynab sat on his right, and I sat on his left, right behind Uncle Ghulam. Murad started asking Sohrab, 'How are you are going to pay for all this?'

'I will work,' he said, 'and I can make arrangements to pay on a monthly basis.'

Then Murad became emotional and pushed Sohrab's head from the backseat. 'What about my car? I want my car!' Murad demanded. Uncle Ghulam laughed. Then Sohrab laughed as well.

Aunt Zeynab said, 'Khan has saved some money with your father, and he will pay fifteen hundred. I already have spoken to him.'

'Khan, Khan … why does he have to pay?' Uncle Ghulam said.

'Khan is my friend. That is why,' Sohrab said.

All of a sudden, Murad punched Sohrab on the back of his head again, and Sohrab's head almost touched the windscreen. It surely would have if he had not been wearing his seat belt. Uncle Ghulam lost control of the car. The car veered to the left. A van honked as it was approaching us. Finally, Uncle Ghulam pulled the car aside. Aunt Zeynab shouted at Uncle Ghulam: 'Do not stop the car! Go home! I am starving!'

In the afternoon, Murad, Sohrab, and I went to the police station to find out where Murad's car was. The officer gave us an address which was more than half an hour's drive away. 'The place your car has been towed to will keep your car for thirty days. They charge thirty dollars a night. So far you owe nine hundred dollars. You must pay in order to pick up your car,' the officer said. 'The other option is to give the car to them. Then you just have to go there to pick up your plates and sign the ownership of your vehicle over to them.' Murad got very emotional and started to scream. He almost punched Sohrab right there in the police station. Murad made fists of his hands then pushed Sohrab. 'Let's go home,' Murad said. The policeman saw Murad push Sohrab. 'Take it easy,' he told Murad.

We walked back home and told the story of Murad's car to Uncle Ghulam and Aunt Zeynab. Uncle Ghulam was not able stop laughing. 'Nine hundred dollars to get back that piece of junk?' The way he laughed made Sohrab and I laugh too. Finally, Uncle Ghulam agreed to drive us there at least to see the car. Uncle Ghulam could not stop talking about how good his car was. 'This is a Toyota Corolla,' he told us. 'It consumes less gas and it is strong as iron. Can you not hear? The engine it runs like clock. Your car is a Nissan, and you bought it for fifteen hundred dollars,' Uncle Ghulam told Murad. 'I bought this one for thirteen hundred, and it is much better than yours, Bachem.'

We arrived the junkyard in Montreal where Murad's car was. After we gave the papers from the police to the man, he opened the gate. We saw hundreds of motor vehicles parked there. Ultimately, Murad found his car. He took the key from the man to start his car, but it did not respond. Then he opened the hood of the car and saw that the radiator was broken. The right front sidelights were broken. The hood, the right wing, and the bumper were crushed. Uncle Ghulam was not able to stop laughing at the car. And then he said, 'Nine hundred dollars to get this car back?' Finally Uncle Ghulam convinced Murad to sign the ownership of his car to the man, and forget the car, because it would have cost him too much to repair it. Murad signed the paperwork, and then we left.

That evening, Aunt Zeynab did not want stop talking about the money that Sohrab had to pay, both to the lady and also for the police fines. Then she asked Sohrab to calculate how much was the total amount. 'Six thousand seven hundred in total,' Sohrab said.

Uncle Ghulam was still laughing and kept on repeating the amount. 'Bachem, how are you going to pay?'

Aunt Zeynab wanted me to pay $1,500 for Murad's car, and pay half of the $6,700, which did not make sense to me. I proposed that I would pay $1,500 for Murad's car and that was all. Aunt Zeynab shouted at me. I had to get up early in the morning; therefore, I asked Uncle Ghulam to pay $1,500 from my saving account to Murad so he could buy another car. Aunt Zeynab wanted me to pay more, because she thought I had made Sohrab drunk. I tried to explain to her what exactly had happened before the accident, but she never accepted my story.

I was not able to sleep that night. I went to the basement to my bedroom. I tried to fall asleep, but I was not able to. After a while, I heard Sohrab come down to the basement. I said, 'What your mother proposes is not fair, and you know that, but I will do exactly what she decides, and I am sure you understand.'

'You are right,' he said. 'Whatever happens, I will find a second job and work hard. It is all good, Khan.' Then he looked at the window. 'Let's go and buy beer,' he said. 'It is ten thirty. We have another thirty minutes before the store closes.'

'Let's do it,' I said. We got out of the house through the basement the window and walked in the cold to purchase beer. We returned to our basement bedrooms via the same route, and we started to drink. As we were drinking, we looked at each other. We were both thinking about what we had experienced over the past two days – his accident, the hospital, the police, the judge's decisions, Murad's car, and Uncle Ghulam making fun of Murad's car. We laughed, yet we were concerned about how we would pay for all the damages we had caused. After all, I had promised Sohrab I would pay half of the total amount.

It was late in the morning when I got up for the next day. Uncle Ghulam and Murad had already left for work. Sohrab was still asleep, and Aunt Zeynab was not home. That afternoon Sohrab and I went to the police station and made the arrangement to pay the police fines on monthly basis. Then we went to the bank and asked for a $2,000 loan each to pay the $4,000 to the lady. The bank agent refused to give us a loan at first, but she gave us an appointment for the next morning to meet with the bank manager.

During our next-day appointment, we explained to the manager the reason we needed the money. Finally, the bank manager agreed to loan us $2,000 each. We would have to pay back the bank on a monthly basis with a 10 percent interest rate. Later on that day, I called my job to explain the reason I had not been able to show up for work. The manager hung up the phone on me.

That evening Sohrab and I went to play billiards at the closest bar to the house. When we came home, Aunt Zeynab shouted at both of us, and then pointed her finger at me. 'You fatherless bastard! You are turning my son to an alcoholic!'

Sohrab tried to tell her, 'We did not drink. We just played billiards. That is all.' But she didn't listen. We went to the basement. We were both angry. Why did she yell at us at all the time? Out anger, we decided to go and buy beer. As we had done before, we got out of the window, purchased beer, and came back into the basement through the same window. We started to get drunk in the basement. I put the empty beer cans under my bed. I was not able to get up early in the morning; therefore, I was late for work. My manager sent me to see the big boss; the boss already had made decision. He gave my last pay cheque. 'Empty your locker. You are fired,' he said.

At home, I explained why I had lost my job. As usual, Aunt Zeynab was mad at me and doubted everything I had to say. 'Don't! Don't mention Sohrab's name. It is your entire fault!' she said. She walked down to the basement and brought all the beer bottles and cans into the living room. 'Look, you are an alcoholic!' she said. I did not mention Sohrab. I was in trouble. I did not want him to be in trouble too. She mentioned my mother's name and said, 'You are just like mother! Your father was killed because of her, and you almost had Sohrab killed,' she said.

I got very offended and shouted at Aunt Zeynab, 'Stop talking about my mother! I already have made agreement with Sohrab to pay half of what he has to pay.'

Then she got close to me and slapped me really hard. 'Don't mention my son's name.'

For whatever reason, I called her bitch, and then Murad got close to me to attack, but Uncle Ghulam stopped Murad while he was laughing. Then my tears came, and I was not able to stop crying. I told Uncle Ghulam, 'I am leaving this house. Since you guys have come, I can't be happy.'

Aunt Zeynab started shouting again. 'You are jealous, like your mother and your grandpa! Of course you are not happy to see us in Canada!' With everything I said, she had the talent to direct my meaning in different directions. It was coming to a point where even Uncle Ghulam seemed to be starting to believe Aunt Zeynab that everything was my fault.

I felt very cold. I went down to the basement with tears in my eyes. I questioned myself. What had happened to the family? Why were there fights and arguments all the time? I packed up my clothes and went up to the living room. I told Uncle Ghulam I had to leave. I did not have any interest in seeing Aunt Zeynab or Murad. Timur was busy with schoolwork.

'Where are you going?' Uncle Ghulam asked.

'I cannot live with you guys,' I said. 'I will find an apartment in Montreal.'

'It is late at night,' he said. 'You must not leave.' Uncle Ghulam tried to convince me to stay. Then he asked me to sit and have tea and something to eat and talk about it.

Aunt Zeynab came in, picked up my backpack, opened the front door, and threw it out into the street. 'Go! Go!' she shouted. 'Leave now!' I looked at Uncle Ghulam and asked to give some of my money. 'No, no! Give him nothing!' Aunt Zeynab said.

Uncle Ghulam walked up the stairs to his bedroom and came back with $1,800. I gave $750 back for Murad's car. 'No! No! You pay all of it, Aunt Zeynab shouted. 'Fifteen hundred!'

'I already spoke to Sohrab,' I said. 'He will pay for half of the damage.'

'Don't you mention my son's name,' she yelled. 'It is entirely your fault!' she yelled. She brought out the bill for the ambulance that had transported Sohrab from the site of the accident to the hospital. 'This is sixty dollars!' she shouted. 'Pay thirty for this!' Then she said, 'What about the rent? You have rented this expensive house for us, and now you are leaving.'

I gave her another $300. 'That is all I can afford,' I said.

'What about Negar?' she said. 'She is waiting for you, and she is your fiancée.'

'She is just a kid,' I said. 'When the time comes, I will send her gifts.'

'When? When? And what do you expect us to tell your widowed mother?'

I was not able to listen anymore. I walked out of the house, picked up my bag off the street, and walked to the bus terminal. Uncle Ghulam had wanted to give me a lift to the bus terminal, but Aunt Zeynab would not allow him to leave the house.

In downtown Montreal, I went to the same building where I had rented my first apartment. I had called the landlord from a pay phone to ask him if he had an apartment for rent. He was on vacation, but his wife came out of the building. 'What has happened to you?' she asked. 'You have lost so much weight!'

'Nothing,' I said. 'I just had a little problem with my family, and now I want to live by myself.'

'Your old apartment has been rented, but I have a better apartment on the first floor, and the rent is four hundred, everything included,' she said. She opened the apartment to me. All I wanted to do was rest. I gave her the first month's rent.

'We will sign the rental lease tomorrow,' she said. 'There is a sofa. I will get you blanket.' She came back with a blanket. 'It is cold take this.' Then she looked at me from head to toe. 'You are not lying?' she asked.

'I don't lie,' I said. 'Why do you ask me that?'

She shook her head. 'It seems like you just have been released from prison, young man.' Then she smiled. 'Don't take it personally,' she said.

Thirty

I slept for three days and nights without calling anyone. I had great anxiety about what had gone wrong in the family. I had called Aunt Zeynab a bitch in the English language in front of her family. My mother, sister, and the rest of the family were in Mazar-i-Sharif. The family that I knew hated me. What was the truth?

Everything I said to Uncle Ghulam's family was rejected, as I had been branded a liar. The light that unites the family under its reflection – where was it? These were the main questions that were keeping me in a state of uncertainty.

In two weeks I found a job and started to work in a factory that produced shampoo, soap, and other products for women to make themselves pretty for the public. I called Uncle Ghulam's house after two weeks. Uncle Ghulam wanted to see me in my apartment. 'You disappeared just like a bird,' he said.

When he visited, I told him, 'I have been seeing your son Sohrab, and I have made the first three-hundred-per-month payment.'

'I know, but how about us?' he said. 'We are worried about you.' I had nothing to say. I was not able to talk about how his wife treated me. All of sudden he mentioned her. 'Every time your aunt makes *Ashak*, she talks about you. We know Ashak is your favourite food,' he said. He picked up the phone. 'I want you to talk with your aunt,' he said, and then he dialled the numbers. 'Here, talk to her,' Uncle Ghulam said.

'Khan, Khan, where are you?' She had changed the tone of her voice. It sounded much softer, and thinner. She said she wanted to see me. 'Come, come, this Friday. I will make you Ashak,' she said.

'Thank you, but I have to work this Friday,' I said.

'Okay, come Saturday then,' she said.

'I work in a restaurant on the weekends,' I said.

Then she said, 'Do you work seven days a week, Bachem?'

I replied, 'Yes.'

'Your mother called from Pakistan,' she told me. 'They want to come to Canada. Don't you want to talk them?'

'Yes, of course,' I said. 'I will come to your house.'

Then she asked me to pass the phone to Uncle Ghulam. 'Okay, okay, lady.' Uncle Ghulam smiled and hung up the phone. I offered to prepare more tea for him. 'No, Bachem, I just wanted to see that you are fine,' he said, and then he smiled. 'I came by bus,' he said, and then he left.

On the evenings at the weekends, I was washing dishes in a bar – The Rock Star in downtown Montreal, five Metro stations away from my apartment on the Green Line. The restaurant was owned by an Italian. I had no idea who the boss was, and everyone who worked there dressed very well. Three line cooks, a salad maker, a pastry girl, and the chef ran that kitchen. I asked one of the cooks, who was in the kitchen at all the time, where he was from. I asked while he was busy putting charcoal in place. When he had finished, he placed a large piece of meat on the cutting board. He was ignoring me.

We never turned off the dishwashing machine until the end of the night. It was my responsibility to pick up the dirty dishes from the line cooks. I had to put the dishes away after washing them. Everyone in kitchen wore white uniforms. My shift started at 4.00 p.m. and ended at 3.00 a.m. From 8.00 p.m. until 11.30 p.m., the kitchen was very busy. Sometimes the manager walked into the kitchen and yelled at everyone. Sometimes the waitresses argued with the line cooks, and the cooks, in response, would say, 'If the customers do not tip you enough, why do you bitches have to take it out on us? You must dress sexier than what you are wearing.' Sometimes the cooks were fired on the spot by the mangers, and sometimes the waitresses were sent home. At around 2.00 a.m., the kitchen stopped taking orders, and twenty-four beers were brought to the kitchen for the staff to drink. By 3.00 a.m. the kitchen was closed and everyone had gone home.

I went to see Uncle Ghulam's family once every three to four months. I spoke to my mother and my sister, and to Grandpa when they were in Pakistan. In 1997 they applied to the Canadian embassy in Islamabad to emigrate Canada. In December 1997, my mother, sister, and Grandpa had decided to go to Quetta from Islamabad to visit Shreen and her family. After staying two days in Quetta, my mother went to a vegetable market to do some grocery shopping. Unfortunately, a suicide bomber exploded in the crowed, and my mother was pronounced dead. After that incident, Grandpa and my sister left Pakistan for Mazar-i-Sharif and merged with Uncle Rustam's family. Uncle Ghulam told me this privately at his house. I was not able to stop crying that day; I left his house in tears and walked in the snow. Sohrab followed me in his car and insisted that he give me a ride home. 'I have never understood what is wrong with the people of Afghanistan and Pakistan,' I said to him. 'Why do they have to kill each other?'

'It is predestined,' he said. 'This is how Allah wants it to be, and we cannot go against his will.'

'I am very sick and tired of living in Canada,' he said. 'Everyone is after money, and I do not like the Western way of life. Within a few months I will be eligible to take my Canadian citizenship exam, and then I will go to Mazar-i-Sharif to marry your sister, Mena. I have been working in factories for the last two years, and I do not like it,' he said. Then he asked me to travel with him. I told him that I would be allowed to take my Canadian citizenship exam in 1999. 'Remember you cannot apply for citizenship until after three years of receiving the Canadian permanent residency. You received yours a year before I did – while you were in Pakistan,' I said.

'Yes, you are right,' he said. Then Sohrab rested in my bed. 'You are very lucky to live alone,' he said. 'My parents argue all the time. Remember that house that you rented for us? It was a very good house because everyone had a private bedroom. But the apartment in which we live right now is small. I sleep in the same room with Timur. When my parents argue, I go out and buy beer and sit in the park and drink. It calms me down. Sometimes I even call in sick, and I sleep all day when Timur is at school.' Then he laughed. 'We are Muslim, and we should not drink alcohol, but beer is okay, because it has only 5 per cent alcohol.' That made me laugh as well. During that visit, Sohrab and I spoke about everything – politics, religion, culture, and especially about our futures in Canada.

Late one night Sohrab came into my apartment. He was all excited. 'Look, look!' he said. 'This is my Canadian citizenship card. Now I can go to Mazar-i-Sharif. I have saved eleven thousand dollars. I spoke to Grandpa. They want me to come. They do business in Turkmenistan and Mazar-i-Sharif. They import gas and sell it to the local gas stations in Mazar-i-Sharif,' he said. 'I will purchase my plane ticket to Turkmenistan, then I will go to Mazar-i-Sharif over land. If I like it there, I will stay and do business with them.'

A week later, Sohrab came back and showed me his Canadian passport and his plane ticket. He flew in the summer of 1998, from Montreal to Turkmenistan. A few weeks later, I heard from Uncle Ghulam that Sohrab had been married to my sister in Mazar-i-Sharif at a big wedding. I spoke to Sohrab, my sister, and Grandpa after the marriage. It was in the month of August 1998. I heard that the Taliban had entered Mazar-i-Sharif. In six days, the Taliban had slaughtered over 13,000 Hazara in Mazar-i-Sharif. Furthermore, the Taliban had warned the northern people of Afghanistan that they would send the Tajiks to Tajikistan, the Uzbeks to Uzbekistan, the Turkmens to Turkmenistan, and the Hazaras to hell (*goristan*). Uncle Rustam called from Turkmenistan and told Uncle Ghulam, 'Everyone is fine. We arrived in Turkmenistan a few days ago. Grandpa, Sohrab, and Mina were in their new house when the Taliban entered Mazar-i-Sharif. I am sure they are fine, but we are not in contact with them.' The major concern was where they may have been. A few weeks later we heard the heartbreaking news from Grandpa that the Taliban were searching for Hazara people door to door. Sohrab had been very happy with his wife. That evening when Grandpa went to search for Sohrab and Mina, he found both had been shot in the head in front of the door on the street.

It was unbelievable. Sohrab had been in Canada only a month before. Everything had changed within a few weeks. I went to the funeral at Uncle Ghulam's house and saw everyone crying. Everyone had tears coming down. Later on that evening, Grandpa called from Turkmenistan and spoke to everyone. He had nothing to say but, 'This is what Allah wanted, so we cannot go against his will, and that is how it is.' He asked me, 'Why do you have to live alone in Canada? Move back to your uncle's house. You must respect them; they are your family.'

After losing my mother and my sister and Sohrab, I had nothing to say. I had to accept Grandpa's proposal. Then he asked me to pass the phone to Uncle Ghulam. Uncle Ghulam looked into my eyes as he listened to Grandpa. He was saying, 'Yes … yes …'

A few days later, Uncle Ghulam came to my apartment. 'Bachem, your grandpa is right,' he told me. 'You must move in with us. Living by yourself is not good for your health. Come and live with us, and everything will be fine, Insha'Allah. We have lost Sohrab and your sister. We need each other. Keep your job, save your money. While you are not married, live with us. You are like my son,' Uncle Ghulam said. In a couple of months our lease will end, and we will rent a bigger apartment. Then you will have your own room,' he said. I had no choice but to accept his idea, because it was originally Grandpa's wish.

In March 2001, these animals destroyed the Buddhas of Bamyan.

I moved in with Uncle Ghulam after they rented a bigger apartment. We all had our own rooms except for Uncle Ghulam and Aunt Zeynab, who shared a room. Uncle Ghulam came up with a myth right in middle of another of Aunt Zeynab's disputes. She was arguing about who should cook dinner.

Here is Uncle Ghulam's story: A fisherman was lying beside a river, his fishing rod in the water. A stranger passed by and asked the fisherman's permission to sit and have a chat with him. The fisherman accepted his request, and then the stranger proposed an idea to the fisherman. "Why don't you find a small boat to get in the middle of the river and fish more?" The fisherman smiled and said, "I have a small family, and I catch enough fish to feed them." The stranger said, "No, you don't understand. Fish more and sell your catch in the market. Then you will have money." The fisherman smiled at the stranger and asked, "What should I do with the money?" The stranger said, "You can buy yourself anything you want. Have employees and make a small fish factory. Smoke the fish and put it in small containers and export them outside of your city, and even your country. I am sure you would make good money." The fisherman asked, "If I get a lot money, then what?" The stranger said, "You will become very rich and popular, and you will gain respect from the people in your city." The fisherman asked again, "If I am well respected by others, then what?" The stranger said, "Not only will you have respect, you will have power, a big house, nice clothes, popularity, and travel around the world. You will be able to get anything you want … I mean anything." The fisherman said, "Let's imagine I have all those advantages you just mentioned, then what?" The stranger stared at the fisherman. "Then you don't have to worry about anything. Just lie down on a beach and enjoy your life," he said. The fisherman started to laugh out loud. Then said, "That is what I am doing right now. Why do I have to do all that shit in order to get where I am now?"

About the Book

Away from this World

(The Afghan hound)

When government corruption becomes a way of life, it is the minorities that suffer the most.

Aftab Hakimi was born into a Hazara family in 1973 in Kabul, Afghanistan. At the age of fifteen, he emigrated to India. After living in India for a year and five months, he was smuggled to London, England. He received his British travel document after living in London for ten months. He decided to live in the United States with his cousin; however, the US embassy in London refused to give him a visiting visa on his British travel document. Aftab obtained a Mexican visa, and from Mexico climbed over the border and landed on US soil. After two and half years, the US immigration did not accept his refugee application and put him on deportation. Aftab decided to start a new life in Canada, so he crossed into Quebec from New York and declared himself an Afghan refugee in Canada.

Throughout his journey Aftab used fake names and dates of birth in order to protect his actual identity. Aftab faced many social challenges, such as cultural shock, jealousy, a materialistic lifestyle, and women.

Printed in Great Britain
by Amazon